WITHDRAWN
HARVARD LIBRARY
WITHDRAWN

Speaking of Gods in Figure and Narrative

Also by Deeanne Westbrook:
Ground Rules: Baseball and Myth
Wordsworth's Biblical Ghosts

SPEAKING OF GODS IN FIGURE AND NARRATIVE

Deeanne Westbrook

palgrave
macmillan

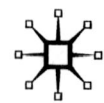

SPEAKING OF GODS IN FIGURE AND NARRATIVE
Copyright © Deeanne Westbrook, 2011.
All rights reserved.

First published in 2011 by
PALGRAVE MACMILLAN® in the United States –
a division of St. Martin's Press LLC,
175 Fifth Avenue,
New York, NY 10010.

Where this book is distributed in the UK, Europe and the rest of the world, this is by Palgrave Macmillan, a division of Macmillan Publishers Limited, registered in England, company number 785998, of Houndmills, Basingstoke, Hampshire RG21 6XS.

Palgrave Macmillan is the global academic imprint of the above companies and has companies and representatives throughout the world.

Palgrave® and Macmillan® are registered trademarks in the United States, the United Kingdom, Europe and other countries.

ISBN: 978–0–230–10811–0

Library of Congress Cataloging-in-Publication Data

Westbrook, Deeanne.
  Speaking of gods in figure and narrative / Deeanne Westbrook.
    p. cm.
  Includes bibliographical references (p.   ).
  ISBN 0–230–10811–3
  1. Language and languages—Religious aspects—History. 2. Metaphor—Religious aspects—History. 3. Narration (Rhetoric)—History. 4. Religion—History. I. Title.
  BL65.L2W47 2011
  210.1'4—dc22

2010030069

A catalogue record of the book is available from the British Library.

Design by MPS Limited, A Macmillan Company

First edition: February 2011

10 9 8 7 6 5 4 3 2 1

Printed in the United States of America.

In Memoriam
Jerry Westbrook
Carol Franks

... there is a time
In which majesty is a mirror of the self. ...
—Wallace Stevens

Contents

Preface ix
Acknowledgments xi

Introduction The Mirror of Heaven 1

1 In the Beginning: Time and the Figurative Forms of Creation 17
2 End-Times and Doom-Eagerness 31
3 The Power and the Glory: Divine Combatants, Heavenly Hosts, and Holy War 49
4 All in the Family: The Secret Sex Lives of Gods 69
5 Fathers and Sons: Violence and Sacrifice 89
6 Look Who's Talking—and Writing: The Language of Heaven 105
7 The Great Figures of Life and Death: Dualism and Divine Judgment 119
8 The Ways of God to Men: Belief, Preordination, Predestination, Rewards and Punishments, Spiritual Economics 137
9 Prophecy and Plot: The Making of the Hero and the Villain 155
10 Prayer, Praise, and the War Plot 171
11 Holy Madness 181
12 Reflections 205

Notes 215
Works Cited 233
Index 239

Preface

> With their capacity to reflect back nearly all incident light upon them and so recapitulate the scene they face, mirrors are like pieces of dreams, their images hyper-real and profoundly fake. Mirrors reveal truths you may not want to see. Give them a little smoke and a house to call their own, and mirrors will tell you nothing but lies.
>
> Angier 1

Twenty-first century citizens are heirs of a religious legacy so ancient that its origins predate history. In the third millennium BCE, Sumerians were telling a story of the gods' creation of man—a lowly creature made of clay and intended to free the gods from laboring for their own food (Kramer, *Sumerian Mythology* 69).[1] Over a millennium later, the Babylonians told a similar tale of man's creation from bloody clay for the purpose of tilling the fields and tending the temples of the gods (Thomas 12). Later still, the Israelites related a version of mankind's creation that incorporates both the earthy material from which the man was made and his purpose as found in the earlier stories. Genesis 2 tells of God's creation of a man from red clay, whose purpose was to till God's garden and keep it. The Qur'an receives and adapts the legacy: "We created you from dust, then a drop of fluid, then a clinging form, then a lump of flesh, both shaped and unshaped . . . then from a morsel, shaped or shapeless . . ." (22:5).

The legacy is a body of figurative language spoken in the silence where ignorance meets fear. As one system of beliefs displaces an older one, the older does not evaporate into the mists of time but leaves its traces in the new system. Lévi-Strauss thought of the myth-maker as a *bricoleur*, a workman who fashions a new thing from the materials he finds lying at hand, constructing, as Boas said, "new mythological worlds" from the "shattered remains of the old" ("Structural Study of Myth" 50). Further, "mythological thought," Lévi-Strauss claimed, is "a kind of 'intellectual *bricolage*'" (*The Savage Mind* 17). As centuries and millennia pass, the old ideas become part of a scarcely noticed worldview crafted of shattered remains, an intellectual *bricolage*. Carried in metaphors, analogies, personifications, and their narratives, the figures and images cross a boundary between the poetic and the real and become "facts," not in some remote place or time, but here and now. The facts are sacred truths. Nor would this reality-making legacy give concern, except for the fact that it can provide license—even sacred duty—to harass, berate, belittle, exclude, control, and even kill one's fellow human beings. Consider, for example, the effects of applying the designation *warrior* to a being conjured, through a name, from the unknown and unknowable. Consider the narrative possibilities that might follow from such naming. Perhaps the divine Warrior is armed with a "terrible swift sword." Perhaps he requires a host, an Army of God, to fight on his behalf. Perhaps he relishes the slaughter of "enemies." In any case, the figurative "realities" induce in many a state of "holy dread"—a condition of hopeful, anxious, unreasoning, and vulnerable credulity.

Acknowledgments

I am grateful to kind and generous colleagues—Sharon Elteto, Shelley Reece, Katya Amato, Peter Reader and John Vignaux Smyth—who read chapters and offered helpful suggestions. And I can never repay Carol Franks, first reader and friend, who read every word and offered only encouragement. Again, I want to thank the fine editors at Palgrave. And, finally, boundless gratitude goes to my mentor in this project, an extraordinary scholar and editor, the friend I have never met, Marilyn Gaull.

Introduction

The Mirror of Heaven

> For now we see through a glass, darkly; but then face to face . . .
> King James Version, 1 Corinthians 13:12[1]

> Your understanding has utterly failed regarding this world, and do you think you can comprehend the way of the Most High?
> 2 Esdras 4:2

> It is not expected of critics as it is of poets that they should help us make sense of our lives; they are bound only to attempt the lesser feat of making sense of the ways we try to make sense of our lives.
> Frank Kermode, *The Sense of an Ending* 3

IN WHAT FOLLOWS I ARGUE THAT HUMANKIND can know absolutely nothing of what may be called the metaphysical heavens, their supernatural inhabitants, if any, and the motives and designs of whatever gods may be. I further argue that, despite that abysmal ignorance, mythmakers have created through figurative devices and other linguistic and narrative maneuvers "realities" whose beneficial or toxic effects are felt day by day in our world. Those created "realities" are not such as may be seen in a spiritual telescope, but rather a looking glass, reflecting our fear and desire, bias, and earthly circumstances.

I write not as a theologian or philosopher (although I call on their testimonies), but as a textual critic who has for decades taught world mythologies, poetry, the Bible as literature, the Bible and literature, related courses in criticism, and linguistics. That experience has taught me that narratives—ancient and modern, religious and secular—and the figurative language in which they are couched help us make sense of our lives; they have, in addition, the often unacknowledged power to shape conceptions of something called "reality."[2] As happens for some—and too often—the "making sense" is poisonous rather than palliative. Sam Harris, for example, is concerned about the suicidal tendencies of religion-fostered action in the world and a "dark current of unreason in our national discourse" (46). Harold Bloom speaks of the "mutual passion" between "nine out of ten of us" who "love God and are loved in return." That "mutual passion," he says, "centers our society and demands some understanding, if our doom-eager society is to be understood at all" (*American Religion* 30).[3]

Whence that suicidal impulse? That doom eagerness? For the most part, religious passions and the sometimes destructive actions they drive arise not, I think, from theologians and philosophers. Such thinkers and interpreters seem quite remote from—and often blind to—passionate popular understandings of God, death, judgment, heaven and hell. Religious critic William James understood that underlying "learned" theological and philosophical pronouncements is a stratum of lived religion—"the feelings, acts, and experiences of individual men in their solitude, so far as they apprehend themselves to stand in relation to whatever they may consider the divine" (36). It is in the realm of lived religion that sacred texts and their figurative language exert their immense power for good or ill.

REALITY AND THE BOOK

The textual nature of the metaphysical is foregrounded in the fact that although today's three great monotheistic religions have their significant differences, they nevertheless share a focus on a sacred text and the distinction of having been born from and achieved their identity and character from something called "the Book." They are "religions of the Book"; Jews, Christians, and Muslims are "people of the Book." Whether that Book is the Torah, the Hebrew Bible, the Christian Bible, the Qur'an, or some spiritual archetype from another world—the heavenly "Mother of Books" (Aslan 99–101) or the "Book of Life" (Revelation 3:5), these world-shaping and world-shaking religions are in many senses "scripted" and "scriptured." Theologian David Tracy observes, "Unlike such traditions as Buddhism, Hinduism, and Confucianism, the three Abrahamic religions understand their sacred written texts not as classics, nor even as sacred texts, but as Scripture and thereby as somehow participatory in what is construed as the revelation of God" ("Writing" 383). Moreover, the revelation of God is a "self-manifestation." The participation of texts in the divine self-manifestation predictably lends an ethereal shining to the very characters and words, phrases, sentences, and plots. Tracy notices the centrality of notions of the Word, the Book, and (more importantly, I think, than has been noticed) *the narrative*—especially to the Christian understanding of God's self-revelation in the different forms of scripture. Tracy observes,

> The recent theoretical work on Western "logocentrism" and writing . . . needs to be explicitly related to a study of Christian self-understanding within . . . theology, the discipline that asks "Greek" (logocentric) questions of Jewish and Hellenistic Jewish scriptural texts, especially . . . narrative "gospel" texts.
>
> "Writing" 385[4]

In the grand plot of the Book and its individual narrative episodes, metaphors, and other figures come alive, move, speak, and act. Thus, texts that participate in "divine self-revelation" are loaded and overloaded with significance, presenting countless occasions for asking "Greek" questions, for linguistic interrogation, and spiritual interpretation.

The language of the Book, in both its encompassing plot and its little narratives, presents a God figured as divine Author, his words conveyed by inspired spokespersons, using a legacy of ancient metaphors and other figurative devices driving the narratives. These have been repeated, edited, revised, and handed down through unnumbered generations, an inheritance in the form of a house of language (maybe a prison house, as some contend).[5] Thinking of its reality-creating power, Wallace Stevens calls this legacy "a ruined mansion house" and declares on behalf of those earlier generations that "what we said of it became a part of what it is" ("Postcard from a Volcano").

As Steven Prickett argues, narratives do not merely tell stories. Each "of itself, constitutes a kind of 'knowledge'—a particular way of understanding the world" (*Narrative, Religion, and Science* 14).[6] The most powerful of reality-creating narratives are referred to as "grand narratives," those that seek to tell the story of everything from beginning to end.[7] Certainly, religions have their accounts of things as they are. The Bible, for example, is a grand narrative that begins "In the beginning" and ends at a moment just before a passionately anticipated End; so is the Qur'an (with its intertextual incorporation and amendment of both the Hebrew Bible and New Testament). So are the Hesiodic epics and the Babylonian Genesis, Enuma Elish—these latter texts concerned not with a plot that culminates at End Times, but rather with the ongoing realities of their world. Such narratives—metaphysical, public, and social—offer their hearers "knowledge" of themselves in the world and realms beyond.

Figuring the Unknown: Narratives as Figures in Motion

The Lord is a man of war. . . .

Exodus 15:3

Behold the Lamb of God . . . !

John 1:29

Praise be to God the Lord of all the worlds.

Qur'an 37:182[8]

I take it as broadly true that figurative language not only creates what people know of the metaphysical, but that it imposes on the everyday world, shaping mundane reality. Speaking of the role of figuration in "knowledge," Taylor observes that, "the imagination *informs* cognitive, *which is not necessarily to say conscious* [my emphasis], processes through the activity of *figuring*" (*After God*). That is, what one "knows" may originate through unconscious absorption of the "truths" conveyed through figuration, a term that covers a multitude of modes and processes. Taylor draws attention to the richness of the term *figure*, and its multiple uses and meanings, many of which are themselves figurative. *Figure,* he points out, can mean, "form, shape; an embodied (human) form; a person considered with regard to visible form or appearance; the image, likeness, or representation of something material or immaterial; an arrangement of lines or other markings forming an ornamental device; to form, shape; to trace, to embellish with a design or pattern . . . " (*ibid.* 20). A common usage, and one of central concern in this study, is "figure of speech." Another word for *figure* is *trope* (designating a linguistic "turn"). Both *figure* and *trope* are names for the imaginative processes whereby an abstract, unknown, or little-understood "something" is brought into the realm of "knowledge" through a concrete, known, understood representation. The use of figures in science, for example, helps make a theory communicable: before anyone had "seen" an atom, its structure was "understood" as being like that of the solar system.[9]

Figuration in the sciences helps to shape understanding of physical reality. A model or metaphor will prevail until a more satisfactory figure comes along. Thomas Kuhn (*The Structure of Scientific Revolutions*) has argued that scientific revolutions occur as a result of paradigm changes, the exchange of one model or metaphor for another that better explains the observed data. In science, the prevailing model or metaphor is continually subjected to scrutiny and discarded (like the earth-centered model of the universe) when an accumulation of data demonstrates its impracticability. In religion, figuration helps to shape understanding of *metaphysical* reality. Yet here figures have alarming longevity. Accumulated data have little influence. Such figures can endure largely intact through millennia, outlasting cultures and empires, traveling unnoticed from primitive to sophisticated systems of thought and belief, and through political and scientific revolutions. The metaphor of the deity as warrior is older than history and as young as today's newspaper. Metaphor, chief among the figures or tropes of resemblance, creates a merging of identity, taking the form, *A (the abstract, unknown, misunderstood) is B (the concrete, known, understood)*; for example, Yahweh is "a man of war."[10]

One might ask, who cares? It's just a figure of speech. Nevertheless, a point to keep in mind is that one's only "knowledge" of the metaphysical is through such devices. If God is a warrior, how does that affect his worshipers' attitudes toward war? A characteristic of all figures of speech, and especially of metaphor, is that insofar as language serves to communicate thought from one person to another, there must be an implicitly shared understanding of the relationship between the language of the figure and a referent, often an image (as of a warrior, for example—what Zoltan Torey calls "primary precept entities"). Figuration, while one of the great treasures of language as a means of advancing thought and enlarging realms of discourse (Johnson, especially 42–44; Corbett 459), has the effect of creating a "loosened nexus" between word and referent. It therefore has great creative power whose dark side is a "latitude for projection" (Torey 68–69).

The Book and its narratives are linguistic structures, *things made exclusively of words*, including those aspects of the stories of which no human being can have empirical knowledge: the running of time, supernatural beings, their nature and attributes, their venues, their motives, preferences, and dispositions. It is a problem to know just what to call this field of topics—the metaphysical, the transcendental, the supernatural, the sacred, the unknown. The sources I cite use all these terms. On this topic, Xenophanes, a Greek philosopher of the fifth century BCE, speaks of this unknown as "Thing." He makes the crucial point that "a Thing whose true description must owe nothing to the characters of those who describe it is beyond our reach: whatever we find it plausible to say It is will be what we find plausible. If it is absurd to think that the Thing is azure-haired and bearded (as it is), must it not also be absurd to think it rational?" (Cited in Stephen R. L. Clark 12). Although Xenophanes' term, "Thing," is fascinating (as is a related term, "Nothing"), I shall not use it. I tend to favor *the Unknown* and will be more or less consistent in my use of it. Nevertheless, the point I wish to emphasize here is that whichever term is used, the Unknown in all its aspects must necessarily be rendered in figurative language and must owe something (plausibility) to those who describe it.

Knowledge, on whatever firm or shifting ground it stands, is limited. Beyond the limits of knowledge one can only send linguistic probes—model, metaphor, analogy, figure—and beyond language is only silence. Gerhart and Russell put the matter this way:

> By means of a theory of limit, all understanding is itself understood to be partial in the sense that it points beyond the known-known and the known-unknown to the unknown-unknown (questions we can ask and answer, questions we can ask and can't answer, and questions we cannot even ask).
>
> 175

What are those questions we cannot even ask? We may push language forward and beyond, but there comes a point when it falters. Gerhart and Russell use David Tracy's term "limit-language" for the boundary beyond which language cannot go, which is a limit described and circumscribed by religious metaphors. The lexicons of ordinary discourse that serve well enough in the day-to-day world take on figurative attire the moment they attempt to cross the boundary into a darkness "which cannot be conceived, grasped, mastered, or controlled," an apt description of Gerhart and Russell's "unknown-unknown," and the sense implied in my term "the Unknown":

> However helpful a later metaphysical language may be [the language of philosophy or theology], *all authentic limit-language seems to be initially and irretrievably a symbolic and a metaphorical one* [my emphasis]. Insofar as the hidden dimension of an ultimate limit is not merely hidden but not even expressible in the language of everyday (as no-*thing*, no object in the world alongside other objects), that language retains the linguistic structure of metaphor and symbol.
>
> Tracy, *Blessed Rage* 108

Paradoxically, the *inexpressible* can only be *expressed* in everyday language. Karsten Harries similarly notices, "Metaphors speak of what remains absent." They point to a lack: "All metaphor that is more than an abbreviation for more proper speech gestures towards what transcends language" (82), including that about which "we cannot even ask." As the only available medium, a figure can serve as a light of sorts shown into the darkness of the Unknown and unknowable, rendering a portion of it speakable—even if only to announce its ineffability. The effect, for example, of projecting the metaphor *father* into the unseen and unknowable beyond the boundaries of nature and language is to *create* a space for a manlike population of one—Father.

Such necessarily figurative language routinely takes on a life of its own. Rhetorician Kenneth Burke analyzes the use of figures (especially metaphor) in religious discourse as terms drawn from the lexicons of nature, society, politics, and language—Lion, Father, King, Word: "Whether or not there is a realm of the 'supernatural,'" Burke argues, "there are *words* for it" (7); that is, figurative language creates "another world." Words, as he puts it, "may be used analogically to designate a further dimension, the 'supernatural.'" As a result, "There is a sense in which language is not just 'natural,' but really does add a 'new dimension' to the things of nature" (8). Inasmuch as "the supernatural is by definition the realm of the 'ineffable'" (15), that is, the unspeakable, any words used for "supernatural" persons, places, conditions, and events must be transported from the natural, sociopolitical, and linguistic orders and made to do figurative work in a "dimension" or realm that gradually assumes a space and shape—a reality—as its elements are figuratively named, for example, the throne of God or the Gardens of Paradise.

Words that move figuratively from the realm of nature to the supernatural (words like *father, creator, king, grace*, etc.), acquire supernatural implications—*Father, Creator, King, Grace*. A connotative load of supernatural meanings then enhances or transforms the words when subsequently they return to natural realms. As with the typical relationship between the vehicle and tenor of metaphor, there is an interaction resulting in an "exchange of particles" between the members of the equation. My favorite metaphor for the interactive aspect of metaphor is the case of the scientist and the fly in the film *The Fly*. The hapless scientist with his molecular disintegration and reintegration machine accidentally disintegrates and reintegrates himself and *the fly* that has entered the machine unseen. When he emerges, the scientist is something new—neither man nor fly but a third thing with characteristics of both. Metaphor has a way of creating that third thing. As with the scientist/fly, sometimes that thing is a monster. Another favorite metaphor—this for metaphor's reality-producing ability—is that of Colin Murray Turbayne, who suggests that metaphor is like the green-tinted glasses presented to the travelers as they arrive at the gates of the Emerald City. They don the glasses before they enter, and when the gates are opened, behold! The city is green, and "they believe they contemplate nothing but the un-made-up face of the truth" (*The Myth of Metaphor* 27).[11] As metaphor for the Unknown, the word *father*, for example, does not go innocently into the supernatural realms, but carries with it a human history and a wealth of associations—its sense of social authority, power, masculine gender, and (pro)creative virility. These particles of meaning necessarily attach to the divine. Once *father* and *Father* are figuratively identified, the status and power of supernatural fathers may be more readily applicable figuratively in enhanced natural situations—Father of his Country, Father of the Atom Bomb, etcetera.

Burke speaks of this phenomenon as a "double process" whereby the figurative application of words from nature to supernatural "things" changes the words so that when they return to the natural realm they carry particles of the preternatural (10). His discussion of the term *creator* provides an example:

> "Create" apparently comes from an Indo-European root meaning simply "to make" and having such Greek derivatives as the words for "strength" and "accomplish" (*krátos, kraíno*). In theology, it comes to have the meaning of production *ex nihilo*—and this in turn gives rise to the semisecularized view of poetic production as (in Coleridge's words) a "dim analogue of Creation."
>
> 8

Thus what began as an analogy projected into the heavens to foster understanding of the Unknown gets reversed and returns in this double process to the natural world, rendering *human* creativity, the original basis of the analogy, a "dim analogue" of God's creativity. Thus words from the human world applied to the Unknown make that Unknown figuratively "known." They speak into being a "dimension" as this or that sort of realm inhabited by this or that sort of being—the Unknown is a Creator, Author, Father. At the same time the language so used gets invested with supernatural sparkle. Through the naming process, the human *creator* (maker) becomes a first *Creator*, reducing human makers to imperfect imitators of the divine.[12] Human creativity thus becomes devalued in a figurative process by which divine creativity is created.

One has only to ask, "Why is there something rather than nothing?" and imagine a being responsible for the existence of "something"—the cosmos and its creatures.[13] God tells Enoch, "All thou seest, all things that are standing finished I tell to thee even before the very beginning, all that I created from non-being.... For before all things were visible, I alone used to go about in the invisible things" (Crane and Guthrie, *The Forgotten Books of Eden* 90). By this means, the unknown and unknowable "being" appears (partially "known") with the metaphor Creator, and with the name arrive associated attributes of elevation, power, mind, and boundless innovation.

THE MARVEL OF NOTHING

Once upon a time there was nothing; then something; then nothing again. But nothing had changed irredeemably.

Anon[14]

In God's account of creation from nothing, he has made use of negative morphemes (for example, *non-*, *in-*), a linguistic device frequently employed for describing the *Un*known. Being ("things") is created from *non*-being ("no-things"); before visible things were created, God went about in "*in*visible things." A negative morpheme helps to distinguish the Unknown sacred realms from the world of nature: they are *in*finite, consisting (in God's paradoxical term) of "*in*visible things"; gods, unlike humans, are *im*mortal; spirit, unlike body, is *in*visible, *in*substantial, or *a*physical (Burke 18–23).[15] St. Paul might be called a master of the negative in his definition of faith: "Now faith is the assurance of things hoped for, the evidence of things not seen. . . . By faith we understand that the world was created by the word of God, so that what is seen was made out of things that do not appear" (Hebrews 11:1–3). *Assurance* and *hope* negate each other, as does the notion of *evidence* ("visibility") of the invisible, "things that do not appear."

I am struck by an intriguing reversal here: with my metaphor of the mirror of heaven, I assert that humans create the Unknown, unseen "world" through *words* drawn from the realms of the seen. In Hebrews, however, the biblical author paradoxically privileges the negative, reversing the process (with Platonic overtones): visible nature is made by the transcendent, *un*seen *Word* (of God) from "no things"—"things" *un*seen—in this way prioritizing heaven and making the world a mirror reflecting an invisible heavenly array. Once "unseen things" have been given priority, the Unknown can be known linguistically through encompassing or superlative forms in partnership with negative designations. God and his acts are not *un*natural, but *super*natural. The *im*mortal is not just powerful, but omnipotent, "all powerful"; God is omniscient, "all knowing," omni-benevolent, "all good"; he is God All Mighty, wisest, best.[16] And if the most powerful, most respected of earthly inhabitants is king, then God is King of Kings.

Parapraxis and the Negative

> Yesterday, upon the stair,
> I met a man who wasn't there.
> He wasn't there again today.
> I wish, I wish he'd go away. . . .
>   Hughes Mearms, "Antigonish"

Yet another linguistic maneuver associated with the negative and used for the Unknown is called *parapraxis*, which was, in modern usage, a Freudian term for an error or "slip." In recent thought, *parapraxis* has come to describe a sort of sacred, purposeful catachresis involving the warping or contortion of language to express the otherwise inexpressible.[17] Taylor describes parapraxical writing as the "praxis of the 'para,'"[18] through which one might create a sort of linguistic edge for the presence/absence of the Unknown:

> This praxis involves the inscription of the boundary, threshold, margin, or limit. To write parapraxically is to write the limit as such rather than to write *about* the limit. . . . [I]n contrast to performative utterance, which always does *something* with words, parapraxis struggles to do *nothing* with words. It succeeds by failing. By doing nothing with words, parapraxical writing *stages* the withdrawal of that which no text can contain, express, or represent.
>
> *Tears* 224–25

Taylor's claim is that parapraxical writing is not exposition, but demonstration. Moreover, his explanation is, ironically but appropriately, a demonstration of parapraxical writing (it *succeeds by failing* or it *does nothing* by doing something—*staging the withdrawal* of the linguistically inexpressible).[19] Parapraxical writing occurs when language arrives at the border of the Unknown and disintegrates.

Parapraxical writing, Taylor adds, "undoes the coherence of signification." Citing Certeau, he explains that such writing "torments words in order to make them say that which literally they do not say" (*Tears* 226). The trope Taylor associates with parapraxical writing is, as mentioned, catachresis—a figure J. Hillis Miller defines as the "procedure of naming by figures of speech what cannot be named literally because it cannot be faced directly" (*Ethics of Reading* 21). Catachresis involves misuse, excessive use, or distortion of words by projecting them into alien situations. In general, one might say that any application of a term from nature to supernature involves the parapraxical, but I want to claim a difference between parapraxical writing (with its use of catachresis) and other figures used for the Unknown. That difference lies in the fact that catachresis is language misuse that is purposeful, artful, self-conscious, and even despairing—a language of last resort—and that it always results in a sort of contortion or mutilation. It frequently implicates syntax in the figurative distortions. Taylor cites a passage from Maurice Blanchot, which may serve as an example: "Now it was certain, something was approaching him, standing not nowhere and everywhere, but a few feet away invisible. . . . He felt ever closer to an ever more monstrous absence that took an infinite time to meet" (1). Or, more simply, "I met a man who wasn't there." In both cases "something" (monstrous, awesome, or frightening) emerges inexplicably from "nothing." It is, as it were, "not nowhere and everywhere," but a "few feet away," "present" even in its absence. St. Augustine quite readily shifts into parapraxical writing in his addressing God as "changeless, ever changing; never new, never old." Jesus resorts to the parapraxical when he proclaims, "Before Abraham was, I am" (John 8:58).

One of the more intriguing negative designations of the Unknown is "The Incomprehensible," meaning "That cannot be contained or circumscribed within limits; illimitable, boundless, infinite; immense" or "That cannot be grasped by the understanding; beyond the reach of intellect or research; unfathomable by the mind" (*OED*). It is hard not to notice the proliferation of negatives in the definition: one "comprehends" the Incomprehensible by understanding that one cannot understand. The paradoxical name suggests not only the futility of such naming, but also the oddness of telling stories about this ultimate mystery. Nevertheless, the moment the name appears it makes a story possible: "In the beginning, the Incomprehensible looked about. . . ." Authors of sacred texts necessarily set metaphor into narrative motion. Thinking again of the question, "Why is there something rather than nothing?" the attempt to bring an imagined *creator* of that something into the human linguistic realm and "comprehensibility" throws the language user into the figurative and the parapraxical, as is poignantly manifest in a third-century Greek text written in Egypt. The speaker addresses the Unknown, the man who wasn't there, as "Invisible Time": "I want you: *Invisible Time outlasting time right here / Kyrie / Lord / in good body for me to see*" (Doria 10–11).

Grammar and the Gods

Whatever has been fixed by a name, henceforth is not only real, but is Reality.
Cassirer, *Language and Myth* 58

Even the grammar in which a narrative is framed can affect the resulting reality. Grammatical gender, for example, plays a part in the figurative creation of the Unknown in personal forms as divine beings. Hebrew, Arabic, and most Indo-European languages (including Greek, the language of the New Testament) designate many nouns, their associated adjectives, and in some cases, their verb forms as either masculine or feminine. Speaking of the effect of grammatical gender in Hebrew and Arabic—the languages, respectively, of the Hebrew Bible (Old Testament)[20] and the Qur'an—Raphael Patai remarks, "With reference to the God-concept this gender-emphatic nature of Hebrew and Arabic has as its consequence that no statement can be made about, and no name given to, the deity without simultaneously designating the divine person referred to as either masculine or feminine" (*The Seed of Abraham* 192). Once the Unknown is designated as masculine, for example, and given a personal name, a number of other mundane metaphors attach almost unnoticed—"father," "king," "warrior," "lord," "husband," "shepherd," and more, depending on the position and disposition of the narrator. Such gender attachment to the Unknown undoubtedly contributes to the almost universal tendency to anthropomorphize deities.[21] In a similar way the Old and New Testament figures of Wisdom (Hebrew *Hokhma*; Greek *Sophia*) and Word (Greek *Logos*), although designating similar "first creations" by God, eventually take on personal forms reflecting the gender of the words in Hebrew (feminine) as the bride or lover of God (*Hokhma*) and Greek (masculine) as the Son of God (*Logos*).[22]

BURDEN OF A LEGACY

But where shall wisdom be found?
And where is the place of understanding?

Job 28:12

In this study, I explore and attempt to understand the tendency of peoples, ancient and modern, to name their "Ineffables" and "Incomprehensibles" and to create narratives about them. My claim is that such names and stories reveal much about the people who name and tell and absolutely nothing about the mysterious Unknown. The human habit of arranging the universe vertically (up is good; down is bad) makes of the space "up there," whether light or dark, sky or soaring mountain, the abode of deities and the scene of their actions.[23] If God is a warrior, there must be a heavenly host and armory; if God is a King, there must be a throne, a throne room, a banquet hall, and divine attendants. That space up there necessarily becomes a mirror reflecting the narrator and his or her natural, sociopolitical, and linguistic milieux created in the devices of language and the art of narrative. It is therefore not handwriting on the wall that concerns me, but that on the mirror of heaven, and the idea to keep in mind about mirrors is that they are always in some sense deceptive. They seem to open up a space behind their flat surfaces; they seem to reverse left and right, but not up and down; they may enlarge or otherwise distort; they may be "clouded" or colored, convex or concave. The reflected face of the beloved may be one's own, but as in the case of Narcissus, unrecognized.

The world's religions, past and present, offer a parade of deities—a crowd peering back from the mirror of heaven. An astonishing fact about them is that, for all the human imagining and linguistic work that produces them, they are seldom paragons of wisdom and virtue and are almost without exception terrifying. Superannuated ideas—primitive, Oriental, and Occidental—contribute to Western religious traditions and modern religious debates. The ancient tales tell of men and societies, anthropomorphic deities, their acts and motives, and life in a world of divinely manipulated events, all of which, taken together, fail to reflect modern ideals of Civilization—enlightened, benevolent, peace-loving societies whose citizens cooperate to eliminate ignorance, poverty, and disease in order to create a serene and prosperous world order. Despite the sophistications of modern theological analyses, the deities change little over the millennia and continue to show traces of ancient thought, a kind of sacred genetic code in which one can discover vestiges of features that endure beyond their usefulness, like the human appendix, that can nevertheless flare up and cause grave damage. Such features have an emotional or psychological appeal that worshipers find compelling. As an example, consider the ancient notion of the god's partiality for a particular individual, group, tribe, or nation over all others. A modern theologian might explain that the deity—by whatever name designated—is "universal," above all human divisiveness and strife, undertaking the care of all people. Against such a benign explanation one notices that believers tend to divide the world into two camps—the faithful and infidels, us and them, the saved and the damned, Protestant and Catholic, Christian and Jew, the House of Islam and the House of War. Such partial gods, protectors of the group, may have at one time emerged naturally from the interaction of species-specific and environmental factors. Alexander Eliot remarks, "People have been fighting since earliest time." What is more "reasonable" than to enlist the tribal deity in such struggles? Eliot continues,

> Eventually human combat grew to be the expected thing. As Edward Gibbon put the case (in his *Decline and Fall of the Roman Empire*), history itself "is a river of blood." So naturally combat has been a recurrent theme in world myth. Some of the earliest stories that we possess concern wars of the elements, of gods, of animals, of men and women, and of all these mixed together in various ways.
> *The Universal Myths* 198

Perhaps it would be fanciful to imagine that, given its verbal, figurative, narrative nature, the mirror of heaven might reflect something other than the enlarged image of human strife and history's river of blood.

Early attempts to name and narrate the story of the Unknown—gods, origins, meanings—serve as powerful explanations for the audiences of the storytellers. They tell them who they are, and describe their place in the universe, their relationship to the gods, their values, practices, origins, and current society. Dudley Young remarks, "Every culture finds its charter—its rules and identity—in the stories it tells of its beginnings." He speculates that "Genesis did this for us until . . . we increasingly looked to science to find out who we were and where we came from." He then raises interesting questions: "Can science replace religion? Can its stories replace the old mythologies?" (5). For many living in the age of Enlightenment, in whose early years the United States was founded, and continuing until a time not so long ago, the answer seemed a necessary "Yes." However, that answer becomes less emphatic now as ancient ideas bubble up from a mythic ooze, manifest in resurgent religious enthusiasm and fierce, even combative, devotion to both old and new grand narratives, revealing once more the power of narrative to create reality and assign meaning to the otherwise meaningless sweep of cosmic time.

In the chapters that follow, I observe the terrifying, grotesque, belligerent, benign, god-faces in the mirror of heaven. I explore the linguistic nature of divine beings in general, and, in particular, Yahweh, Allah, and Jesus, the gods who hold sway now in the Western world. These modern god-figures do not emerge *ex nihilo*. Samuel Noah Kramer identifies the predecessors of the West's modern deities as known through the sacred texts:

> [I]t is quite . . . obvious that for the history of the progress of our civilization as we see and know it today, it is the tone and temper, the word and spirit of the ancient mythologies, those of the Greeks and Hebrews, of the Hindus and Iranians, of the Babylonians and Egyptians, which are of prime significance. *It is the spiritual and religious concepts revealed in these ancient literatures which permeate the modern, civilized world.*
>
> Sumerian Mythology 27–28; emphasis supplied

From the earliest written accounts of the Unknown and the figures through which their narrators attempted to make it comprehensible until the present moment, that history is a record of metaphors, other tropes, and the narratives spun from them, supplemented, appropriated, and modified age after age. The earliest biblical stories appropriate the figures and plots of earlier texts; later Old Testament texts appropriate and supplement earlier ones; the New Testament appropriates, supplements, and modifies Old Testament figures and themes; Islam, likewise, appropriates, supplements, and modifies this entire tradition. Jesus saw himself as continuing or fulfilling the tradition of Mosaic law: "For truly I say to you, till heaven and earth pass away, not an iota, not a dot, will pass from the law" (Matthew 5:18). Likewise, Muhammad understood his revelation as confirming and supplementing biblical accounts. "We believe in God," he asserted, "and in what has been sent down to us and to Abraham, Ishmael, Isaac, Jacob and the Tribes. We believe in what has been given to Moses, Jesus, and the prophets" (Qur'an 3:84). As Aslan points out,

> The Qur'an, as a holy and revealed scripture, repeatedly reminds Muslims that what they are hearing is not a new message but the "confirmation of previous scriptures" (12:111). In fact, the Qur'an proposes the unprecedented notion that *all* revealed scriptures are derived from a single concealed book in heaven called the *Umm al-Kitab*, or "Mother of Books" (13:9).
>
> 99

A seldom-acknowledged fact, however, is that the old texts—insofar as they are held to be sacred—freeze time. Unchanged and unchanging, they reveal in the mirror of heaven ancient attitudes, prejudices, unexamined assumptions, limited concerns, and ignorance. The superannuated ideas and attitudes are thus verified and validated for a world vastly different from those from which they emerged. In what follows, I examine ancient literatures to demonstrate their influence on and presence in the Book, drawing primarily on Mesopotamian texts from Sumer and Babylon as well as Indo-European texts from Persia, Greece, and Rome. I give attention to the divine predecessors of Yahweh, Jesus, and Allah. I explore the metaphors and other figures by which the Unknown comes to be known, the narratives of sacred acts, the recurring topoi of divine lives and deeds, and details of their places of abode. I examine the realities created through the "plots" of unfolding divinely ordained human history from beginning to terrific, bloody, apocalyptic end.

THE CHAPTERS

I devote each of chapters 1 through 11 to a single type of figuration, its resulting narratives, and its implications. Chapters 1 and 2 explore various figures for time, the notion of narrative as time shelter, the problem of beginnings, the various figurative sorts of divine creation and procreation, the notion of time as a book produced by a divine author, and the evolution of a figure of eternity to be reached at End Times, anticipated by a certain, rather common "doom eagerness."

Chapter 3 focuses on the warrior metaphor for the divine, his officers' club heaven, and his battles against divine and human enemies.

Chapters 4 and 5 explore the metaphor of the human family, family relationships, and interactions as projected into the skies and reflected in the behavior of the gods. In connection with the father-son relationship, Chapter 5 examines the recurrence of sacred violence, the figurative basis for rituals of sacrifice, and the motifs associated with father murder and son sacrifice.

Chapter 6 takes up the figures of divine language—both spoken and written, including divine law codes—and the transformation of language at End Times. Chapter 7 is concerned with what I call the great figures of life and death, the development of dualist thought resulting from the merging of ideas from both East and West and, along with dualism, the emergence of a divine adversary.

Chapter 8 examines the economics of belief, traced through various covenants, systems of rewards and punishments associated therewith, and the relationship of contract to plot. Chapter 9 takes up phenomena associated with prophecy and their relationship to the plot of the divine text, the question of human freedom, and the logical improbability of heroism and villainy in the always already written story of human history. Chapter 10 raises questions concerning the uses of prayer and the efficacy of human petitions. Chapter 11 explores the "prophetic experience" and phenomenon of holy madness, its frequently debated, defined, and redefined relationship to reason and to epistemology. Chapter 12, "Reflections," offers an overview and attempts to draw conclusions from the work as a whole.

CHAPTER 1

IN THE BEGINNING: TIME AND THE FIGURATIVE FORMS OF CREATION

> In the beginning God created the heavens and the earth. . . .
> Genesis 1:1

> This is God, your Lord, there is no God but Him, the Creator of all things. . . .
> Qur'an 6:102

> [Augustine] wants to say that time began at the point at which the world was created.
> Wood 3

HOW DOES A MERE HUMAN BEING, limited in time and space, break into an eternal sweep of events in order to say, "In the beginning . . . "? As one author put it, "you will never reach the beginning, because behind every beginning there's always another 'Once upon a time'" (Gombrich, *A Little History of the World* 2). A narrator may resolve the difficulty by invoking an immortal informant who makes the decision for the storyteller. In his *Theogony*, the Greek theologian/poet Hesiod tells that the muses of Mt. Helikon, immortal daughters of Zeus and Mnemosyne, breathed a voice into him, granting him "power to sing the story of things of the future, and things past," including the birth of the gods (*Theogony* 29–32). An omniscient author tells the Babylonian epic of beginnings; he begins (as do Hesiod's muses) with the birth of the gods (Pritchard 31). The problem is solved in the Old Testament by hearing the story from

Yahweh himself, who inscribes the stories of beginning on tablets of stone (Exodus 31:18). Allah dictates to Muhammad the story of beginnings.

What does it mean—the beginning of time? Time, a human artifact, is among the most elaborate, influential, yet mysterious of things made of words. Philosophers recognize two orders of time: first, they use the term *cosmological time* for the fourth dimension of the physical universe; and second, they speak of *phenomenological time*, time as experienced and generally considered to encompass the past (personal and collective), the present (the razor's edge on which we attempt to stand, even as it disintegrates), and the future (the immense or brief duration of "unused" time streaming toward us).[1] Sometimes terms of more clearly theological import are substituted for these two sorts of time: *Chronos* and *Kairos*. Chronos corresponds to cosmological time, the billiard-ball progress of bodies reacting to physical laws of motion, cause and effect—mindless, determined, and meaningless. It is, Frank Kermode explains, "passing time," "that which according to Revelation, 'shall be no more.'" By contrast, Kairos is "the season, a point in time filled with significance, charged with a meaning derived from its relation to the end" (*The Sense of an Ending* 47). Contemplating the absurd, immeasurable running of cosmological time, and considering the infinitesimal brevity of an individual life or even of human history, one's vision can darken. Ovid's meditation on the relentless movement of time as process resorts to the ancient metaphor of time as a river that sweeps away everything and everyone: "Time like a river in its ceaseless motion; / On, on, each speeding hour cannot stand still . . . / The flying moment gone, what once seemed never, / Is now, which vanishes before we say it. . . . " (*Metamorphoses* 15, 419).

THE SEASON OF SIGNIFICANCE

Is there no change of death in paradise?
Does ripe fruit never fall?
                         Wallace Stevens, "Sunday Morning" vi

One means of responding to the mindless motion of Chronos is to create by means of narrative something that can be called a "time shelter," a "sense-making paradigm"—the "imposition of a plot on time."[2] Imagine a small house in a desert at night: the desert is Chronos; the interior of the house is Kairos, the season of significance. The house itself is the story. It interrupts the senseless flow of time and shelters those within from absurdity. Outside the structure, in obedience to physical law, a relentless wind drives sand through darkness across an endless landscape. Faced with the sweep of cosmic time, an ancient narrator begins, arbitrarily, with the first wall of the time shelter—"When there was nothing but fire and ice . . . " (Crossley-Holland 3); "When above . . . " (the opening words of the Babylonian creation epic); speaking as the Egyptian god Ra, "I made a platform in my heart talking it into act / there came / the many living things . . . " (Doria 83); "In the beginning God created the heavens and the earth . . . " (Genesis 1:1)—once upon a time. What is clear, given the metaphor of time shelter, is that both beginning and end are temporal metaphors for essentially spatial concepts. It is perhaps a happy accident that *plot* has both spatial and temporal implications. The beginnings and ends of plots are narrative walls beyond which cosmological time stretches forever into insignificance.

The space between beginning and end is that in which Kairos, the season of significance, dominates. In this space, histories are written and stories are told: "It was probably toward the end of the fourth millennium B.C., about five thousand years ago, that the Sumerians . . . "; "There was a man in the land of Uz, whose name was Job . . ."; "In the days when the judges ruled there was a famine in the land. . . . "[3] Grand narratives tell the whole story of the season of significance from Alpha to Omega. By this means, Kairos seeks ultimately to destroy Chronos—not merely to pause the flow of time's river, but to stop it dead. In apocalyptic accounts of End Times, the architectural metaphor of time shelter morphs into a time-evading, eternal "place"; as time transforms into space it is frozen. Those eternal places—Blessed Islands, Gardens of Paradise, or the perfectly symmetrical City of God—annul the effects of time. Individuals do not age or sicken or die; ripe fruit never falls. Concerning the architecture of Revelation, Steven Goldsmith argues that here prophecy is transformed into apocalypse, "when Revelation merges its own linguistic order with the sacred space of the New Jerusalem and makes both sites, verbal and architectural, *antithetical to history*" (*Unbuilding Jerusalem* 44; emphasis supplied).

What this maneuver suggests is that in addition to cosmological and phenomenological orders of time, there is available in narrative a third order—call it frozen time, or time-become-space, or, simply, eternity. But the subject is not exhausted even by three orders of time. The paradoxical term *timelessness* takes the spatialization of time even further, identifying a landscape of *omnitemporality*. Keith Ward explains:

> [S]ome Christian thought takes the supremacy of timelessness over temporality so far that even life after death is conceived as a sharing in timelessness. The thought of an experience somehow including the whole of time all at once recurs in more recent thought. Jurgen Moltmann has written that "in the eschatological moment all times will be simultaneous." That

is, at the end of linear time, the whole life of the universe will be wholly present, and so there will be "a future for what is past."

114

This notion of timelessness has its analogue in narratives enclosed within the covers of a book, or the Book. The book has a first page and a last page, a beginning and end, contained *within the space* or physical boundaries of its covers. Thus beginning and end and everything between are contemporaries and share "one equal coexistence."

The figurative nature of time and its forms complicates human attempts to create a coherent account of the place of humans—in time or out of it. Time is generally acknowledged to be a destroyer of all things mortal and all things crafted by human beings, including their plans, hopes, and aspirations. Ovid observes that "Time and Old Age eat all the world away— / Black-toothed and slow, they seem to feast forever / As all things disappear in time, in death" (*Metamorphoses* 15, 421). And Shakespeare observes that as time brings to fruition, it also kills:

> And so, from hour to hour, we ripe and ripe,
> And then from hour to hour, we rot and rot;
> *And thereby hangs a tale.*
> *As You Like It* 2:7:26–28; emphasis supplied[4]

"AND THEREBY HANGS A TALE"

Recognition of the inexorable passage of time and one's own extreme jeopardy within it fosters a majority of tales, including sacred narratives. The individual's progression from birth to death prompts speculations about origins and destinations, of persons, of cultures, nations, and empires, and ultimately of the universe. Through a narrative, a sense-making paradigm can be transferred figuratively from phenomenological time (the life of the individual) and superimposed on cosmological time, so that it becomes possible to create a cosmic shelter with walls at the beginning (birth) and the end (death) of time.

THE LINE AND THE CIRCLE

All things fall and are built again . . .
William Butler Yeats, "Lapis Lazuli"

A time to break down, and a time to build up . . .
Ecclesiastes 3:3

The pattern of existence may be represented by one of two figures—the line and the circle. In the linear view, human life proceeds "rationally" from birth (beginning) to death (end). Societies that understand human existence to be like that of animal life tend to work with the metaphor of the line—for human life, but also for history. They will favor cremation for their dead and consign them to a perpetual state of nonexistence in a place called Hades, Nifelheim, or Sheol—a place inhabited, in Homer's phrase, by "afterimages of used-up men" (*The Odyssey* 200). These places of crepuscular existence are populated by all the dead, just and unjust alike. At times one of the denizens of gloom may be roused from an endless sleep through a ritual in which charms are chanted or the dead are fed blood (considered the medium of the "life"). Odysseus performs such a ritual in Book 11 of *The Odyssey* so that he can consult the dead prophet Tieresias. Saul instructs the witch or medium of Endor to perform such a ritual in order to consult the dead prophet Samuel (1 Samuel 28:8–19). Odin rouses a long-dead seeress from her cold grave to discover Balder's fate (Crossley-Holland 148).

By contrast, the cyclical view (inspired by the vegetation cycle in which new "birth" emerges from the burial of "dead" seeds) finds that human existence includes a circling of a life essence through birth, death, and "rebirth." This metaphor transforms the linear birth-death configuration by adding a third phase—rebirth—either within nature or out of it. If within nature, the metaphor leads to the concept of reincarnation, if out of it, to eternal existence in a timeless place. This second possibility is in effect a synthesis of line and circle, and is characteristic of apocalyptic texts.[5] Hunters and herders tend to favor the metaphor of the line, farming cultures, that of the mystical cycle.

IN THE BEGINNING

So Eden sank to grief.
                    Robert Frost, "Nothing Gold Can Stay"

"Why is there something rather than nothing?" Apparently simple, the question nevertheless poses complex theological/philosophical problems for those who tell the story of beginnings. The answer usually evades realities of the universe in its unimaginable scope and duration and invokes the notion of creation: if there is something, "someone" must have made it. The answer requires adroit manipulation of the resources of language. This "something" about which one asks encompasses the empirical world—the earth, its flora and fauna, its human inhabitants, the phenomena of climate and weather, the visible heavenly bodies, and their movements. Where and why did it all originate? What force or power produced it? And for what purpose? Of what material does it consist? The creation analogy applies human making to divine beings: human beings are craftsmen, making things with their hands—pottery, weapons, houses, gardens—or they produce things out of their bodies—babies, excrement, spit, sweat, semen, breath, thoughts, words. Hence the reply: inasmuch as this immense "something" exists, some incomprehensible "someone" must have *made it or produced it*. In other words, the speculation is that there must be a first Creator (making things out of the materials at hand or of nothing) or Procreator (producing this "something" out of him- or herself). This maker or producer will be someone like a human but unimaginably grand in size or power. Given the two sorts of human creativity, figurative application dictates that the stories of beginnings will fall into two groups—procreators and creators. Among the world's narratives of origin, creators tend to be masculine; procreators tend to be feminine, although there are numerous exceptions. Procreators in some accounts are androgynous or come in pairs—male and female.

Procreators

> Now sound out the holy stock of the everlasting immortals
> Who came into being out of Gaia....
> Hesiod, *Theogony* 105–6

Some procreators, although figuratively, nominally, and predominantly male, appropriate the power of the womb.[6] An Egyptian account from c. 2300 BCE tells that in the beginning Ra, the sun-disc lord, became Khepera, a dung beetle rolling the "shitball sun." Khepera's hieroglyphic can be translated as "to come into being," "to become," or "to transform." Ra "conceives" through internal talking (thought) a platform in his heart, from which emerge the seeds of many living things. Subsequently, the sun-disc procreating lord self-inseminates, raining semen ("seedwater") into his mouth, and giving birth from his mouth and other orifices to the various conceptions in his heart, including divine and human beings (Doria 83–86).

Other procreators are found in Zoroastrian (Zurvan "Time"), Babylonian, Greek, and Norse tales of beginnings. Zoroastrian and Norse procreators (Zurvan and Ymir) are androgynous; the Greek Gaia (Earth) is female as is the Babylonian Tiamat. Zurvan produces twin sons, hypostases of good and evil; Gaia (with her son/consort Uranus) and Ymir (androgynously) produce broods of supernatural giants. Tiamat mates with Apsu and produces a generation of gods. From the original Nothing, Chaos, Time, Fire, Ice, or watery void, a procreator emerges, and produces a "platform" for the rest of creation. Ra "conceives" a platform in his heart; the living earth, Gaia, serves as an "unshakable foundation / of all the immortals" (Hesiod, *Theogony* 117–18). The corpses of Tiamat and Ymir serve as platforms (Thomas 12; Crossley-Holland 3). Within a generation or two ever more manlike deities emerge—Zeus and the Olympians, the Babylonian Marduk and his court, the Norse gods, Odin, Vili, and Ve.

Common in the world's tales of beginning is the identification of the birth-giver with nature or the earth, envisioned as a vast female body from which everything that lives is born: She is "Mother Earth." Greek (Gaia), Sumerian (Ashratum), Canaanite (Asherah), and Roman accounts include this figure, who bears the children of the divine sky-father. Her name in Hebrew is Adamah, from whom her substance (earth) is taken and combined with divine mist to produce the first clay man.

In his story of beginnings, Hesiod begins with Chaos (a fluid, "masculine" concoction of all the elements—fire, air, earth, and water)—a meaningless, timeless anticosmos. The first firewall is erected and the narrative begun as Gaia (Earth) extricates herself from Chaos (leaving fire, air, and water [*Theogony* 117–18]). Another offspring emerging from Chaos is "black Night," a terrible female who gives birth to a host of abstractions and horrors. The process, as in the Norse tradition is to move in steps toward the emergence of ever more manlike gods. Here the progression is from primordial matter (Chaos), to personified Earth and Heaven, to the giant generation of Titans, and finally to the anthropomorphic Olympians whose lives and realms mirror the Greek sociopolitical ideal—a patriarchal family led by Zeus, "Father of Gods and Men," the ultimate ruler, warrior, and propagator.

The ruling idea of Hesiod's account (as in other tales of procreators) is that the "something" all about him, including heaven and earth, is the product of sexual generation. The Enuma Elish, for instance, also begins with a chaotic mixture of sweet and salt water and mist that form an "immense, undefined mass in which were contained all the elements of which afterward the universe was made" (Heidel 3). The story of beginnings almost immediately personifies salt water and sweet as the sea monster Tiamat and her consort, Apsu, who, like Hesiod's Gaia and Uranus, produce divine offspring and initiate a series of generations that results in a crowd of boisterous, anthropomorphic gods. Their energy and noisy conviviality anger the monstrous matriarch and patriarch. This situation prompts a conflict in which a young god, Marduk, defeats the ancient Tiamat (watery chaos monster). At this point the rule of procreators ends, as Marduk, a creator, begins to bring order to chaos and construct the world of the Babylonians from the corpse of his great-grandmother.

The metaphor, earth is body, is common, whether the body be dead (Tiamat, Ymir) or "living" (Gaia, Adamah)—"Mother Earth," the matter of creation. In Ovid's flood narrative, the goddess Themis instructs the surviving man and woman (Deucalion and Phyrra) to regenerate the human race by scattering the "mother's bones." Deucalion recognizes that "our Great Mother is the Earth, her bones / Are guiltless stones we throw behind us." Having scattered the pebbles as they go, they find an autochthonic race emerging from the "Great Mother":

> Pebbles grew into rocks, rocks into statues
> That looked like men; the darker parts still wet
> With earth were flesh, dry elements were bones,
> And veins began to stir with human blood. . . .
> Ovid 42

The earth mother leaves traces as well in the name Adam gives the woman after the Fall—Eve, "mother of all living," another epithet for Mother Earth or Mother Nature.

Genesis presents two accounts of creation. In Chapter 1, Yahweh is a procreator who, like the Egyptian Ra, "thinks" and then "talks" things into being. And like both Ra and Marduk, he confronts a dark, watery chaos—the deep (*Tehōm*), the "Hebrew counterpart" of the Babylonian Tiamat (Forsyth 48). Like Ra and the Zoroastrian Ahura Mazda, Yahweh is associated with light, and his first divine fiat is to command, "'Let there be light'" (Genesis 1:3). But as in Ra's primordial scene, there is no "platform" in the formless void, and so Yahweh speaks the firmament into being—a way of containing the primordial waters: "Let there be a firmament in the midst of the waters, and let it separate the waters from the waters" (Genesis 1:6). Yahweh names the firmament Heaven, envisioned as a dome arching over the nether waters like an umbrella, holding at bay the "waters above the firmament," and thus creating a space for the placement of sun, moon, and stars in a subsequent fiat. Further control of the deep is accomplished when Yahweh commands, "Let the waters under the heavens be gathered together into one place and let the dry land appear" (Genesis 1:9). Having achieved control of the chaotic water,[7] he then proceeds to speak into existence the vegetation, heavenly bodies, birds, great sea monsters, fish, and land animals. The procreativity of Yahweh rivals that of Ra. Although the narrative contains no explicit notion of Yahweh's self-inseminating his "conceptions," later Christian texts will hint at the possibility through the figurative personification and designation of God's Word (Logos) as Son:

> In the beginning was the Word, and the Word was with God, and the Word was God. He was in the beginning with God; all things were made through him, and without him was not anything made that was made. In him was life, and the life was the light of men.
> John 1:1–5

The figurative "facts" of the situation are complex. God conceives, speaks, and what he names *is*: light, firmament, vegetation; the words are/become things—the substance of the "something" about which one inquires. Substance—the word as thing—emerges from the Insubstantial, as in Yahweh's announcement to Enoch that he created "all things" from "non-being" (Crane, *The Lost Books of the Bible* 90).[8] Yahweh confronts nonbeing in its figurative form as a dark, watery chaos and defeats it by speaking: "Let there be light." In the quotation from John (an intertextual reference to and interpretation of the Genesis passage), the speaking (word) and the thing (light) are identified with the Son, known metaphorically as the Word and the "Light of the World" (John 8:12).[9] A shift occurs at the end of this Genesis account, as Yahweh speaks to unidentified others, "Let us *make* man in our image." It is an arresting moment, for not only does God transform from procreator to creator just then, but simultaneously the text offers a glimpse in the mirror of heaven of the "appearance" of God in the image of man, a reflection of man "in the image of God."

CREATORS

> Then the Lord God formed man of dust from the ground. . . .
> Genesis 2:7

> It was He who created all that is on the earth for you, then turned to the sky and made the seven heavens. . . .
> Qur'an 2:29

Some creation narratives depict primordial beings who have emerged from primordial matter or have been coeternal or even identical with it, and who contain the universe *in potentia* within themselves, thinking, speaking, sweating, ejaculating, birthing, or otherwise producing the universe from within. A common pattern is to proceed from processes of procreation to those of creation (Norse, Babylonian, Genesis 1). In many cases the metaphor of procreation leads to the birth (beginning) of an evolved being in a subsequent generation who then becomes a creator, a craftsman or artisan who takes a hands-on approach to the making of man and world. In the Norse tales, the procreation of Ymir is ultimately succeeded by the creation of the world and humankind by Odin and his brothers. For this task, the three gods attack and kill Ymir, and like human builders—*bricoleurs*, to use Lévi-Strauss's term—construct from his corpse a world in the gap between fire and ice. The Norse "firmament" consists of Ymir's skull, held in place at four corners by dwarfs. The three gods then place sun, moon, and stars in their places. Soon after, the gods discover two fallen trees, from which the divine artisans carve the first man and woman; then, "Odin breathed into them the spirit of life," along with feeling hearts and perceptive minds (Crossley-Holland 5). The Norse reality offered an understanding of humankind in sharp contrast to the Babylonian view. After constructing the earth and heavens from the corpse of Tiamat, another *bricoleur*, Marduk, ordered that a race of puppet-men be formed from the blood or life substance of the rebel god Kingu for the sole purpose of serving the gods (Thomas 12).

Hesiod's account of the creation of the first woman reveals much about himself, his culture, and his contemporaries. He tells the story twice, the only narrative appearing in both *Works and Days* and *Theogony*. In each case, however, the motive given for the creation of woman is to punish men. Hesiod describes a time before her creation when the earth-born "races of men" lived in a sort of masculine paradise "free from all evils, free from laborious work, and free from all wearing sicknesses." (There may be a suggestion that while they were happy and healthy, they were uncivilized, unmotivated, and not very bright.) Prometheus angered Zeus by changing the dynamics. He gave men fire (figuratively: consciousness, culture, and passion) that Zeus had withheld. In retaliation Zeus commanded the other gods to create/construct a beautiful evil—made of earth and water, with a "face like the immortal goddesses." She would have the "mind of a hussy, and a treacherous nature." Her human voice would utter "wheedling words of falsehood." When all was finished Hermes gave her "the name of woman, / Pandora," bearing the gods' "gifts" to be a "sorrow to men."[10] She arrives on the masculine scene with a great jar containing all the ills of existence, which with malicious intent she spills into the world, "and her design was sad troubles for mankind" (*Works and Days* 57–95). In retelling this narrative in the *Theogony*, Hesiod adds the detail that "this sheer deception is more than mortals [i.e., men] can deal with, / For from her originates the breed of female women" (589–90).

Hesiod's powerful tale permits the gods and heavens to reflect both his own and his society's biases, here given figurative existence and a narrative that legitimizes for posterity his reality, including his misogyny. Created as a punishment, women enter and destroy an ideal world. They are a necessary evil, required to propagate the species (after men are no longer "earth-born"),[11] but nevertheless the cause of untold suffering—"troubles by thousands that hover about men, / for the earth is full of evil things, and the sea is full of them" (*Works and Days* 100–101). Hesiod makes their role a divinely mandated one—to bring evil into the world and remain for all time a troubler of men.

Ovid provides another creator in the classical tradition. As do others, he begins with Chaos, a brew of potential life: "[A]ll Nature was all Chaos, / The rounded body of all things in one, / The living elements at war with lifelessness." His God, "whichever God he was, created / The universe we know." Ovid's unnamed God (like the Old Testament Yahweh) calms the seething elements, separating earth from sky, air from water, and makes the earth, a "delicately poised" sphere with all its waters, winds, valleys and meadows, mountains and climactic zones; he creates weather in all its manifestations. He sets the stars aflame and enlivens the whole, creating fish, beasts, and birds. Finally, he creates man, "a creature that had hints of heaven":

> So man was made.
> Whether He who made all things aimed at the best,
> Creating man from his own living fluid [divine semen],
> Or if earth, lately fallen through Heaven's aether,
> Took an immortal image from the skies,
> Held it in clay which son of Iapetus [Prometheus]
> Mixed with the spray of brightly running waters—
> It had a godlike figure and was man.
> While other beasts, heads bent stared at wild earth,
> The new creation gazed into blue sky. . . .
>
> Ovid 31–33

One is struck by Ovid's diffidence. He does not claim to know the name of the creator God; he does not know how man, the "godlike figure," came to be—whether made of divine fluid by God (a procreator) or of clay and water by Earth and Prometheus (creators) in an "immortal image from the skies." As mentioned, the Enuma Elish and the first account of creation in Genesis both describe the making of humankind in what Ovid might have called "an immortal image from the skies." The notion of a divine image persists in modern religions.

In the second and older biblical account of creation in Genesis 2,[12] Yahweh is first procreator, and then creator. The initial situation is one not of too much water (as in Chapter 1), but of too little, suggesting the tale's origin in an arid region. Before God causes it to rain, there are no plants, no animals, and no humans. There are only Yahweh and Adamah, "earth," a dyad similar to that in the Greek tale of Uranus (heaven) and Gaia (earth). In this account Yahweh is undeniably anthropomorphic, a god in the image of man. At this beginning moment of divine insemination, the life-giving divine waters appear as a "mist" that "watered the whole face of the ground" (Genesis 2:6). Then, like a human sculptor, God takes earth and water and fashions a clay man. In an almost comical act he breathes "into his nostrils the breath of life; and man became a living being" (Genesis 2:7).[13] The metaphoric sculptor-god is common in the world's accounts of beginnings and includes not only Yahweh but also Marduk, Hephaistos (maker of Pandora), the Egyptian Ptah (Leeming 148), Prometheus (Ovid 33), and Allah.

When it seems prudent to create a human counterpart for the man, the Yahwist's creator God turns from sculpting to scrimshaw, crafting a woman from one of Adam's ribs, an act similar to that of the Norse gods' carving the man and woman from trees. In an "unnatural" reversal of human procreation, where the man comes from the woman, in the case of Adam and Eve, Adam's "priority" and superiority are elaborated in countless interpretations of the narrative. A particularly explicit statement is found in the Second Book of Enoch where God describes for Enoch the creation of Eve:

> And I put sleep into him [Adam] . . . . And I took a rib from him, and created a wife for him that death should come to him by his wife, and I took his last word and called her name mother, that is, Eva.

As in the Greek narrative of Pandora, the woman enters a world of masculine perfection bringing danger, sorrow, and death. God goes on to explain to Enoch that the Devil "nurtured thoughts against Adam," so "he entered his world and seduced Eva but did not touch Adam" (Barnstone 6). In Genesis, Adam is condemned to death for having "listened to the voice of [his] wife" (2:17–19).

This Western foundational tale with its acknowledgement of death and misogynistic bias has deep roots, for an ancient Sumerian motif is evident in the Genesis account. One of the epithets for earth (Adamah) is "mother of all living," the title Adam gives to Eve ("living"), because she is "the mother of all living." Kramer has noticed that the narrative of the rib and the naming of the woman were carried over from a Sumerian tale involving a pun on the Sumerian homonyms *rib* and *live*, a pun that must have originally fostered a narrative about the creation and naming of woman, but that loses its double entendre when translated into Hebrew (*History Begins at Sumer* 144). In any case, the metaphors of the rib and the male birth reverse and comment on the numerous tales that make Mother Earth primary, and the man her child. In Genesis, Eve, "living," actually brings death into Yahweh's pristine garden-world.

SOMETHING, RATHER THAN NOTHING

The question, "Why is there something, rather than nothing?" seeks a purpose for existence. In response, authors of grand narratives break into the sweep of cosmological time, creating time shelters—"In the beginning . . . "—presenting "sense-making paradigms" that must necessarily mirror the human condition, human fears, cultural biases, and physical and social conditions of the world in which and to which the author speaks. J. M. Bernstein defines grand narratives in terms that delineate them from narratives-in-general: "Typically, a grand narrative will make reference to some ultimate originating principle [beginning] or ultimate *telos* [end]; it will seek to place existing practices in a position of progress toward or regress from the originating principle or ultimate end" (102). Grand narratives, figurative in nature and endlessly interpretable, work not despite the absence of empirical corroboration, but rather because of it. They enjoy a reality-creating power ascribed so often to God or the gods. Their figurative constitution requires that we ask about the sorts of satisfaction they provide to those who live, struggle, work, and die in their shadows. One might do well to ask, why adopt these particular figures? Why impose this particular plot or time shelter on the running of cosmological time? Why embrace this particular language-made image of history, of life, of humankind? Why *this* something?

I have been arguing for the language-made nature of heavens and earth, "the way things are." Humankind uses and reuses figurative language to create the gods and heavens, its persons and places, to reflect and validate its own peculiar world and ways, and authorize its continued subservience to ancient metaphors and the tales in which they are set in motion. Human time is figurative for universal time. As one begins, so the world begins—abruptly, dramatically—born into light and the running of time from a dark, watery womb. The defeat of the chaos water signals the beginning. As one dies, so dies the world—abruptly, dramatically. I turn my attention next to the end of the grand narrative.

CHAPTER 2

END-TIMES AND DOOM-EAGERNESS

> If anyone's name was not found written in the book of life, he was thrown into the lake of fire.
>
> Revelation 20:15

> God promises the Fire of Hell as a permanent home for the hypocrites, both men and women, and the disbelievers: this is enough for them.
>
> Qur'an 9:68

> Apocalypse depends on a concord of imaginatively recorded past and imaginatively predicted future, achieved on behalf of us, who remain "in the middest."
>
> Kermode, *The Sense of an Ending* 8

CRITICS FROM THE TIME OF ARISTOTLE speak of the doctrine of narrative inevitability: stories that begin must end, and end in a way that is congruent with their beginnings and their middles. Frank Kermode refers to this relationship as "consonance." In the preceding discussion of beginnings, I have noted that in grand narratives the beginning is problematic and often abrupt (like a birth), initiating the running of time (analogous to a human lifetime); the middle will tell of time, all of human history; and, as seen from the narrative perspective, the end (corresponding to death) will follow *necessarily* from the beginning and the middle. This is the "imposition of plot" (*The Sense of an Ending* 5).[1]

TIME IS A BOOK: GOD IS ITS AUTHOR

The metaphor, God is an Author, becomes pertinent when one considers the "Plot of Plots." Yahweh dictated and engraved "the two tables of the testimony, tablets of stone, written with the finger of God" (Exodus

31:17–18). God's authorship and plot make the Book a book of destiny (or truth, or life). Religious grand narratives require not only divine authors but also a perspective on time from "outside time," from which the whole design may be plotted from beginning to end. The narrative's structural concordance is partially responsible for one's sense of the outcome's inevitability. Speaking of the progress of a plot, Forsyth makes this point: "We owe the *notion of fate* to analogy with the shape of narrative inevitability; one projects onto the cosmos the shape that personal events have achieved once they become narrative events, once the tale is told. In a Christian context . . . God is understood as the ultimate author of this narrative reasonableness" (16). On this subject of divine authorship and narrative inevitability, early theologian and philosopher, Boethius, questioned his Christian muse, Philosophy, about the possibility of deviation from the "plot":

> "I want to know whether thou deemest that there is any such thing as chance at all, and, if so, what it is." . . . [Philosophy] made answer: . . . "I roundly affirm that there is no such thing as chance at all, and consider the word to be altogether without meaning. . . . What place can be left for random action, when God constraineth all things to order?"
> *Consolation of Philosophy* 173–74

In a Christian context, this metaphor of divine authorship (of the book and human history) and the inevitability of its progress are referred to as Providence, which directs the course of events from the momentous (for example, the Flood) to the trivial: "Are not two sparrows sold for a penny? And not one of them shall fall to the ground without your Father's will. But even the hairs of your head are numbered" (Matthew 10:29–30).[2] Several matters converge here: (1) the concept of narrative (book, plot and the imposition of structure on unsorted, insignificant events); (2) a required congruence of beginning, middle, and end; (3) inevitability of events; (4) relationship of plot (beginning, middle, end) to time and space; and (5) writing it all, God, Author of authors. As discussed in Chapter 1, in its temporal dimension plot unfolds in time (as told, or read), but the tale *as book* (especially *the* Book) is an object in space; its end and beginning are always copresent and their relationship fixed. Within the written book, all times become present, taking on the character of space. The idea suggested by a theory of End-Times is that the human story has already been "written," although we remain "in the middest," still reading, living.

Leland Monk, addressing the matter of narrative inevitability, remarks:

> [C]hance marks and defines a fundamental limit to the telling of any story: *chance is that which cannot be represented in narrative.* . . . [Yet this

study's] operating premise is the conviction that without chance there would really be no stories to tell.

9–10; emphasis supplied

If one considers this claim in regard to the grand narrative of the Bible and the Qur'an, one encounters, quite early on, what might be called not chance exactly, but the *semblance* of chance, or, if you will, a garden of forking paths. My claim is that the *semblance* of chance is all any tale can offer.

In this regard I think of the darkly comical story of the Fall in Genesis 2–3. It tells of a time in the beginning when two humans lived in a garden-world, free of toil, pain, sorrow, and mortality, at home with the animals and freely conversing with Yahweh, their creator. As God places the newly formed clay man in the garden he has planted, he seems to announce the existence of two paths, and hence choice and chance: "You may freely eat of every tree of the garden [including the tree of life]; but of the tree of the knowledge of good and evil you shall not eat, for in the day that you eat of it you shall die" (Genesis 2:16–17). The two mythical trees apparently offer a choice: life or death. However, even ignoring the matter of God's motive for placing the tree of forbidden fruit in the center of the garden and his apparent plan for history, a simple consideration of plot requires that the man eat the fruit of knowledge and death. Without that act, there would be no story. As Joseph Campbell points out, the tale contains a motif well known to folklorists—the "one forbidden thing" motif (*Occidental Mythology* 110). Readers recognize it and see that the one forbidden act is exactly that which the protagonist must perform—whether or not inadvertently. Theologians and exegetes have nevertheless long attempted to decide whether the eating of the fruit was necessary to God's purposes. But of course it was. With the plot set in motion and God's constraining all things to order, human time unrolls, an already-written scroll. In the course of that history no chance occurrence can intervene to alter the text of God's authorship—no sparrow fall without the Father's will; no hair be lost.

Many naive plots end in perpetuity. "And they lived happily ever after" is, of course, the fairy-tale ending, but also that of the Bible: "God . . . will wipe away every tear from their eyes, and death shall be no more, neither shall there be mourning nor crying nor pain any more" (Revelation 21:3–4). The language of the Qur'an is similar, with a promise to those who are "foremost in good deeds": "they will enter lasting Gardens. . . . They will say, 'Praise be to God, who has separated us from all sorrow. . . . He has, in His bounty, settled us in the everlasting Home where no toil or fatigue shall touch us'" (Qur'an 35:32–35).[3] In keeping with narrative congruence, the timelessness, ease, absence of strife, and community with

God of the first garden will return, and, unlikely as it seems, humans who have written their history in blood, exalted their warriors and warrior-gods, and inhabited a world of endless strife will—so the apocalyptic story has it—find eternal peace satisfactory.

Inasmuch as humans are creatures of and in time, the narrative impulse to end time is peculiar. Kermode comments, "[T]he End is a figure for [one's own] death." Men "fear it, and as far as we can see have always done so" (*The Sense of an Ending* 7). Perhaps only a bold figurative maneuver can have neutralized that fear and account for the apocalyptic longing that characterized the end of the Old Testament period, flourished in the intertestamental period, colored the tone of Jesus' ministry and the Pauline epistles, achieved its extreme statement in the book of Revelation and the Qur'an, and remains alive among countless Christians and Muslims today. The figurative maneuver that encourages End-Time longing calls on the ancient metaphor of the vegetation cycle: what dies and falls into the ground will live again—will be resurrected, like Tammuz, Dumuzi, Osiris, Adonis, Dionysus, Persephone, and Jesus.

Life and Death in the World before the Figure of Resurrection

Thou turnest man back to the dust . . .

Psalms 90:3

The vegetation metaphor plays little role in Old Testament thought concerning life and death. Its texts accept a linear view of human existence and the universal destiny of creatures to be born, live, and die.[4] Therefore, in general, value resides in the pleasures of long life, health, family, and possessions. In this regard, the texts follow the precedent of millennia of thought. The *Epic of Gilgamesh,* dating from "the turn of the second millennium" BCE (Pritchard 40), not only exhibits the terror aroused in the protagonist by the death and physical corruption of his friend, but also the futility of seeking immortality. After a long, bitter quest for the secret of eternal life, Gilgamesh learns from a wise woman, Siduri (a sort of divine barmaid), that he will not find the immortality he seeks because the gods "set aside / Life" for themselves (Pritchard 64). Ecclesiastes delivers a similar message: Man and beast "all go to one place; all are from the dust and all turn to dust again" (3:20). Yet this life is intended for pleasure: "Go eat your bread with enjoyment and drink your wine with a merry heart; for God has already approved what you do" (9:7). In a similar vein, proverbial wisdom promises *earthly* rewards for just or wise behavior: long life (Proverbs

10:27), offspring, and prosperity (Proverbs 13:21; 24:3–4). In a reality in which Sheol is the common destination all, God must bestow rewards for righteous behavior *in this life*. Similarly, the unjust or foolish must suffer punishment for their behavior *in this life*—illness, poverty, and loss of land.

THE FIGURES OF RESURRECTION AND ETERNITY—NO END IN SIGHT

> Their hope was rich with immortality.
> Wisdom of Solomon 3:4

> It is for you that paradise is opened, the tree of life is planted, the age to come is prepared, plenty is provided, a city is built, rest is appointed, goodness is established and wisdom perfected beforehand.
> 2 Esdras 8:52

Among Old Testament books, only Daniel offers the possibility of immortality, mentioning briefly that the righteous will "awake to everlasting life" (12:1–3). Still, the direction taken in Daniel will flourish. A somewhat later (first century BCE), deuterocanonical author, influenced by Greek philosophical speculations on the soul's immortality, articulated at greater length the doctrine of immortality introduced in Daniel: "For God created man for incorruption, / and made him in the image of his own eternity" (Wisdom of Solomon 2:23; see Stephen L. Harris 301–2), and other apocalyptic texts continued to expand and specify the doctrine. The Wisdom of Solomon, composed during the intertestamental period (c 165 BCE–150 CE), is indicative of a world-changing shift away from a strict linear view of existence resulting from adoption into biblical literature of a vegetation metaphor; assimilation of Greek philosophical ideas of a dualistic universe consisting of the ideal and the material, or, as translated into New Testament terms, spirit and body; and an idea popular in Greek mystery religions of a transformed vegetation god who offers his or her initiates the secrets of resurrection of the dead and immortality of the soul.

Along with these developments comes a revision of ideas of divine justice. If the soul is immortal, divine justice will operate not in this world, where the suffering of the virtuous and felicity of the wicked may be apparent, but in the "next world," where rewards and punishments are awarded in a final, irrevocable, and eternal Last Judgment. Old Testament notions of the blessings of life, health, and prosperity in the world of time are rejected and replaced by contempt for all things worldly, whose condition is pitifully brief in comparison with "eternity." In this vein, Jesus instructs his followers to "go, sell what you possess and give to the poor, and you will have treasure in heaven"; indeed earthly riches may be a detriment, rather than a blessing. Pleasures of the world and physical bodies are now understood as not only of brief duration and therefore of little account, but actually evil, drawing the soul away from its contemplation of eternity. "It will be hard for a rich man to enter the kingdom of heaven" (Matthew 19:21, 23). Similarly, the Qur'an will instruct, "Striving for more distracts you until you go into your graves.... You will most definitely see Hellfire" (102:1–6). From such attitudes and the acceptance of immortality emerge a privileging of death (of the body) and apocalyptic longing—for the end of a flawed world, the material of which it is made, and the corruptible bodies that inhabit it

In a world dominated by the figure of vegetal renewal, death is to be desired as the gateway to Life; life is existence in a world of Death. The Jewish author of the Wisdom of Solomon rejects the linear view of the "ungodly" as reasoning mistakenly that "[s]hort and sorrowful is our life, and there is no remedy when a man comes to his end, and no one has been known to return from Hades." These "ungodly ones" expect that dead means dead: "When [the spark of reason] is extinguished, the body will turn to ashes, / And the spirit will dissolve like empty air" (Wisdom of Solomon 2:1–3). In an early version of the *carpe diem* theme, the "ungodly" say, "Let us crown ourselves with rosebuds before they wither" (Wisdom of Solomon 2:6, 8). The author is one of many who adopt a modified vegetation metaphor (along with notions of rebirth, final judgment, and eternal life). With the shift of metaphors the plot of plots takes a direction from which, thus far, it has not swerved.

END-TIMES AND THE ETERNAL GARDEN

> The age is hastening swiftly to its end.... For the evil ... has been sown, but the harvest of it has not yet come.... For a grain of evil seed was sown in Adam's heart from the beginning, and how much ungodliness it has produced until now and will produce until the time of threshing comes!
> 2 Esdras 4:26–30

Biblical authors are not unique in their awareness of living in a world of suffering and injustice and thinking that things might have been different. Humans in many times and places have imagined perfect existence as residence in a lush land or garden with clement weather, where the worthy individual is immortal, and labor is unknown. The earliest Sumerian and Babylonian texts already speak of Dilmun, a distant locale described as "the place where the sun rises" and "the Land of the Living." As a place of immortality, the imagined land is necessarily timeless and seasonless, where "Snowfall is never known" and "the West Wind always blow[s]" (Homer, *Odyssey* 69). Nature produces its riches without human labor (Hesiod, *Works and Days* 167–72); "Corn will ripen in fields that were never sown" (Crossley-Holland, "Ragnarok" 175). This land of immortality may be an island, a place at the world's end, like the Greek Elysion (Homer, *Odyssey* 69; Hesiod, *Works and Days* 168), in "the Faraway," beyond the borders of the world on the other side of the "waters of death" as in the Sumerian/Babylonian home of Utnapishim (Pritchard 64), or it can be removed to an Underworld, as in Virgil.

What is important to know about the perfect place is not where it may be found, but *for whom it is provided*. The ancient Sumerians, Babylonians, Greeks, Romans, and Norsemen understood that there was no escape from time and death. The few exceptions to the universal law—for example, the Sumerian/Babylonian Utnapishtim, the Old Testament's Enoch and Elijah, a Greek half-god, or a Norse hero—are just that, exceptions. Dilmun, Elysion, and Heaven remain out of reach for humanity.

The Old Testament accepts this common understanding and provides for the dead a mere warehouse, Sheol (Greek Hades). It does, however, offer a representation of timeless perfection—closed to human beings since the beginning of time, gated and guarded through all of history. The biblical narrative begins and pauses a brief moment in the perfect garden; the Old Testament ends with predictions of a restored Jerusalem, fruitful land, and close association with Yahweh—all aspects of that state of beginning; the New Testament gathers up the Old Testament pattern and predictions and returns humans to the perfect place, the garden which is also a city—New Jerusalem. Similarly the Qur'an provides for the blessed eternal Gardens. Given this beginning, and the common complication of disobedience and fall, these plots, each in its time, proceed to congruent endings. Inasmuch as the loss of the garden is the precipitating event, the place of beginning does not fade away or become irrelevant, but haunts the plot and imposes requirements on the progress of the narrative.

Thus, in some later Old Testament texts, aspects of the ancient garden reappear in conjunction with God's restoration of a remnant of his people to a rebuilt Jerusalem. New Testament authors, after a crucial shift of figurative thinking, project the image, transformed, into the future, at "the end" of the story. Between the first garden and its reappearance, the plot unfolds; time (God's season of significance) runs through the world and human history with destructive force, annihilating individuals, peoples, nations, and empires in accordance with God's authorship. Eden as the biblical site of original existence works on the analogy of childhood as a time/place of innocence, leisure, and happiness. Many traditions create a story of such a time and place, beginning with a Golden Age. Hesiod tells of a time without labor, pain, or old age, when men were "on friendly terms with the blessed immortals" (*Works and Days* 113–20). Ovid, too, speaks of a first Golden Age, characterized by peace, ease, innocence, a perpetual spring—when "The innocent earth knew no plow," but "gave her / Riches as fruit hangs from the tree" (*Metamorphoses* 33). The Greek and Roman Golden Ages pass naturally, yielding to the effects of time, to be replaced by increasingly less desirable ages until one arrives at the present—the Iron Age, a time of hard work, pain, and contention, when there "is no defense against evil" (Hesiod, *Works and Days* 175–202), for, inevitably, "golden ages turn to years of iron" (Ovid 421).

Nevertheless, iron-age storytellers can imagine some sort of ultimate cycle of destruction and renewal. Frequently the renewal consists of resetting the clock, or eliminating its influence. These are, generally speaking, universal tales of renewal *within time*—for the earth or an age. In this vein, the Old Testament prophets, regional and tribal in their focus, predict a renewal in time, concentrating not on the earth or the age, but on the chosen people and Jerusalem, the city of Yahweh's habitation. The theme of Hebrew narrators, early or late, produces congruence in the tale as a whole by reflecting the pattern of their earliest events—perfection, disobedience, punishment or destruction, followed by restoration. The prophets reiterate one story: the chosen people have been disobedient (as were Adam and Eve); they have abandoned the proper worship of Yahweh and observance of his law, worshiping the gods of other peoples; and God's anger will be (or has been) directed against them, leading first to destruction and tribulation of the vast majority, and then to a renewal of the covenant and restoration of a remnant in a rehabilitated (earthly) Promised Land, or Holy City. For such authors, renewal does not mean return to the timeless perfection of Eden, but rather to the strict observance of the covenant between God and his people, with all the blessings that relationship entails *within the realm of history.*

Amos, earliest of the Old Testament writing prophets, establishes the prophetic theme destined to be repeated many times by succeeding prophets. Amos's God accuses his people and announces destruction: "Behold, the eyes of the Lord God are upon the sinful kingdom, / and I will destroy it from the surface of the ground...." (9:8). The announcement of annihilation is followed by the promise of partial renewal: "I will restore the fortunes of my people Israel, and they shall rebuild the ruined cities and inhabit them... ; / I will plant them upon their land, and they shall never again be plucked up out of the land which I have given them" (9:14–15). Similarly, Hosea's God declares, "I will be to them like a lion, like a leopard

I will lurk beside the way . . . / and there I will devour them like a lion. . . ."
(13:7–9). And after the destruction, restoration: "They shall return and dwell beneath my shadow, they shall flourish as a garden" (14:7).

This pattern receives interesting elaboration in the prophetic books of Ezekiel and Isaiah, in whose writings apocalyptic elements begin to appear. Ezekiel's message is that Yahweh, angry with his people, has handed them over to the Babylonians, orchestrated their defeat and exile, yet promised an ultimate return to Jerusalem. God will return his people to the Holy City, where God's dwelling will be rebuilt: "Son of man, this is the place of my throne and the place of the soles of my feet, where I will dwell in the midst of the people of Israel for ever" (Ezekiel 43:7). Elements of the restored city are reprised from Eden: the waters of life will flow from the sanctuary, and eternally bearing fruit trees will nourish and "heal" (Ezekiel 47:1–12), but these will be waters and trees in time and the world; there is no suggestion of individual human resurrection and immortality.

Isaiah 24–27, known as the "Isaiah Apocalypse," begins with a prediction of God's destruction of the entire earth; "few men are left" (24:6). After the destruction, the survivors among the Chosen will return, "will come and worship the Lord on the holy mountain at Jerusalem" (27:13). Second Isaiah (chapters 40–66) likewise has an apocalyptic tone. It depicts God not only as creator and destroyer, but also as architect of a new creation. The prophet suggests that while destruction is imminent—"heavens will vanish like smoke, the earth will wear out like a garment, and they who dwell in it will die like gnats"—so too is deliverance: "but my salvation will be for ever, and my deliverance will never be ended" (51:6). Anticipating the language of Revelation, Yahweh announces, "For behold, I create new heavens and a new earth; and the former things shall not be remembered or come into mind." In the renewed creation, there will be no sorrow, no *untimely* death, no strife or privation, but peace and plenty where the "wolf and the lamb shall feed together" (65:17–25). As in Ezekiel, the new creation is one for humans who die. Yahweh merely promises these mortals endurance through their children and remembrance: "For as the new heavens and the new earth which I will make shall remain before me, says the Lord; so shall your descendants, and *your name shall remain*" (66:22; emphasis supplied).

APOCALYPSE—THY KINGDOM COME

> The God of heaven will set up a kingdom which shall never be destroyed, nor shall its sovereignty be left to another people. It shall break in pieces all these kingdoms and bring them to an end, and it shall stand forever. . . .
> Daniel 2:44

Reading the Bible through from Genesis to Revelation, one realizes that the two testaments were produced for two different realities. It is as if one were to attend a play and watch a drama unfold until intermission, but discover, when one returned to the theater, another play in progress with new characters and a new plot, reflecting a different set of assumptions about the nature of God, justice, humankind, nature, life, death, heaven, and earth.[5] This fact makes the appropriation, interpretation, and revision of the Old Testament by New Testament authors, so as to lend a sense of consonance to the biblical plot, all the more remarkable. As mentioned, only the book of Daniel, with its brief assertion of resurrection, eternal life, and final judgment, is genuinely apocalyptic. Yet this book is merely an early example of an apocalyptic genre consisting of numerous texts produced from around the time of the settling of the Old Testament canon, continuing during the intertestamental period and into the first century CE. By the time the first of the New Testament texts were produced, apocalyptic thought and themes had become so common that they pervaded virtually all New Testament narratives, whose focus, of course, is on the death and resurrection of Jesus as paradigmatic of the apocalyptic theme of death and resurrection for believers.

The extraordinary contrast in thought that separates Old and New Testaments reflects primary shifts of figurative "knowledge" that developed during the intertestamental period. The first, as mentioned, involves a shift away from the linear metaphor for time as representing the course of human life and history. This metaphor is modified to include a recursive component realized in the concept of resurrection (death is not the end, but the beginning) and the dualistic doctrine of "two ages" (This Age, in time, perishable and terminable, and the eternal "Age to Come") (Vielhauer 588). With the two ages comes a change in the figurative understanding of the governance of the universe, from monism to dualism,[6] manifest in a change from ascribing to Yahweh all power as the source of good and evil, to the emergence of an entity separate from Yahweh, an autonomous (or semi-autonomous) figure of embodied nastiness whose sole mission is to oppose Yahweh, his law, and his design. Dualistic thought involves not only the notion of the two ages and a separation of cosmic powers, but a concomitant division of the individual human being into mortal and immortal components. It is for possession of the immortal soul that Yahweh and his Enemy (the devil or Satan) vie, albeit in a contest whose end has always been written.

For a period of nearly 300 years apocalypse was "in fashion," a popular literary genre whose authors knew the literary form, saw its relevance to the times, and depended upon certain conventions and intertextual allusions in their composition of texts.[7] Philipp Vielhauer succinctly defines *apocalyptic* as designating "first of all the literary genre of the Apocalypses, i.e., revelatory writings which disclose the secrets of the beyond and especially of the end of time, and then secondly, the realm of ideas from which this literature originates." The word came into use in Christian writings, and was then applied retroactively to Jewish texts, becoming the common designation of the genre (Vielhauer 582).

To see how these generic developments are realized in the narratives, it is useful to have a more detailed sense of the formal peculiarities of an apocalyptic narrative. In general, the narratives will share some or most of the following features: (1) a pseudonymous[8] narrator who claims to have been transported, often in a dream-vision or state of ecstasy, usually by an angel, into heaven where he learns about the nature of the cosmos and End-Times (hence *apocalypse*, "unveiling"); (2) expectation of the *imminent* destruction of the world, preceded by disruptions in the natural order (Vielhauer 582, 584); (3) acceptance of the doctrine of the eternal nature of the soul; (4) anticipation of the resurrection of believers to eternal life; (4) description/prediction of End-Time events, including a great battle between good and evil, frequently rendered in symbolic or allegorical images characteristic of nightmare, dominated by descriptions of composite or monstrous beasts and a suggestively Freudian preoccupation with horns; (5) creation of a new heaven and new earth; (6) announcement of a messiah (the anointed one), often as "son" (in the line of King David) or "Son" (of God)—Jesus; (7) final judgment and sorting of souls; and (8) transformation or elimination of time.

Apocalypse emerged and flourished in politically, socially, and religiously beleaguered times, an expression of those who felt that this age had grown old, corrupt, and absurd and was waning toward a necessary end to make way for a new age. Marked by intense utopian longing, its premise is that justice will prevail in the age to come, and that if one just follows the rules, if one merely *believes*, one can obtain immortality and eternal life, peace, and absence of sorrow and pain in a heavenly community of the blessed. To exemplify the characteristics of End-Time narratives, I draw my material chiefly from three texts—the Old Testament book of Daniel, the influential intertestamental book of 2 Esdras, and the New Testament book of Revelation.

The book of Daniel sets the tone for subsequent elaborations of his themes. In his first vision, Daniel sees the phases of history symbolically embodied in four monstrous beasts emerging from the sea of time and representing successive foreign kingdoms. The first three fall, after which the fourth (an enemy of the "Most High") is to be confronted, defeated, stripped of power, and consumed, its power awarded to the Israelites (Daniel 7). In Daniel's world, nations have patron gods and angels.

Gabriel (with his companion Michael) appears to Daniel to reveal what is "inscribed in the book of truth" containing God's world plot (Daniel 10:21), at the end of which "many of those who sleep in the dust of the earth shall awake, some to everlasting life, and some to shame and everlasting contempt" (12:2). Gabriel explains that the end of time is imminent (perhaps 490 years [9:24] or three-and-a-half years [12:7]) before destruction of the Holy City. He leaves assuring Daniel that he will survive: "[A]nd you shall rest, and shall stand in your allotted place at the end of days" (12:13). This early apocalypse displays several of the features listed above: a vision of God's throne and God's emissaries, a view of events depicted in symbolic images of nightmare, disclosure by an angel of events leading to End-Times, a prediction of last battles and the imminent end of the world, resurrection, and judgment of the living and dead.[9]

The book of 2 Esdras will serve as exemplary of intertestamental apocalyptic texts. The author assumes the name Esdras, the Greek form of Ezra, Old Testament prophet. The first-composed and main portion of the text (chapters 3–14) describes human history in seven visions during which Ezra is instructed by the angel Uriel in the mysteries of heaven and earth, time and eternity, man and God. Foremost in Ezra's mind is the Joban preoccupation with divine justice. He wants to know why God's chosen people suffer while their enemies prosper: "Are the deeds of Babylon better than those of Zion?" (3:31). More elaborately, he asks why "the people whom you loved has been given over to the godless tribes . . . ; why we pass from the world like locusts, and our life like a mist, and we are not worthy to obtain mercy" (3:23–25). Uriel responds with a prophecy and a promise. The end of the age is near; Hades (Sheol) will soon give birth to the dead committed to it "from the beginning"; the end will be preceded by "great terror"; Babylon (as symbolic of ruling earthly power) will be destroyed, and unnatural events will occur: "the sun shall suddenly shine forth at night and the moon during the day. / Blood shall drip from wood, and the stone shall utter its voice; . . . / and the stars shall fall (5:4–5). Nevertheless, Uriel explains, God's ways are inscrutable, and Ezra cannot hope to understand the divine plan or its justice. God reveals through Uriel the nature of his divine authorship, asserting that he had planned everything "at the beginning of the circle of the earth"—"then I planned these things, and they were made through me and not through another, just as the end shall come through me and not through another" (6:1, 6). The voice of God, "like the sound of many waters"[10] announces the imminent disclosure to the world of his plot, saying, "[T]he books [Ezra's version of Revelation's seven scrolls] shall be opened before the firmament, and all shall see it together" (6:17, 20).

Afterward a general terror and destruction will eliminate most of the world's population: "Whoever remains shall see my salvation and the end of my world"; they will be transformed—"changed and converted to a different spirit" (6:25–28).[11]

Ezra hears details of the last judgment, rewards for the righteous, and punishments for the wicked (7:36, 47). He learns that after the world has been "turned back to primeval silence" the dead will be resurrected, and divine "compassion shall pass away," as the many are condemned to the pit (Sheol) and the few are awarded residence in the paradise of delight. "The day of judgment will be the end of this age and the beginning of the immortal age to come" (7:34, 113). Blessings of the saved are enumerated for Ezra who, not surprisingly, is to be one of the few: "It is for you that paradise is opened, the tree of life is planted, the age to come is prepared, plenty is provided . . ." (8:52–54).

The figure of an eternal city (Jerusalem) becomes fused with the chosen people in the figure of a woman (Esdras 11–12). Ezra experiences a completion of Daniel's vision of history (12:11). He sees Daniel's fourth kingdom (the Roman empire) destroyed under the authority of the Messiah (in the form of a lion) who begins to assume a supernatural form as he arises "from the posterity of David" (12:32) and takes on the role of judge to destroy the majority of the Israelites and "deliver in mercy" the remnant (12:33–34). In a subsequent and duplicating vision, the Messiah appears from the sea of time as a "figure of a man," flying with the clouds, terrifying everything on which his gaze falls and "all who heard his voice" (13:1–4). This figure, kept by the Most High "for many ages" until "the end of time," emerges promptly as written in God's book, destroys the multitude ranged against him with a stream of fire and storm of sparks from his mouth, and welcomes the peaceable ones (13:8–13; 26, 52).

I have described at some length the apocalypse of Ezra for several reasons. First, it is apparent that the pseudepigraphal author sees himself as part of a literary tradition whose precursors include the author of Job and biblical prophets Ezekiel and Daniel, from whom he borrows. Second, the text offers evidence of certain literary conventions associated with the genre of End-Times narratives (the dream-vision, the angel guide/interpreter, symbolic animals, composite beasts, themes of resurrection and judgment). Third, the work offers a deuterocanonical link between Old and New Testament apocalyptic narratives, having been written by a Palestinian Jew and subsequently edited and augmented twice in the next two centuries by Christian editors and authors. Finally, Esdras shows the tendency of the genre to elaborate upon, augment, and revise earlier texts. This propensity is apparent in the evolving, increasingly important role and power of the Messiah figure. In the process, the Messiah is transformed from an earthly king (the anointed one) to an eternal figure, the "Son" of the Most High whose mission is not only to rule the restored Jerusalem, but to judge, punish, and reward. Revelation will take this evolution even further, making the Messiah, rather than God, the central figure in the drama of apocalyptic events.

The Revelation of John shares Ezra's literary enterprise, the apocalyptic tradition, and prophetic impulse. Whereas 2 Esdras is generally excluded from Protestant Bibles (although included in the Catholic Vulgate), Revelation is afforded more broadly the "authority" of canonized texts. Revelation manifests its dependence on the conventions of the genre that I have examined, but repeats them if not in a higher tone, with rather more extravagant and fanciful vision, more eager anticipation of an imminent end (its theme—"what must soon take place" [1:1]), and rather more enthusiasm for and graphic description of the suffering of countless "others," who will ultimately be consigned forever to the lake of fire. Some have found John's text hopelessly chaotic and his passion for divine punishment of enemies excessive. Typical apocalyptic features found in Revelation include dream-vision, transport to heaven, description of God on his chariot-throne, instruction by angels, vivid images of monstrous horned beasts, death, destruction, resurrection of the dead, judgment, creation of a new earth and heaven, revelation through symbols, including personification of the cities of Babylon and Jerusalem, respectively, as whore and bride.

Of all the biblical texts, Revelation offers the most detailed description of heaven (compare Enoch's intriguing new house filled with sheep). John's heaven is a place where one might experience sensory overload. The scene is dominated by a figure seated on a gemstone-encrusted throne, surrounded by an emerald rainbow. This central throne is further encompassed by twenty-four other thrones on which are seated white-clothed, golden-crowned "elders." From the throne itself issue flashes of lightning, voices, and peals of thunder; before it burn seven torches which are the "seven spirits of God," and surrounding it is a "sea of glass, like crystal" (4:1–6). While the reader is still attempting to visualize this scene, more is added—a revision of the composite creatures (cherubim, seraphim) described in Ezekiel and Isaiah. Now the four faces are each assigned to a separate creature—the face of a lion, an ox, a man, and an eagle, and each has six wings and is "full of eyes all round and within." The scene adds further noise and action: the four living creatures "day and night . . . never cease to sing, 'Holy, holy, holy, is the Lord God Almighty, / who was and is and is to come!'" To this "never-ceasing" chorus is added an antiphonal chant and action by the twenty-four elders: "whenever the living creatures give glory and honor and thanks to him who is seated on the throne, who lives for ever and ever, the twenty-four elders fall down before him who is seated on the throne and worship him . . . ; they cast their crowns before the throne, singing, 'Worthy art thou, our Lord and God, / to receive glory and honor and power, / for thou didst create all things, / and by thy will they existed and were created'" (4:6–11). An insistence on the eternal nature of these figures, their stations, and actions—the visual and auditory excess—"for ever and ever"—renders this "heaven," to say the least, less than serene. The metaphor, God is King, dictates that his throne-room may take to extremes the ambience of earthly throne-rooms, where a sovereign receives praises from his obsequious citizens, except that here, alas, there is and can be no end to it.

As in 2 Esdras, the enthroned God holds the book of truth—sealed scrolls on which is written the whole of human life and history, God's eternal grand narrative. The single figure who steps forward to unseal the scrolls and reveal the end of the plot is the Messiah, called the "Lion of the tribe of Judah" and the "Root of David," who strangely appears "between the throne and the four living creatures" in the form of a monstrosity—a seven-horned, seven-eyed Lamb, "standing as though it had been slain." This bizarre figure takes the scroll (in his hoofs? in his mouth?), prompting the living creatures and the elders, "each holding a harp, and with golden bowls full of incense, which are the prayers of the saints," to fall down before the Lamb and sing "a new song" (5:1–9). It is here that the central figure of Christianity—the sacrificed Jesus—in the form of an unnaturally deformed and slaughtered lamb becomes the chief actor of John's End-Times narrative.

His subsequent opening of the seals has the effect of moving the plot to its conclusion—destruction of This Age, time itself, and creation of the Age to Come, eternity. From the first four scrolls emerge four horsemen, riding four symbolic horses—the white horse of power (of the Messiah), the red horse of war, the black horse of famine, and the pale horse of pestilence and death. The fifth seal reveals the Christian martyrs—"souls of those who had been slain for the word of God"—who are told to "rest a little longer" awaiting the final judgment (Revelation 6:9–11). The opening of the sixth seal brings destruction of heaven and earth in the day of wrath (*dies irae*): "for the great day of their [God's and the Lamb's] wrath has come, and who can stand before it?" (6:1–17). In Revelation, Yahweh's Old Testament wrath endures, shared here by the Lamb.

As in Esdras, the coming of the Messiah, the "first-born of the dead," will strike terror in human hearts (1:5, 7). Here the Messiah seems merged with God, encompassing all of time—the linear time of worldly events, and the "eternal" before and after: "'I am the Alpha and the

Omega,' says the Lord God, who is and who was and who is to come, the Almighty" (1:8). The Messiah, usually referred to in Revelation as "the Spirit," ("one like a son of man") or the Lamb, speaks directly to the author, causing great fear, as well he might, for "his eyes were like a flame of fire, his feet were like burnished bronze . . . , and his voice was like the sound of many waters . . ." (1:13–16). The figure announces again that he is "the first and the last": "I died and behold I am alive for evermore, and I have the keys of Death and Hades" (1:17–18). As was Esdras, John is instructed to write the Messiah's words from dictation.

Elaborate details are provided of the slaughter of many and of the salvation of few (expressed often as 144,000, 12,000 from each of the twelve tribes, or those "who have not defiled themselves with women, for they are chaste; it is these who follow the Lamb wherever he goes," the first redeemed [14:4–5]). Gradually the "kingdom of the world has become the kingdom of our Lord and of his Christ" (11:15). In the process the world is personified as the whore of Babylon,[12] its citizens metaphorically the harvest that the Lamb will cut down with his "sharp sickle" (14:14). After an extended description of the fall of Babylon, there is rejoicing by a multitude in heaven who celebrate the fact that "the smoke from her goes up for ever and ever" (19:3). At the last judgment, Satan (the embodiment of Ezra's "sin," refashioned as a supernatural opponent), along with the beast, the false prophet, and all those whose names were "not found written in the book of life" are consigned to the lake of fire where they "will be tormented day and night for ever and ever" (20:7–15).

New elements enter Revelation, which appear to be tropes for (1) a challenger of God's supremacy, and (2) sin—an embodied faithlessness. The first of these, a supernatural opponent in the form of a "dragon," emerges among the heavenly host: "[A] great red dragon, with seven heads and ten horns, and seven diadems upon his heads." After a battle in heaven between Michael, leading an angelic force, and the dragon and his (unspecified) forces, the dragon is defeated: "[T]he great dragon was thrown down, that ancient serpent, who is called the Devil and Satan, the deceiver of the whole world" (12:3–9). There are two more brief mentions of the dragon, concerning his binding for a thousand years and, following a final battle, his ultimate confinement forever in the lake of fire and sulphur (20:2, 7–10).

The narrator pays more attention to a figurative form of Ezra's "sin," or human infidelity and disobedience, personified as the "great harlot," the "whore of Babylon." His "human" and "female" enemy seems the primary object of devastating divine wrath—that of God, but also of the Messiah, the sword-tongued horseman who will "tread the wine press of the fury of the wrath of God" (19:16),13 and the Lamb who opens the seals and releases the horsemen, including himself riding the white horse, who will devastate the earth (6:1–8). In its female embodiment sin finds its metonymy in "fornication," the sin of sins. The figurative designation of human evil as feminine and sexual will resonate through millennia in religious, theological, and philosophical treatises, social attitudes, and political institutions emerging from these texts—indeed the whole of the history of Western civilization will be haunted by the whore of Babylon. The narrator's imagination is clearly engaged by the "great harlot." He depicts her riding on a seven-headed, ten-horned "scarlet beast"; she is richly dressed and holds a golden cup "full of abominations and the impurities of her fornication." (One can only speculate about the exact nature of this substance.) She appears more formidable even than the great dragon, for on her forehead is written the word *mystery*; and whereas Michael and his angelic host defeat the dragon, Babylon and her people receive the attention of the Messiah and are thus conquered by the Lamb himself, the "Lord of lords and King of kings" (17:1–14).

With the defeat of the dragon (Satan) and Babylon, and the destruction of heaven and earth, all that remains is to make a new heaven and earth, administer the Last Judgment and consign the sinful to eternal torment, eliminate time, reconcile the perfections of Eden and the Holy City, and reunite God and redeemed humans. Time no longer exists, as indicated by the fact that the earthly markers of time (the sea, the sun, and the moon) have been excluded from the new creation, which is illuminated perpetually by God and the Lamb, and "night shall be no more" (22:5). The holy city, New Jerusalem, has come "down" out of the new heaven to the new earth, "prepared as a bride," the "wife of the Lamb" (21: 2, 9). New Jerusalem is a perfect cube of a city, shining with gems and gold. The river of life and the tree of life, hidden since the exile from Eden, reappear in the city. The river flows from the throne through the city; the tree of life grows on its banks, and God and the Lamb "shall reign for ever and ever" (22:1–5). The plot is complete and congruent from beginning to middle to end.

END-TIMES AND DOOM-EAGERNESS

And so, in Revelation, the last and most overtly figurative book of the Christian Bible, apocalyptic themes introduced in the Old Testament and developed in the intertestamental period achieve their extreme expression. The book has proven to be one of the most controversial and most frequently interpreted of the New Testament texts. It has been incalculably influential on Western thought, art, and literature. Its influence is apparent throughout the Qur'an, which accepts and revises many of the premises of Revelation. Allah warns of universal destruction and final judgment as written in "the Book," that is, the Bible: "[T]here is no community We shall not destroy, or punish severely, before the Day of Resurrection" (Qur'an 17:58). As in Revelation, the "disbelievers" will "stay in Hellfire, where they will neither be finished off by death, nor be relieved from Hell's torment" (35:36). The Islamic faithful, like the Christian faithful, look forward to resurrection and an existence of peace, ease, and plenty (35:33–35).

The Islamic Paradise is rather more pastoral than urban, but, like the New Jerusalem, has its opulence. It also has a degree of sensuality absent from Revelation: "Gardens of lasting bliss with gates wide open. They will be comfortably seated; they will call for abundant fruit and drink; they will have well-matched [wives, or maids] with modest gaze" (38:49–54; cf. 52:17–27). End-Times "may well be very soon" (17:51).

Revelation ends in a hurry, anticipating the quickly approaching end of time—the logical end of human beings who are, after all, creatures of time, yet who hope to find existence beyond the end, a permanent home in the unchanging, unchangeable fields of eternity. John's motif as the book ends is "coming soon." Christ tells him, "Behold, I am coming soon, bringing my recompense, to repay every one for what he has done. I am the Alpha and the Omega, the first and the last, the beginning and the end. . . . Surely I am coming soon." John replies, "Amen. Come, Lord Jesus" (22:7–20), thus bringing to a close God's book, whose end has been shown to be always present from the beginning. And the paradox at the heart of it is that in their doom-eagerness humans can longingly anticipate such a nightmarish vision of destruction, eternal suffering, and endless chanting of praise.

John's vision of heaven is shaped first by the metaphor "God is King," and the superlative, "King of kings." Heaven is an embarrassingly opulent throne-room, its inhabitants suitably obsequious. However, another metaphor is at work shaping John's heaven, for as the scrolls are opened, heaven takes shape as an armed camp, headed by a divine general, and inhabited by a population of supernatural warriors and their monstrous mounts. The metaphor that makes the Unknown a warrior is the focus of the next chapter.

CHAPTER 3

THE POWER AND THE GLORY: DIVINE COMBATANTS, HEAVENLY HOSTS, AND HOLY WAR

> Thy right hand, O Lord, glorious in power,
> Thy right hand, O Lord, shatters the enemy.
> Exodus 15:6

> From the days of John the Baptist until now, the kingdom of heaven suffereth violence, and the violent bear it away.
> Douay Bible, Matthew 11:12

A COMMON FIGURE FOR THE UNKNOWN is the metaphor of God as warrior. The power and reach of the metaphor and the reality it has created and sustains cannot be overestimated. Through millennia the mirror of heaven has revealed an uninterrupted series of martial models. Effects of the metaphor encourage a combative ideal, emphasize the masculine nature of the divine, privilege aggression, and glorify warriors. Through the metaphor one's human enemies are readily made God's enemies and the horrors of war sanctified. Our texts, as often as not, reveal heaven to be an armed camp.

OFFICERS' CLUB HEAVENS

In Valhalla, the Norse god Odin ("War Father") presides over the Einherjar, dead warriors who pass the time fighting and killing each other by day and reviving and feasting by night. Their hall is roofed with shields, and its rafters are spears. Odin selects the bravest and best of fallen heroes to inhabit Valhalla, where they await a final battle, Ragnarok. In his *Aeneid*, Virgil reserves a special district of the Underworld, the "Groves of Blessedness," for fallen Trojan heroes, their priests, and their poets: "A gracious place. The air is generous; / the plains wear dazzling light; they have their very / own sun and their own stars." These heroes participate in wrestling and other martial sports, dance, sing, and listen to the priest-poet Orpheus sing of their military might. Observing these, Aeneas is amazed to see "their phantom / armor and chariots" and their spears and horses: "The very same / delight that once was theirs in life—in arms / and chariots and care to pasture their / sleek steeds—has followed to this underneath (Virgil 6:847–68). Value and delight attach also to the heroes' arms, armor, and equipage.

In both traditions, warriors occupy an honored position, the only members of society afforded an afterlife of sorts. The Old Testament, from which the prospect of an afterlife is noticeably absent, offers a darker tribute to ancient heroes—the "fallen mighty men of old"—who have their own separate place in Sheol and the cold comfort of their weapons and armor:

> They [dead enemies, the "uncircumcised"] do not lie with the fallen mighty men of old who went down to Sheol with their weapons of war, whose swords were laid under their heads, and whose shields are upon their bones. . . .
>
> Ezekiel 32:27

In Homer's Hades—like the biblical Sheol, a universal destination—heroes wander mindless among the dead, unless a blood sacrifice restores temporarily their ability to speak. Yet heroes are notable exceptions to the rule of universal death: Heracles, whose "phantom" drifts about Hades, abides on Mt. Olympus in the halls of Zeus (*The Odyssey*, Book 11), and Menelaus, son-in-law of Zeus, is promised a home in the paradisiacal islands of the blessed (*The Odyssey*, Book 4). Hesiod, too, exempts a few favored heroes from the common fate and envisions for them an afterlife of ease, "apart from human kind, at the end of the world" where they live with "hearts free of sorrow in the islands of the blessed" (*Works and Days* 165–72).

The heaven of Revelation, likewise, has a decidedly masculine and heroic population—Yahweh's heavenly host or army, the cherubim and elders who surround the throne, and the pervasive theme of battle. Then there are the "redeemed"—the "hundred and forty-four thousand who have not defiled themselves with women" (Revelation 14:3–4). Add to these Yahweh's war chariot, warrior angel Michael, the four horsemen of the apocalypse, and Jesus' two hundred million mounted warriors.

Heavenly Horses

The warrior's steed is frequently a resident of heaven. Odin owes his excellence as War Father in part to his possession of the gifted eight-legged horse, Sleipnir, who travels easily between realms of the gods and the dead. The dead Trojans have their "sleek steeds." Heracles, the Greek hero who achieves apotheosis, possesses immortal horses. Helios, the sun god, drives a horse-drawn chariot across the sky each day. Bellerophon tames the winged horse Pegasus, *an offspring of Poseidon*. Attempting to fly to Olympus, Bellerophon perishes, and Pegasus, Zeus' equine nephew, is taken into Zeus' stables (Moreford and Lenardon 154, 614–15). Yahweh praises the "natural" battle-readiness of horses: "[The horse] paws in the valley, and exults in his strength; he goes out to meet the weapons. / He laughs at fear and is not dismayed; he does not turn back from the sword" (Job 39:21–25). A Hebrew version of the ubiquitous sun chariot appears in the story of the passing of the prophet Elijah: "And as they still went on and talked, behold, a chariot of fire and horses of fire separated the two of them [Elijah and Elisha]. And Elijah went up by a whirlwind into heaven." Elisha recognizes the fiery apparition as "the chariot of Israel and its horsemen!" (2 Kings 2:11–12).

Jesus is also associated with war and warhorses. At the last days, four horsemen will ride to accomplish eschatological tasks in an approaching conflict. The rider of the white horse, leader of the "armies of heaven," is "the Word" (Revelation 19:11–15). According to the Qur'an and traditional commentary, in his "Night Journey," Muhammad was visited in the Kaaba by the archangel Gabriel, who brought a winged, heavenly steed (a horse or mule) al-Buraq that would carry Muhammad on a two-part journey, first to the "farthest mosque" and then into the heavens.[1]

The prophet Habakkuk sees Yahweh riding in a horse-drawn chariot, shooting arrows toward the earth (3:8–9, 15). A more astonishing variation on the heavenly chariot and its driver is found in the Merkabah (Hebrew "chariot"), the throne-chariot of God elaborately described in Ezekiel's vision (Ezekiel 1), and revised in Revelation (Revelation 4). Ezekiel sees that the Merkabah is drawn not by horses, but by composite beasts ("four living creatures"), and the driver sits on what appears to be a throne. The creatures are part man, part beast and part bird (Ezekiel 1:5–10).[2] These "living creatures," known as cherubim, are associated with clouds and depicted as mounts,[3] companions, or signals of the presence of Yahweh,[4] who as cloud-rider is like both the Canaanite god Baal and the Babylonian Marduk.[5] In Psalm 18, for example, God rides not on a flying horse, but on one of these composite beasts: "He rode on a cherub and flew" (10).[6] Cherubim, as clouds, function not only as monstrous steeds or draft animals, but also as a metonym for Yahweh, signaling the divine presence. In the wilderness, God guides the Israelites by day as a pillar of cloud, and on completion of the Tabernacle the divine cloud-presence fills the tent and hovers over it (Exodus 40:34–38).

The theme of flight runs through these accounts of divine heroes and their mounts—either through an ethereal medium of heaven or as transport between earth and heaven. Many of these "steeds" are composite beasts; many, logically enough, are winged (Pegasus, Buraq, the cherubim, and perhaps the horses that draw sun chariots), but wings appear unnecessary for the four horses of the apocalypse or the two hundred million lion-headed horses of Revelation 9.

Celestial Armory

When the goddess Thetis pleads with the divine craftsman to make new armor for her mortal son Akhilleus, Hephaistos hurries to his bellows, anvil, and hammer and employs his artistry to make armor and weapons of unequalled beauty and splendor (Homer, *The Iliad* 18). One of the most ancient of the armed gods is the Canaanite storm god Baal, who carries a club or mace fashioned for him by the craftsman god Kothar-and-Khasis. The Babylonian chief god, Marduk, appears to fashion his own arms—a bow, arrow, club, net, lightning, and winds—with which he rides to meet the monstrous Tiamat in his storm chariot, drawn by a team of four creatures.[7] The tendency in many of the traditions was for a figure originally associated with rain (divine semen) to evolve into a storm god, then into an armed storm god, and finally into a war god.

Yahweh is an armed storm god/warrior (hanging up his bow after he destroys the world with a flood) (Genesis 9:13), as is the Greek Apollo, who showers the Greeks with his arrows of plague: "Apart from the ships / he halted and let fly, and the bowstring slammed / as the silver bow sprang, rolling in thunder away" (Homer, *Iliad* 13). Isaiah graphically depicts Yahweh in his storm god aspect as the Lord of armies, advancing against Jerusalem's enemies: "[Y]ou will be visited by the Lord of hosts with thunder and with earthquake and great noise with whirlwind and tempest, and the flame of a devouring fire" (26:6).

In these examples, the gods' weapons are associated with meteorological events, merging the naturally destructive power of lightning, hail, rain, and wind with the storm god's crafted weapons. Although in historical times Zeus has lost many of his storm god attributes, he remains armed with the lightning bolt and becomes manifest through thunder and lightning. Homer describes a moment of calm in the Trojan War, when the ominous presence of "Zeus the Profound," wielder of the lightning bolt, makes himself known, as "all night long Zeus made thunder overhead / while pondering calamities to come, / and men turned pale with fear" (*Iliad* 177). The warrior/storm god's majesty and terror are represented similarly in a paean to Yahweh, "who hast stretched out the heavens like a tent, who hast laid the beams of thy chambers on the waters, / who makest the clouds thy chariot, who ridest on the wings of the wind, / who makest the winds thy messengers, fire and flame thy ministers" (Psalm 104: 2–4). In Revelation the ancient storm god aspect returns in the "flashes of lightning, and voices and peals of thunder" that issue from the throne (4:5). In his perhaps most memorable epiphany, Yahweh appears to Job as a personification of the storm itself—a whirlwind, emblem of his overwhelming destructive power. Allah threatens unbelievers with "sandstorms," "violent storms," and drowning (Qur'an 17:68–9).

THE WAR METAPHOR

> Then shall the Lord go forth and fight against those nations, as when he fighteth on a day of battle.
>
> Ezekiel 14:2

Narratives of divine warriors begin with a simple metaphor, for example, "The Lord is a man of war" (Exodus 15:3). Once that figure is projected onto the Unknown, it invites—even necessitates—elaboration. If the gods are warriors, there must be terrible enemies, natural or supernatural; they will need celestial weapons (and what could be more appropriate than lightning, hail, wind?); the god and his "host" will need armor, armories, forges, mounts and chariots, bridles and reins, stables, divine wranglers and artisans, and probably celestial oats (fertilized, one supposes, with celestial dung). The metaphor *God is Warrior* vies with *God is Father* as the most frequently encountered in the Western tradition of mythological and religious narratives. This fact prompts the question: what is it about human existence that results in this sort of privileging of a combative ideal?

Clearly war gods must emerge from and exist among a cluster of related ideas and attitudes, perhaps fundamental to human nature but especially prominent in the early social, political, and religious narratives of the West. Whatever the case, narratives extolling combative prowess attach alike to divine and human actors. Whether man or god, the "hero with a thousand faces" (Campbell) or "the hero of tradition" (Raglan) enacts a narrative pattern apparently imposed through human desire and need. Forsyth makes a convincing argument that there is a narrative imperative for the pattern. He argues that the "old enemy" or Adversary (known especially in the Christian tradition as Satan) serves a narrative function and without whom there would be no story. As Forsyth points out, the title of Adversary "defines a being who can only be contingent: he must always be a function of another, not an independent entity. His character is, in this sense of the word, a *fiction*" (Forsyth 4). Or, more precisely, his character is a *figure*, a personification or embodiment, just as divine *warrior* is a figure, for the Unknown. The narrative follows from the initial creation of the figure.

And so, therefore, why is this particular figure of the adversary or enemy included in tales of the Unknown? What factors produce this odd reflection in the mirror of heaven? Can the Ineffable be opposed? Can the Incomprehensible be "comprehended" through an Adversary? Does an Adversary enhance or diminish the Incomprehensible? Inasmuch as I have largely restricted my inquiry to the backgrounds and texts out of which the three monotheistic religions emerged—those of the Near East, the Middle East, and the Mediterranean—exploring the human situation of the ancient narrators provides a starting place from which to answer these questions.

THE MEETING OF TWO MYTHOLOGIES—THE CIRCLE AND THE LINE

Beat your plowshares into swords and your pruninghooks into spears. . . .
Joel 3:9–11

Two ancient orders of religious experience dominate prehistory and manifest their individual characteristics and the results of their meeting in recovered artifacts and texts in two parallel cultural transformations—one in Mesopotamia and one in Greece. Joseph Campbell calls the two orders "The Way of the Seeded Earth" and "The Way of the Animal Powers." The first is characteristic of early agriculturists and the second, of ancient nomadic or semi-nomadic hunter-warrior-herdsmen. Different sorts of culture are associated with these two ways. Farming permitted a settled existence, the building of villages and towns, the development of technologies, arts, crafts, and, in time, writing; it fostered the veneration and propitiation of gods whose powers might assure the fertility of the plants and animals on which the society depended. Fertility deities usually included an Earth Mother, from whose womb all life emerged, and to which returned, in a mystic cycle patterned figuratively on the circling of seasons, the cycle of vegetal growth and decay, the waxing and waning of the moon. Ecclesiastes, a remarkable, anachronistic biblical aberration, offers a bleak view of this ever-repeating round in his magnificent opening poem in which the cycles of nature, repeating endlessly, produce a situation in which "All things are full of weariness." "What has been done," he says, "is what will be done; / and there is nothing new under the sun" (Ecclesiastes 1:4–9). In this nonhistorical view, the earth that "remains for ever" is personified as Mother Earth; her consort—husband, son, or brother—is at times associated with the moon (which took the animal form of the bull) or the anthropomorphized sky, a figure who not only inseminated the Earth Mother with celestial rain/semen, but typically enacted in his own birth, sacrificial death, and resurrection the cycle of existence over which she ruled. Burial, suggested by a planting metaphor and the cycle of vegetation, was the typical means of caring for the dead, with the expectation of renewal or resurrection. Jesus, anticipating his own death, employs this sort of metaphor to explain resurrection: "Unless a grain of wheat falls into the earth and dies, it remains alone; but if it dies, it bears much fruit" (John 12:24). Osiris, worshiped in Egypt for over three thousand years, is said to be killed and dismembered annually by his brother Seth and his body parts scattered in the fields. Isis, his sister-wife, through a surrogate priestess, ritually mourning his death, recovers the parts and reassembles them. Once reassembled, Osiris is strong again, and from the underworld can renew the vegetation—especially grain—in its yearly cycle (R. T. Rundle Clark 109–18). Worshipers enacted the insemination of nature through a ritual marriage between a "king god" (or a substitute) and a priestess of the goddess. The hierogamy itself could result in the ritual death of the sacred god-king. Homer reaches deep into old ritual to depict the vegetation-restoring power of the mating of the sky god Zeus and the earth goddess Hera on top of Mount Ida. As he embraces his wife, "under them earth flowered" (*Iliad* 340–41). Or the ritual pair might be depicted as Mother goddess and ritual bull,[8] embodiment of male virility—figures that were to retain their influence through thousands of years. Joseph Campbell quotes Anton Moortgat to this effect, "[T]he mother-goddess and sacred bull—the earliest tangible, significant spiritual expressions of farming village culture—represent thoughts that were to retain their form in the Near East through Millenniums" (*Oriental Mythology* 45).[9]

By contrast, hunting and herding required different sorts of gods and different metaphors. Hunting and herding encouraged a nomadic existence, as people necessarily pursued game or followed the seasonal movements of herds. A Sumerian myth relates the story of a Semitic god of nomadic shepherds, Martu, who performs a heroic deed and asks for the hand of a Sumerian (hence farming) princess as his reward. The Sumerian princess agrees to wed, but friends advise against the union, pointing out the extreme differences in lifestyle: "He lives in tents, buffeted by wind and rain, / Eats uncooked meat, / Has no house while he lives, / Is not brought to burial when he dies. (Kramer, *Mythologies* 119). Nevertheless, the princess persists in her choice of the shepherd-hero.

Proficiency with implements used for hunting and butchering was easily employed against human prey as need or desire dictated. Value was placed on the skills of hunters and warriors—strength, speed, courage, endurance, and adroit handling of animals and weapons. It is understandable, therefore, that figures in the mirror of heaven reflected the ideal hunter, the perfect shepherd, the ultimate invulnerable warrior with irresistible weapon and supernatural mount. It is through the sacred experience of such people that officers'-club heavens are created, and it is ultimately through that experience, too, that the privileging of warriors and warfare and their figurative projection onto the Unknown occurs. Existence for those who follow the way of the animal powers is not cyclical, but linear: like the animals, humans are born, they live, struggle, and die. Just as animal carcasses are dismembered and cooked, so are human carcasses cooked up—cremated. (One of the objections to the marriage of the Sumerian princess is that the Semitic Martu "is not brought to burial when he dies.") The cooking metaphor replaces the planting metaphor to represent the course of existence. There is no resurrection, no mystic cycle of existence. Such a view is evident in the early Greek texts and in the Old Testament. That is what Odysseus learns in Hades, the realm of "after images of used-up men" (*The Odyssey* 200). Odysseus' dead mother, temporarily revived by the blood sacrifice, explains a universal truth about mortals: "No flesh and bone are here . . . since the bright hearted pyre consumed them down . . . to ash" (*The Odyssey* 192). Such attitudes toward death placed value on the span of human life, its pleasures and achievements—the "name" one made for oneself. As the writer of Ecclesiastes puts it, "Whatsoever thy hand findeth to do, do it with thy might; for there is no work or thought or knowledge or wisdom in Sheol, to which you are going" (9:10). Even more poignantly, he comments, "he who is joined with all the living has hope, for a living dog is better than a dead lion. For the living know that they will die, but the dead know nothing" (9:4–5).

The two competing views embrace radically different realities: the mystic theme of birth, death, and rebirth, and the rational theme of birth, life, and death-as-extinction. Views of time are likewise contrasted: on the one hand, endlessly returning cycles of existence in which there is "nothing new under the sun"; on the other, the linear march of time and history toward some far goal—often End-Times or the Last Day. Our received stories of the Unknown show evidence of encounters between these two sorts of culture, a subsequent struggle for dominance, and greater or lesser degrees of accommodation between radically different ways of approaching life and death. Several tales will exemplify the meeting of these orders.

Two of these are Sumerian tales dating from approximately 2000 BCE, which Kramer names "Emesh and Enten: Enlil Chooses the Farmer-God" and "Inanna Prefers the Farmer." Already in ancient Sumer in these tales and others, one finds evidence of competition, but also reconciliation, between the mythic visions of village-farming culture and nomadic-herding culture (apparent in the tale of the shepherd Martu and the Sumerian princess). "Emesh and Enten" is a story of two brothers who compete for the title of Farmer God, who will become god of both shepherd and farmer. Both brothers have caused the land and animals to produce richly. Chief god Enlil chooses Enten as Farmer God on criteria that remain obscure, yet the two brothers afterward become reconciled. Parallels with the Cain and Abel story are obvious. Even closer is a story concerning the goddess Inanna. She is the tutelary deity of the city of Erech (Kramer, *Sumerian Mythology* 42). In this story, a shepherd, Dumuzi, and a farmer, Enkimdu, court the goddess. She prefers the farmer, saying, "The much-possessing shepherd I shall not marry." Nevertheless, despite Inanna's preference for the farmer, the shepherd makes an eloquent case for himself, which results in his victory; once again the contenders are reconciled (Kramer, *Sumerian Mythology* 101–3). The goddess's preference for the farmer suggests her old agricultural associations, and reasons for the shepherd's victory remain unspecified. In each tale, however, the cultural bias of the narrator appears to contribute to a "resolution" of a power struggle between competing lifestyles.

The Sumerian tales predate the story of Cain and Abel by more than a millennium, during which period Mesopotamian farming culture was transformed by a series of invasions—first by Akkadians (Semitic, nomadic aggressors), who seized control and established an empire under Sargon I (2330 BCE) and, some 600 years later, in a period known as the "age of biblical patriarchs," by people known as Amorites, of whom, perhaps, Abraham was one (Stephen L. Harris 49). The Amorites were Semitic, nomadic shepherd-warriors, who succeeded in wresting control from the Akkadians and establishing three centers of power, the most famous at Babylon under King Hammurabi. When read with the Sumerian precursor tales in mind, the story of Cain and Abel, sons of Adam and Eve, can be seen to reflect this meeting of two mythologies and two lifestyles. Such a reading, too, helps shed light on some of the puzzles presented by the biblical tale in which Yahweh, unlike Inanna, prefers the shepherd. As in the Sumerian tale, the reasons for Yahweh's "regard" for the shepherd are open to speculation. Here is the biblical text:

> Now Abel was a keeper of sheep, and Cain a tiller of the ground. In the course of time Cain brought to the Lord an offering of the fruit of the

ground, and Abel brought of the firstlings of his flock and of their fat portions. And the Lord had regard for Abel and his offering, but for Cain and his offering he had no regard.

(Genesis 4:3–5)

Unlike the Sumerian tale, this story shows no reconciliation between the brothers but results instead in Cain's murder of his shepherd brother, sterility of Cain's fields, and exile. In this way, the story represents in miniature the great master theme that runs through the remainder of the Old Testament narratives—which might be called the shepherds vs. the farmers—including the conflicts implicit in the Covenant with Abraham, the Exodus from Egypt, and the conquest of Canaan. Such conflicts pit Israelite shepherds against agriculturists; the Israelites' warrior-sky God against the farmers' fertility gods, and a linear view of time against a cyclical view. Yahweh's promise—of a land "flowing with milk and honey"—is to give (at a point in the distant future) the nomadic, herding Abraham and his descendants the land of the settled, agriculturist Canaanites. In Egypt, the Israelite shepherds occupy a separate "land"—Goshen, the "best" region in all Egypt (Genesis 47:6). They have deceived the Pharaoh by pretending to be cattlemen, for "every shepherd is an abomination to the Egyptians" (Genesis 46:34). When Yahweh sends his devastating plagues against the Egyptians, Goshen is spared (Exodus 8:22, 9:26). Yahweh makes his regard for his shepherds clear: "[T]he Lord makes a distinction between the Egyptians and Israel" (Exodus 11:7). When Joshua leads the wandering Israelites into Canaan, it is with intent utterly to destroy its farmer inhabitants (Joshua 3:10).

With this in mind, Yahweh's "regard" for the shepherd Abel and his lack of regard for the farmer Cain are not at all mysterious. In exile, Cain settles in the land of Nod, where he marries and becomes the founder of cities, sedentary cultures with their farmers, shepherds, musicians, and smiths (Genesis 4:16–22). Biblical narrators distinguished their shepherd-warrior-heroes (e.g., Abraham, Isaac, Jacob, Moses, Joshua, and David) from more highly cultured farmers, on the one hand, and the apparently less civilized hunters (e.g., Isaac from Ishmael, Jacob from Esau), on the other. They venerated Yahweh, the God who prefers the shepherd, who is called a shepherd (Psalm 23), leads his people as battle commander (Exodus 15), and rejects the fertility religions of village, town, and city.

In the various literatures I am examining, Old Testament tales are to be distinguished by their rejection and devaluation of The Way of the Seeded Earth, the fertility gods of neighboring peoples, especially the Canaanites' Baal and Asherah, and a resulting xenophobia directed against the farming inhabitants of the land. Both fear and hatred of the religious practices of farming-urban centers are evident in God's question to Jeremiah:

> Seest thou not what they do in the cities of Judah and in the streets of Jerusalem? The children gather wood, and the fathers kindle the fire, and the women knead their dough, to make cakes to the queen of heaven [Asherah], and to pour out drink offerings unto other gods [especially Baal], that they may provoke me to anger.
>
> Jeremiah 7:17–18[10]

The series of invasions by Semitic nomads in Mesopotamia was paralleled in Greece when Indo-European hunter-herder-warriors made a series of incursions into Minoan farming-fishing villages. The invaders arrived with their armed sky god, Zeus, their patriarchal social organization,[11] and their language—a form of Indo-European that would evolve into classical Greek. As in Mesopotamia, the newcomers learned from the more highly civilized people they came to dominate (to employ swords against plowshares almost assures victory).[12] Two Greek tales will serve to illustrate the meeting of the two mythologies in Greece and the Aegean islands. The first is an episode in Book 5 of The *Odyssey*, a text committed to writing within a century of the Yahwist's tale of Cain and Abel. It concerns a marginalized, pre-Greek goddess, Kalypso, and the Greek warrior Odysseus. Kalypso has rescued Odysseus after a shipwreck and kept him a virtual prisoner on her isolated garden-island of Ogygia ("navel") for seven years. At the behest of the sky god, Zeus, his messenger, Hermes, orders Kalypso to let Odysseus go. Kalypso, with her Earth Mother associations, is not happy to receive orders from the sky gods. Her reply makes mention of the ancient farming ritual of sacred marriage intended to fructify the fields and often involving the death and dismemberment of the fertility goddess's consort:

> Oh you vile gods, in jealousy supernal!
> You hate it when we choose to lie with men—
> immortal flesh by some dear mortal side.
> So radiant Dawn once took to bed Orion
> until you easeful gods grew peevish at it,
> and holy Artemis, Artemis throned in gold,
> hunted him down in Delos with her arrows.
> Then Demeter [goddess of grain] of the tasseled tresses yielded
> to Iasion, mingling and making love
> in a furrow three times plowed; but Zeus found out
> and killed him with a white-hot thunderbolt.
>
> *The Odyssey* 84–85

The pattern here is one of the fertility goddess's mating with a figure who represents the vegetation in its cycles, but instead of the *ritual death*, dismemberment, and scattering of the male sacrifice, the sky gods (Artemis and Zeus) preempt the ceremonies and destroy the male participant. One implication is that Odysseus is at risk in his "ritual" mating with the goddess, and therefore the sky gods interrupt the ritual, this time extricating Odysseus from his participation in it. Kalypso, as representative of the ancient earth goddess, describes the blessings she has bestowed on Odysseus: "I fed him, loved him, sang that he should not die / nor grow old, ever, in all the days to come" (*The Odyssey* 85). Warrior-hero Odysseus wants none of it. He rejects her seemingly sinister gift of (cyclical) immortality, even after having already viewed the "after images of used-up men" in Hades. He finds that the linear existence of struggle and strife is preferable to the goddess's cycles (which seem, perhaps, full of weariness): "Let the trial come," he says (*The Odyssey* 87).

A second example concerns the conflict between Zeus (sky) and Demeter (earth), which like the Sumerian tale results in a reconciliation of two ways of mythic thought. In the Homeric "Hymn to Demeter," Zeus has exercised his patriarchal prerogatives and given his and Demeter's daughter Persephone to his brother Hades for a bride. Hades has unceremoniously claimed her by abducting and carrying her off (in his war chariot) to his underworld domain. Hearing Persephone's screams, Demeter searches the earth for her and eventually, in grief and anger, prevents the crops from growing, threatening to starve the human population. Zeus reaches the ironically pragmatic conclusion that gods cannot exist without worshipers: "Now [Demeter] would have destroyed the entire human race by cruel famine and deprived those who have their homes on Olympus of their glorious prestige from their gifts and sacrifices, if Zeus had not noticed and taken thought in his heart" (Moreford and Lenardon 314). Zeus, Hades, and Demeter reach a compromise by which Persephone will spend one-third of the year in Hades (the winter season) and two-thirds on earth (the growing and harvest seasons). When Persephone descends into Hades, plants lie lifeless on the earth; when she returns in the spring, new plants sprout and flourish. Clearly, here the deities of the two mythic orders reach a reconciliation that acknowledges the powers of both the gods of war and the gods of life, yet, as in Mesopotamia, the warriors retain the upper hand, with a resulting elevation of a warrior aristocracy, and a greater or lesser degree of fear and hatred directed toward the distaff side, whether represented by goddesses or human women.

The meeting of the two mythic orders resulted, then, in transformations reflected in the ascendance of combat metaphors destined to have incalculable and enduring effects on the reality embraced by early forms of Judaism, Christianity, and Islam; these figures would be carried along in revered texts and exert their influence even into the present. The most powerful of these is the metaphor that is the focus of this chapter, *God is a Warrior*, and its corollaries—God has enemies, and heaven is an armed camp.

WARRIOR GODS

> So the angel swung his sickle on the earth and gathered the vintage of the earth, and threw it into the great wine press of the wrath of God. . . .
> Revelation 14:19–20

In Bible lands the transformation began about 2350 BCE, when the Akkadians, a relatively uncivilized Semitic people, entered Sumer, captured the region and established, under King Sargon I, with the blessing of his warrior gods, the world's first empire (Stephen L. Harris 48–49). The result is a "historically conditioned idea" that the Unknown, to which "neither words nor minds can reach" (Campbell, *Inner Reaches* 22), the ineffable, unimaginable, incomprehensible "God" *is a man of war*. It is then a small step to tell the story of this Commander in Chief who not only participates directly in battles, but also directs his worshipers to wage war with him and on his behalf:

> Hear, O Israel, you draw near this day to battle against your enemies: let not your heart faint; do not fear, or tremble, or be in dread of them; for the Lord your God is he that goes with you, to fight for you against your enemies, to give you the victory.
> Deuteronomy 20:2–4[13]

The Akkadians did not, of course, initiate human conflict when they conquered Sumer. The human tendency to identify an object of fear and/or hatred and demonize it is no doubt as old as humanity. What the Akkadian victory in Sumer, and the subsequent Amorite defeat of Akkad, did achieve, however, was to vest power in a military elite whose images were then reflected in the mirror of heaven and whose heavenly battle leaders achieved unprecedented status among the gods. The process is displayed in the Babylonian Enuma Elish—among other things, an account of Marduk's ascension to power among the gods. Because of his willingness to accept Tiamat's challenge, the gods "conferred upon him the powers of the supreme position in the pantheon and gave him 'kingship over the totality of the whole universe'" (Heidel 3–7). A parallel tale tells of Zeus' consolidation of power as king of the gods. After defeating his father and his father's generation of gods (the Titans), Zeus confronts Typhoeus, a dragon-like monster and youngest child of Mother Earth, the ancient Gaia. Armed with thunder and lightning, Zeus defeats the figure of monstrous disorder. Following the battle at the advice of Gaia, the gods "promoted Zeus, the Olympian, . . . to be King and to rule over the immortals" (Hesiod, *Theogony* 883–85). The Norse king of the gods, Odin, was also a warrior and storm god who supplanted the Indo-European god Tyr (or Tiwaz), "the god of the sword and of justice" and Thunor, "the god of thunder and of the protection of property" (Jones and Pennick 143). Odin's appropriation of the roles of Tyr (combat) and Thunor (storm) may suggest earlier contests in which Odin was victorious. Riding across the sky on his eight-legged horse, Odin was followed by battle-maddened troops. In Odin's last battle, Ragnarok, he, together with other gods and heroes, will confront giants and their spawn (including Jormungander, a serpentine, Leviathan-like creature).

Each of these tales involves the king of the gods in a struggle against some sort of serpentine, aquatic, or fiery dragon-like monster—Tiamat, Typhoeus, Jormungander. Their element, water, is primordial, representing a chaotic mixture of the elements; fire too is associated with the mythical old serpent. In each case the enemy is "lawless," destructive, and antagonistic to human life. Therefore, the god's defeat of the chaos monster, as embodiment of the sea and/or destructive fire, enhances human existence by assuring order in the state or the proper progress of nature.

Ancient tales of Baal and his warrior-sister Anant anticipate these sorts of confrontation. Baal's dragon battle is against the monster called "the crooked serpent." Of this battle, Forsyth observes that the name of the dragon, Lotan, is "recognizable as the biblical Leviathan" (Forsyth 62). Leviathan is a figure for that which opposes Yahweh, whose battle Isaiah describes: "In that day the Lord with his sore and great and strong sword shall punish leviathan the piercing serpent, even leviathan that crooked serpent; and he shall slay the dragon that is in the sea" (Isaiah 27:1–3).

Biblical allusions to Yahweh's battle with the monster indicate appropriation of the ancient and widespread combat tales, modified for attribution to Yahweh. In the first chapter of Genesis, the monster is absent, but traces of its presence remain in watery, dark formlessness: "In the beginning the earth was without form and void, and darkness was upon the face of the deep" (1:2). The Hebrew word *tehōm*, "the deep," corresponds to the Babylonian word *Tiamat*, the serpentine embodiment of the sea. Yahweh's task is to control the formless, primordial element, which he accomplishes not by physical combat, as does Marduk or Baal, but by simple command: "And God said, 'Let there be a firmament in the midst of the waters, and let it separate the waters from the waters'"

(Genesis 1:6–8). Although the metaphor of the watery enemy has been to some extent "defigured" here, the process is reversed again in the book of Job. God's boast of his control of the birth of the sea (as an opponent) and its subsequent imprisonment (Job 38:8–11) as well as his long discourse on his control of Leviathan ("Can you fill his [leviathan's] skin with harpoons, or his head with fishing spears? / Lay hands on him; think of the battle!" [41:7–8]) associate Yahweh's warrior persona with ancient hero gods in confrontation with what Forsyth names "the old enemy."

In the early narratives of Yahweh, he is the greatest warrior among a pantheon of gods. Praising Yahweh for his defeat of the Pharaoh and his human armies, the speaker asks, "Who is like thee, O Lord, *among the gods? Who is like thee, majestic in holiness, terrible in glorious deeds, doing wonders?* (Exodus 15:11–12; emphasis supplied). Like Marduk and Baal before him, Yahweh assumes his position as Warrior of warriors and King of the gods. Repeated motifs, images, and plots reveal the *bricoleur's* handiwork in Old Testament narratives as one more divine warrior confronts a nearly invincible opponent in the cause of preserving or creating natural or civic order, "law," and/or life.

While tales of Marduk, Baal, Zeus, Odin, and Yahweh pit a god against a supernatural chaotic force, other tales make humanity as a whole the god's enemy, relating how armed deities, for whatever reason, decide to eliminate the human race. Sumerians, Babylonians, Hittites (Güterbok 144–48), Greeks, and Romans told versions of the myth of the divine destroyer; the destruction takes the form of calamities sent or caused by a warrior/storm god. In the Sumerian version, the gods decide to eradicate humankind for unknown reasons; Ziusudra, a pious king, the "Sumerian Noah," having been warned by one of the gods, builds a boat, survives the flood, and is later deified. The Babylonian version closely follows the Sumerian. Gilgamesh hears the tale from the Babylonian "Noah," Utnapishtim, who (with his wife) is sole survivor of a universal flood. His is an account of gods who wish to destroy all life. Combat language describes how the "storm gods" send the tempest with "the flood-weapon, / Like a battle force" to destroy mankind; "Even the other gods were afraid of the flood-weapon"; at the end of seven days, "all mankind had returned to clay" (Stephen L. Harris 52–53). According to Hesiod, a Greek universal destruction results when Zeus desires to protect immortals from the pain of seeing their half-divine offspring die. He wishes to separate immortals and mortals once and for all. To achieve this end, he plans "monstrous events," a "confusion of tempests" in order to destroy the demigods, "so the children of the gods might no longer mate with wretched mortals, / and so look forward to doom" (Hesiod 10). Ovid relates the Roman version of a universal destruction prompted by Jove's disgust at the evil of mankind. Since it is his duty to protect "nymphs, fauns, satyrs, and small gods who wander / The village streets," he decrees that "The lands they live in must be cleared of evil," for "All men have joined in Hell's conspiracy" (Ovid 36–37). As in other versions, a single favored, god-fearing man and woman (Deucalion and Pyrrha) are preserved from the universal destruction.

These tales of armed storm gods who direct their weapons against mankind provide a context in which to read the biblical flood story. Genesis 6–9 offers two accounts woven together in such a way that they form a single rather incoherent text (see Stephen L. Harris 90–91). The biblical editors introduce the flood narratives with an intriguing mythological narrative:

> When men began to multiply on the face of the ground and daughters were born to them, the sons of God saw that the daughters of men were fair; and they took to wife such of them as they chose. Then the Lord said, "My spirit shall not abide in man for ever, for he is flesh, but his days shall be a hundred and twenty years." The Nephilim were on the earth in those days, and also afterward, when the sons of God came in to the daughters of men and they bore children to them. These were the mighty men that were of old, the men of renown.
>
> Genesis 6:1–4

This "heroic-age" myth of the origin of half gods, their might, and renown eerily echoes the Greek tales of offspring fathered by gods upon human women.

The relationship between the mythic prologue to the biblical flood narratives and Yahweh's motive for destroying the human population is lost in the break between verses 4 and 5. Following the prologue, the first verse of the Yahwist's flood narrative states, "And the Lord saw that the wickedness of man was great in the earth, and that every imagination of the thoughts of his heart was only evil continually" (Genesis 6:5). Readers commonly assume a connection between the "wickedness of man" and what has been said of the birth of the Nephilim. An apocryphal text, the Book of Enoch, attempts to specify the relationship, linking "wickedness of man" with the sexual union of divine beings and human women. In the Enoch text, God tells the "sons of God" (also called "Watchers"), "you defiled yourself with the blood of women, you begot children with the blood of flesh, and like the others you have lusted after flesh and blood as do those who die and perish." The explicit linking of sexuality and death supposedly accounts for the fact that the bodies of "giants," offspring "of spirit and flesh," "emitted evil spirits because they were born from human women and the holy Watchers." Such children "afflict, oppress, destroy, attack over the earth" (Barnstone 487). Unlike

Hesiod's Zeus, who wanted to keep the gods from sorrow, Enoch's God is intent on punishing both the Watchers and their half-divine offspring, whose "evil" appears to originate in miscegenation.

In any case, God's observation that "the wickedness of man was great in the earth, and that every imagination of the thoughts of his heart was only evil continually" is not only a devastating appraisal of humankind, but it also provides a motive like that of Ovid's Jove: universal destruction will rid the earth of evil.[14] Just as Utnapishtim found favor with the Babylonian god Ea, Noah finds favor with Yahweh; he is warned and instructed to build a boat, load it with a pair of "every living thing of all flesh," take as passengers his wife, three sons, and their wives, and a store of food. Whether the flood continued for forty days or one hundred and fifty (Genesis 7:17; 7:24) is irrelevant. The point is that the warrior god has once again sent his destructive "flood-weapon" against humanity, apparently in the form of rain-arrows, for after the flood Yahweh decides not to destroy the earth again (in any case, the destruction failed to eliminate man's "evil imagination" [Genesis 8:21]), and he hangs up his weapon: "I set my bow in the cloud, and it shall be a sign of the covenant between me and the earth" (Genesis 9:13–15).

HOLY WAR—"ARE ALL THESE TALES OF THE GODS TRUE?"

> For their sake I have overthrown many kings; I struck down Pharaoh with his servants, and all his army. I have destroyed all nations before them, and scattered in the east the people of two provinces. I have slain all their enemies.
>
> 2 Esdras 10–11

> Socrates: And do you really believe that the gods fought with one another, and had dire quarrels, battles, and the like, as the poets say . . . ?
>
> Plato, "Euthyphro"

Very often Socrates' questions are answered in the affirmative. More troubling is the fact that an odd phrase attaches to divinely sanctioned wars—Holy War. The tales depict warrior gods engaging actively in battles among themselves, against human beings, and in tribal and national conflicts. While the various warrior gods seem to enjoy a good conflict, and to meddle in the ebb and flow of martial events, and while it is true that the narratives of the warrior-storm gods have recorded the deaths of countless human opponents (the population of the earth or "enemies" either of the gods or the preferred human community), Yahweh alone may be distinguished by the extent to which he participates directly in the wars of his people and by his divinely mandated genocide. He permits no *human* hero, insisting on taking credit for Israelite victories. In Exodus, God is chief combatant and acknowledged victor, devastating the Pharaoh, his magicians, and his people in the plague contest, and drowning the entire Egyptian army in the sea. Allah, identified with the Yahweh of the Old Testament, takes pride in this defeat of the Egyptians: "So he [the Pharaoh] wanted to drive them [the Israelites] off the [face of the] earth, but We drowned him and those with him" (17:103). In one of the numerous battles waged against the Moabites and Amonites, Yahweh informs the army of Judah that it need not fear the multitude of its opponents: "You will not need to fight in this battle; take your position, stand still, and see the victory of the Lord on your behalf . . . " (2 Chronicles 20:17). Both Yahweh and Allah make distinctions between insiders and outsiders that justify killing the outsiders. Yahweh distinguishes Israelites from Egyptians and Canaanites, and Allah distinguishes his believers from "misbelievers." He instructs Muhammad, "Give to those who misbelieve glad tidings of grievous woe!" and "Kill the idolaters wherever ye may find them" (9:4, 5).[15]

As the Israelites' long period of wilderness wandering comes to an end, Yahweh prepares them to take the land he has promised them, land inhabited by Israel's agriculturist "enemies" (Exodus 4:8). Yahweh gives explicit instructions for waging holy war both outside the Promised Land and within it. Outside Canaan, the Israelites may, like the Greek warriors of the *Iliad*, kill all the males and take "the women and the little ones, the cattle, and everything else in the city . . . as booty" and "enjoy the spoil . . . of enemies" (Deuteronomy 20:14–15). The rules are different for conquests inside the Promised Land. There, Yahweh instructs, "you shall save alive nothing that breathes . . . that they may not teach you to do according to all their abominable practices which they have done in the service of their gods" (Deuteronomy 20:16–18). Thus, when the Israelites, led by Yahweh, breach the fallen walls of Jericho, they follow the divine mandate: "[T]he people [Israelite warriors] went up into the city, every man straight before him, and they took the city. Then they utterly destroyed all in the city, both men and women, young and old, oxen, sheep, and asses, with the edge of the sword" (Joshua 6:20–21). For many of a modern disposition, such behavior, to use a favored biblical term, is an abomination.

The old narratives take the metaphor, God is a warrior, literally. The metaphor establishes the God of the Old Testament not only as warrior, but more than that, as Warrior of warriors. He has his enemies—the sea, Leviathan, and other gods (Pharaoh, Baal, Dagon, Asherah). In these respects his battles are like those of his mythic predecessors and gods of "other peoples." He has his own forces—the heavenly host—that he directs against human opponents, even at times his own chosen people. Even as Yahweh fades into the New Testament's heavens and Jesus, his avatar, becomes the textual focus, the narratives that depict so graphically the militance, the partiality, and the jealousy of the Old Testament's Yahweh are not repudiated; rather they are carried forward, as the New Testament incorporates, appropriates, interprets, and revises the precursor texts (John 3:36, Romans 2:5). The angels who announce the birth of Jesus are accompanied by a military chorus, "a multitude of the heavenly host praising God and saying, 'Glory to God in the highest / and on earth peace among men with whom he is pleased!'" (Luke 2:13–14). *Peace among those with whom he is pleased.*

The End-Times narrative of Revelation reprises the military metaphors of the Old Testament—with a vengeance. Not only is the warrior Yahweh ensconced on his war-chariot throne preparing the final devastations, but his son, Jesus, is his primary battle commander and destroyer, clothed in a cloudy mantle and mounted on the steeds of the storm: "Behold he is coming with the clouds, and every eye will see him, every one who pierced him; and all the tribes of the earth will wail on account of him" (Revelation 1:7; cf. 1 Thessalonians 4:16). If the Old Testament narratives of the destruction of Jericho and other cities in the Promised Land rival in horror the worst of modern abominations, surely this much-anticipated slaughter must eclipse all of them, as divine warriors in their glory, with their weapons, armies, horses, and trumpets, wreak havoc among "all the tribes of the earth."

Those who enthusiastically embrace the reality of the metaphor—God is a Warrior—inevitably see themselves and their band of like-minded fellows in the mirror of heaven, congregated as the "saved," and destined to live forever, free of sorrow and pain. At the same time, they are prepared to see (and take satisfaction in) eternal agonies of the unlike-minded. As they understand the situation, the warrior God grants neither amnesty nor reprieve. Allah reveals to Muhammad concerning those who have gone "astray," "We will gather them upon the resurrection day upon their faces, blind, and dumb, and deaf; their resort is hell; whenever it grows dull we will give them another blaze! That is their reward for they disbelieved in our signs . . . " (17:99). Muhammad's Night Journey in some ways parallels the experience of Moses on Mt. Sinai,[16] but also of John of Patmos as recorded in Revelation, in that during the night Muhammad receives a view of heaven and warnings regarding End-Times: "There is no community We shall not destroy, or punish severely, before the day of Resurrection—this is written in the Book [the Bible]" (17:58).

At one point during the forty-year wilderness experience, Yahweh instructs Moses to "Avenge the people of Israel on the Midianites." Moses sends twelve thousand warriors against Midian. Victorious, the Israelites kill all the Midianite men, burn the cities, take "booty and spoil," and return to camp. Moses, however, is not pleased:

> Moses said to them, "Have you let all the women live? Behold, these caused the people of Israel to act treacherously against the Lord. Now therefore, kill every male among the little ones, and kill every woman who has known man by lying with him. But all the young girls who have not known man by lying with him, keep alive for yourselves."
>
> Numbers 31:14–18

The authority of the metaphor (the Lord is a man of war) sanctifies plunder, infanticide, child rape, and indiscriminate slaughter. In Exodus, God calls Israel a "holy nation" (19:6), and in the Talmudic tradition, Moses was named as one of seven holy men responsible for bringing the physical manifestation of God back to earth (Patai, *The Hebrew Goddess* 101). Is a man holy who directs the slaughter of women and children and the rape of girls? Is his nation holy? Are his wars holy?

CHAPTER 4

ALL IN THE FAMILY: THE SECRET SEX LIVES OF GODS

> Royal dignity
> And love are seldom known to go to bed
> Together—therefore the Father
> Of all Gods
> . . . .
> dropped his royal scepter and
> Became a bull.
>
> Ovid 81

THE SOCIAL UNIT OF FAMILY furnishes a common metaphor for the Unknown. Human families typically include a husband-father, one or more wives-mothers, and children; the sexual relationship between husband and wife produces offspring; generations within a family may cooperate or quarrel; siblings may vie with each other for position; husbands may take multiple wives and concubines; wives may take lovers.

This powerful metaphor has determined the shape of countless narratives of divine beings throughout the world's myths and religions. Gender, again, is of central importance, for once a deity is designated male or female and once that figurative realm is available, various familial relationships and sexual behaviors enter effortlessly. Themes associated with the metaphor include marriage, sexual intercourse, pregnancy (male as well as female), birth (legitimate and illegitimate), incest, rape, fidelity, infidelity, love, hate, jealousy, revenge, intergenerational conflicts—all the common, grand, and terrible motifs that repeat in the music of the human family. Foremost among family metaphors, and one that dominates most of the narratives, is that of the heavenly Father.

HEAVENLY FATHER

Zeus, father of gods and mortals . . .
Hesiod, *Works and Days* 174

Yet, O Lord, thou art our Father . . .
Isaiah 64:8

When ye pray, say, Our Father which art in heaven . . .
Luke 11:2–3

Godhead and fatherhood are inextricably linked in the Indo-European family of languages, including Sanskrit, Greek, Latin, and others. As the languages of these patriarchal peoples evolved from a common ancestor, the name of the chief god appeared routinely as a compound: *Dyaus pitar* (Sanskrit), *Zeus pater* (Greek), *Diespiter* and *Juppiter* (Latin)—each designating the chief god and meaning something like "sky-father" (Barfield 84–85). The patriarchal Semites also designated "god" by a masculine noun—*El*, "lord" (used in both Canaanite and Hebrew texts for the high god, father of lesser gods, including the Canaanite Baal and the Hebrew "sons of God" or *bene Elohim*). Hebrew writers borrow other Canaanite names for Yahweh, their cultural father god: the plural form of El (Elohim), El Elyon ("God Most High"), and El Shaddai ("God of the Mountain," or "God Almighty"); another name, Avinu, simply means "our Father." The designation "father" for the Hebrew God therefore arises naturally, influenced by both Hebrew grammar and Semitic precedent (Patai, *Seed of Abraham* 193; Gordon, "Canaanite Mythology" 183–217; and Stephen L. Harris 73, 6–12).

The Greek god, Zeus, offers an extreme example of the father god. He is justly called "father of gods and mortals," for his sexual exploits are numerous, and his offspring include divine sons (e.g., Apollo and Dionysos), divine daughters (e.g., Athena, The Muses, Persephone), mortal sons (e.g., Perseus and Heracles), and a mortal daughter, Helen. The old fertility god lives in the designation "father," and an unabashed sexuality operates in the role of the father god not only in Zeus' activities, but generally. An intriguing example is the previously mentioned mating of Zeus and his consort, Hera, on Mount Ida, a fertility ritual that repeats the ancient mating of Earth Mother and Sky Father resulting in the flowering of nature (*Iliad* 341). "Golden droplets" represent divine semen, as in the shower of gold with which Zeus impregnates Danaë in the tale of Perseus' conception. A Sumerian narrative describes the "courtship" and rape of the divine maiden Ninlil by Enlil, chief god of the Sumerian pantheon, the "father of the gods," the "king of heaven and earth." Divine intercourse, and at times merely divine ejaculation, predictably results in progeny,[1] and this occasion proves no exception, as Ninlil becomes pregnant with the moon god Sin, patron deity of Ur, Abraham's city (Kramer, *Mythologies of the Ancient World* 96–97).

Like Zeus and Enlil, the Canaanite god El, chief of the gods, is a father of lesser gods—seven in number who "establish the seven-year cycle of abundance" (Kramer, *Mythologies of the Ancient World* 185). In some of his narratives, El is an aging god-king whose virility is questioned. His worshipers believed that if he became impotent, that fact would signal "the onslaught of lean years," whereas his ability to copulate and impregnate would usher in a long period of plenty (Gordon 187–88).[2] Among El's children is the fertility god Baal, who in narrative and ritual struggles against Mot ("Death") and undergoes cycles of death and rebirth, and although Zeus in historic times shows mere traces of a largely superseded fertility-god aspect, he does, nevertheless, father the fertility gods Dionysus and Persephone. The history of El and Zeus demonstrates a tendency in ancient narratives for worshipers of a war god to appropriate to their divinity a fertility function from a subjugated agricultural system of belief, so it is common to find a war god who also controls the fertility of the land, the animals, and the people.

The biblical Yahweh fits this pattern. God's first commandment to the birds and sea creatures, the land animals and humans, was the reiterated, "Be fruitful and multiply" (Genesis 1: 22, 28).[3] The very first conception and birth (of Cain) prompts Eve to declare, "I have gotten a man with the help of the Lord" (Genesis 4:1). Yahweh will continue to play a role in conception, intervening either to close or to "open the wombs" of women (including Sarah, Rebekah, Rachael, and the mothers of Samuel, Samson, and John the Baptist, among others), so that they might bear sons. As Patai comments, "[I]t is God who gives children," citing 1 Chronicles 28:5, Isaiah 8:18 and 66:9, Hosea 9:14, and Psalms 127:3 (*Sex and the Family* 74). Indeed one of Yahweh's two covenant promises to Abraham concerns an extraordinary fertility (Genesis 15:5). Fertility resulting in sons is a reward for righteous behavior: "Lo, sons are a heritage from the Lord, / the fruit of the womb a reward" (Psalm 127:3). The same logic dictates that childlessness is a punishment for sin or disobedience. Yahweh's appropriation of earlier gods' fertility function may make explicable to some extent the covenant's preoccupation with reproduction and the male organ of reproduction.

Yahweh's role in furthering fecundity extends to both human and natural realms. Sterility in nature, as barrenness in humans, is caused by human sin (Patai, *Sex and the Family* 84).[4] If it is a contest between Yahweh and Baal, the most prominent of Canaanite fertility gods, to withhold or restore fertility to the land, Yahweh prevails, besting the fertility god at his own game. An example occurs in the narrative in which Yahweh, angry about his people's worshiping the Canaanite fertility gods, Baal and Asherah, withholds rain (the divine semen) from Israel for an extended period until the land grows barren and people are in danger of starving (1 Kings 17). The contest pits Yahweh (and the prophet Elijah) against Baal (and his 450 prophets) on Mount Carmel. Two bulls are sacrificed and placed on altars—one for Yahweh and one for Baal.[5] The contest is designed to reveal which god can send fire to ignite the sacrifice. Baal fails to answer his prophets' entreaties, while Yahweh responds with fire, which "fell, and consumed the burnt offering, and the wood, and the stones, and the dust, and licked up the water in the trench" (1 Kings 18:38). God's display of power impresses the people, who return their allegiance to Yahweh: "The Lord, he is God."

Emulating some of his Semitic precursors and neighbors by assuming control of fertility—of plants, animals, and humans—Yahweh is "Father," a virile producer of life. Moreover, as with neighboring gods, his fatherhood extends into the heavenly realms. Just as the Babylonian Anshar was "father of the gods" (Heidel 28), and Canaanite El was a father god, each with his children—lesser gods, composing a divine court and counsel—so Yahweh fathered "sons of God," the *bene Elohim* (a designation found in both biblical and Canaanite texts[6]). The sons of God are a group of offspring who serve as functionaries in Yahweh's court. Psalm 82 presents the psalmist's vision of Yahweh in divine council condemning to death some of the lesser gods in his heavenly court: "I say, You are gods, sons of the Most High [El Elyon, one of Yahweh's designations], all of you / nevertheless, you shall die like men and fall like any prince" (6–7).

The sons of God appear first in the Old Testament in the mythological heroic-age fragment discussed in Chapter 3 that serves as prologue to the Flood narratives. There the sons of God emerge as sexual beings, who "saw that the daughters of men were fair" (Genesis 6:1), and they proceed to marry human women and father children. Although the narrative makes no overt connection, these acts of the sons of God appear to have provided at least some of God's motivation for destroying his creation along with their half-divine progeny. As discussed, this fragment bears intriguing similarities to a Greek fragment in which Zeus decides to destroy the demigods (Lattimore 10). The two situations are parallel: divine beings have been mating with humans and producing (male) offspring who, although half-divine, are mortal. In both cases, the sons of such couplings are legendary heroes—the biblical "mighty men . . . of renown" or the Greek figures of the heroic age. Both narratives present matter-of-factly sons of God as sexual beings who, in the mirror of heaven, reflect the image of men who find the daughters of men fair. The responses of Zeus and Yahweh, too, are similar—both decide to send a violent natural upheaval to destroy earth's population.

In the pseudepigraphal Book of Enoch, these particular sons of God, also called "Watchers," have asked Enoch to intervene with God on their behalf. God replies with a question: "Why did you leave lofty, holy Heaven to sleep with women, to defile yourselves with the daughters of men and take them as your wives, and like the children of the earth to beget sons, in your case giants?" (Barnstone 487). God goes on to explain that wives and children are needed only by those who die; celestial beings have no need to "live" through their progeny.[7] The tale attributes to God an association of sex with sin and death and an overt disregard for those who "defile" themselves with the "blood of women." It further expresses abhorrence toward women in general, their "blood" in particular, and the sexual converse they inspire.

THE MARRIAGE METAPHOR

So influential is the metaphor of family in Classical, pre-Semitic, and Semitic religions that the supreme god is usually provided one or more heavenly consorts: El has Asherah, Zeus has Hera (and others), Jupiter has Juno, Baal has Anath, and so on. The "motherly" goddess Asherah was wife of El and mother of all his seventy children. She was venerated throughout Canaan, and may have evolved from an ancient Sumerian goddess (Ashratum). Given the ubiquity of her worship, as Patai remarks, "It was almost inevitable that the cult of the great Canaanite mother goddess . . . should penetrate Hebrew religion as well." Evidence suggests that "the worship of the goddess must have been extremely popular in all segments of Hebrew society" (*The Hebrew Goddess* 38, 39). It was a small conceptual step, given the various titles of Yahweh that include *El*, and in view of Asherah's status as wife of El, to associate Asherah with Yahweh as his consort (Dever 183). A recently discovered pottery shard, "Yahweh and his Asherah," apparently represents an ithyphallic Yahweh in a bull mask accompanied by his consort in a cow mask (Stephen L. Harris 73). The tendency to provide God the Father a feminine mate or counterpart is revealed as well in the successive representations of the Cherubim, which in early texts appear as cloud-beings, mounts for Yahweh or draft animals for the divine chariot. A ubiquitous symbol of the divine presence, they assume representation in the Second Temple as "a man and a woman in sexual embrace"—a Hebrew representation apparently associating Yahweh with the divine connubium of ancient times (Patai, *The Hebrew Goddess*, "The Cherubim" 67–95).

The metaphor of family fostered the Hebrews' understanding that inasmuch as Yahweh was male, he was a sexual being; that he superseded the fertility gods of neighboring peoples (e.g., Baal) and fertilized the human and natural realms with divine seed; that in these endeavors he had a divine consort in the form of a goddess (Asherah), who received the divine seed and gave birth to his "children"—including a "son," the "visible creation" (Patai, *The Hebrew Goddess* 77), the flourishing vegetal and animal worlds, as well as the heavenly "sons of God."

Yahweh and the Harlot-Wife

With this figurative context in mind, it becomes possible to begin to sort out the many mysterious and enduring implications of the biblical marriage metaphor (and its companion figure, harlotry), their roles in religious thought, their identification of "spiritual" with physical passion, and association of these with the broad categories "good" and "evil."

Hosea, Old Testament prophet of the eighth century BCE, provides an early, intriguing, yet, troubling example of the marriage metaphor. His story begins abruptly with Yahweh's instruction: "Go, take to yourself a wife of harlotry and have children of harlotry, for the land commits great harlotry by forsaking the Lord" (1:2). In effect, God commands Hosea to become a living human metaphor for Yahweh himself as figurative husband to Israel, ambiguously both land and people, as harlot-wife. The ancient covenant between God and the Israelites is figured in the human marriage contract (in Hosea's case, obscenely entered into in full knowledge that it must be broken).

The interactive theory (discussed in the Introduction) holds that making a metaphor results in a transfer of particles of meaning between the referent and figure. The multiple facets of this metaphor present a figurative snarl in which divine and human meet and merge. So extensive is the transfer between figure and referent that each becomes both and neither: neither God nor man, land/people nor wife/harlot, divine covenant nor marriage contract, neither spiritual nor physical passion—neither *and* both. Gone is separate conceptual existence of any of its elements: the scientist and the fly are one.

In this use of the marriage metaphor, the narrator has Yahweh assume a covenantal/contractual relationship with his *wife*, Israel, in which he plays a specifically sexual role of begetting children, some of whom are bastards, as were the cuckolded Hosea's children. Hosea, as living metaphor *for a metaphor*, must enact and transpose all such implications from the divine to the earthly plane: he must "realize" the metaphor in a purposeful embracing of infidelity, jealousy, anger, and revenge. Gomer, too, is a living metaphor for a metaphor, her "harlotry" a figure for Israel's apostasy. Hosea's account continues: "So he went and took Gomer . . . , and she conceived and bore him a son. And the Lord said to [Hosea], 'Call his name Jezreel'" (1:3). The name *Jezreel* means "God sows," suggesting the legitimacy of this first child. Clearly that is not true of the next two children—a daughter, "Not Pitied," and another son, "Not My People." The anguish and anger of the betrayed husband—neither and both Yahweh and Hosea—appears in a command to Jezreel to act as intermediary: "Plead with your mother, plead—for she is not my wife, and I am not her husband—that she put away her harlotry from her face, and her adultery from between her breasts;

lest I strip her naked . . . and slay her with thirst" (2:2–3). By pronouncing, "she is not my wife, and I am not her husband," God/Hosea has divorced Israel/Gomer, for as Patai points out, these words constitute "a legal divorce formula," which in this complex figurative situation amounts to nullifying both the ancient covenant and Hosea's marriage contract (Patai, *Sex and the Family* 113). In addition, God/Hosea threatens to "strip her naked" and "slay her with thirst"—both punishments applicable to Gomer, the human wife of Hosea, but also figuratively to Israel, the land/people from which Yahweh will withhold his procreant rain. The harlot-wife's crimes include, most importantly, worshiping Baal and attributing to him the gifts of bread, water, wool, flax, oil, and drink. In response, Yahweh/Hosea vows to "hedge up her way with thorns; and . . . build a wall / against her, so that she cannot find her paths. / She shall pursue her lovers, but not overtake them . . . ." Then she will say, "I will go and return to my first husband, for it was better with me then than now" (Hosea 1:5–8).[8]

The Bible offers ample evidence that the ancient Hebrews remained polytheistic, worshiping Baal and Asherah (and others) alongside Yahweh. Greater accommodation was made for Asherah worship, at times making her the wife of Yahweh. Baal worship, however, presented the monotheistic writers and editors greater problems. Inasmuch as the Canaanite Baal was primarily a fertility god, Hebrew farmers routinely participated in the rituals of his worship. These would have involved sexual rituals conducted in sacred precincts. Such ritual "prostitution" was widespread, and extended to sanctuaries dedicated to Yahweh.[9] As Patai shows, "in the early days of the Hebrew tribes after they had conquered Canaan, and undoubtedly under the influence of indigenous Canaanite practices, [sacred] prostitutes [both male and female] were attached to local sanctuaries, serving the visitors and pilgrims." Further, the practice of sacred prostitution persisted, even to the time of the Babylonian Exile (586 BCE) (Patai, *Sex and the Family* 149, 151).

Therefore, God's/Hosea's diatribe against Israel/Gomer is focused on her sexual rituals in propitiation of Baal to whose influence she attributes the fruitfulness of the land. Yahweh/Hosea insists that it was he, rather than Baal, who produced the abundance, "who gave her the grain, the wine, and the oil." As a result of her Baal worship, understood as "marital" infidelity (pursuing her "lovers" and engaging in sexual rituals), Yahweh/Hosea will punish Gomer/Israel by withholding fertility and thus demonstrating that it is Yahweh who fertilizes the land. Yahweh plans her punishment:

> Now I will uncover her lewdness in the sight of her lovers, and no one shall rescue her out of my hand. And I will put an end to all her mirth . . . . And I will lay waste her vines and her fig trees, of which she said, "These are my hire, which my lovers have given me."
>
> 2:9–13

In this passage the voice and the passions express an all-too-human agony, jealousy, and anger, a dark desire to avenge the betrayal, a need for self-promotion—it was I, not Baal, not your other lovers, who lavished abundance on you.

The story reveals violent mood swings, as the protagonist moves suddenly from a desire for vengeance to an impulse to win back the "wife's" affection: "I will allure her, and bring her into the wilderness and speak tenderly to her." Then, it seems, all will be well: "And in that day, says the Lord, you will call me, 'My husband,' and no longer will you call me, 'My Baal.' For I will . . . betroth you to me in faithfulness; and *you shall know the Lord*" (2:14–20; emphasis supplied). The divine/human husband intends to reconcile with the wayward harlot-bride, to betroth her to himself "for ever" and "in faithfulness." His final declaration, "and you shall know the Lord," announces explicitly the sexual nature of the reconciliation.[10]

JERUSALEM, THE HARLOT-BRIDE

> I have seen your abominations, your adulteries and neighings, your lewd harlotries on the hills and in the field.
> Woe to you, O Jerusalem!
>
> Jeremiah 13:27

Hosea's narrative of Yahweh and his bride Israel reveals in the mirror of heaven a human situation in which people, anxious for their crops, their animals, their very lives, propitiate gods whom they believed might assure fertility and life. The belief systems of two of those gods, Yahweh and Baal, manifest radically different attitudes toward women, marriage, and sexual practices. Hosea's figure of the harlot-wife captured the imaginations of the three major prophets, Isaiah, Jeremiah, and Ezekiel, each of whom appropriated the metaphor and applied it to the relationship between Yahweh and the southern kingdom of Judah with its city of Jerusalem, supposed dwelling place of Yahweh. Of the three prophets, Ezekiel developed the metaphor most elaborately, and made it his own:[11]

> Again the word of the Lord came to me: "Son of man, make known to Jerusalem her abominations, and say, Thus says the Lord God to Jerusalem: . . . on the day you were born your navel string was not cut, nor were you washed with water to cleanse you . . . . [Y]ou were cast out on the open field for you were abhorred on the day that you were born.
>
> 16:1–5

Yahweh's biography of Jerusalem depicts an unwanted girl-child of mixed ancestry[12] exposed in a field to die. Yahweh commands her to "Live and grow up like a plant of the field," and she does so, in time reaching "full maidenhood," an explicitly sexual creature with breasts and pubic hair. God continues:

> When I passed by you again and looked upon you, behold, you were at the age for love; and I spread my skirt over you, and covered your nakedness: yea, I plighted my troth to you and entered into a covenant with you, says the Lord God, and you became mine.

The spreading of the skirt over the woman indicates entering into a sexual relationship (c.f. Ruth 3:8–9),[13] validated here by the plighting of troth and the covenant as marriage contract. God continues to describe his care for Jerusalem and the wealth he has given her, who "grew exceedingly beautiful," her beauty "perfect through . . . [God's] splendor" (16:9–14).

Jerusalem proves to be of the same ilk as Hosea's Israel. Addressing Jerusalem, Yahweh says, you "trusted in your beauty and played the harlot . . . and lavished your harlotries on any passer-by" (16:15). She has taken "Yahweh's wealth" to make shrines, upon which she "played the harlot" (16:16), and she has made idols, "images of men" and plays the harlot with them, giving them Yahweh's oil, incense, and bread, and even sacrifices her sons and daughters to the gods of the Canaanites, the Egyptians, the Assyrians, and the Chaldeans: "Adulterous wife who receives strangers instead of her husband!" As a result, God promises to gather her lovers against her in a military/sexual assault. They will "uncover [her] nakedness," or, in other words, engage in a gang rape. God promises to bring upon her "the blood of wrath and jealousy" so that the former lovers will stone her and "cut [her] to pieces with their swords" (35–41).

The tirade and catalogue of punishments finished, Yahweh offers a wife-abuser's conclusion, "So will I satisfy my fury on you, and my jealousy shall depart from you; I will be calm and no more be angry" (16:42), but then he remembers to be angry again, accusing Jerusalem of worse sins than those of all the neighboring peoples, even her "sister" Sodom. And then again the divine mood shifts, and he promises to remember the covenant/marriage contract, and forgive Jerusalem "all that [she] has done" (16:42–63).

THE SEXUAL NATURE OF EVIL

> Then the eyes of both were opened, and they knew that they were naked; and they sewed fig leaves together and made themselves aprons.
> Genesis 3:7

Satan whispered to them so as to expose their nakedness, which had been hidden from them. . . .

Qur'an 7:20

Among the Abrahamic religions, the clash of deities responsible for the fertility and prosperity of worshipers foregrounds sexuality as central to morality. The Bible tells of the twin birth of sex and evil. Adam and the woman disobey the first commandment and eat the fruit of the tree of knowledge of good and evil. According to both the serpent and Yahweh, the fruit brings God-like wisdom (Genesis 3:5, 22). As the narrative reveals, however, the nature of divine knowledge is not an intellectual enlightenment, as one might imagine, but sexual knowledge. Whereas at first, the man and woman are "both naked and not ashamed" (Genesis 2:25), once they have eaten the fruit, their eyes are opened, and they become sexual beings—"they knew that they were naked." They are now ashamed of their bodies (in particular their genitals), and make aprons of fig leaves to hide them. Thus, in a single archetypal moment several ideas converge—disobedience or sin, gaining of sexual (God-like) knowledge, and an inevitable fusing of sex and evil. However mythological the event, implications of this bit of text are incalculable.

Sexuality and sexual behavior emerge as primordial figures for sin as well as rubrics under which various forms of "evil" can be organized and condemned (for example, apostasy as "harlotry"). Both humans and angels *fall into sexuality*. In time sex became a metonymy for biblical evil and its near synonym. This fact helps account for the obsessive focus on human reproduction (the basis of God's covenant), being fruitful and multiplying, opening and closing wombs, sexual chastity and promiscuity, the sexual behavior and rituals of "enemies," circumcision, and the numerous details of God-sanctioned or prohibited sexual behavior. All this taken together becomes a prurient subtext whose covert messages underlie dozens of "laws" (for example, the law concerning building stairs to Yahweh's altar [Exodus 20:26]) and form the plot points for narrative after narrative.

God's preoccupation with sex is odd. The idea that the incomprehensible architect of the unfathomable universe should concern himself with the mechanics, processes, and practices of human sexuality is almost (but never quite) humorous. In the first account of creation, having made human bodies (in the image of God) and judging them "very good" (Genesis 1:31), God's first words to humans were, "Be fruitful and multiply, and fill the earth and subdue it" (1:28). All this sounds pleasant enough. It offers an image of God watching proudly as his new creations frolic in green pastures, similar to the way a rancher might observe his breeding herd. Nevertheless, in the second account of creation, not only does shame at their nakedness attach to sexuality in the newly opened eyes of Adam and Eve, God himself is offended by it, as if nakedness were the visible image of sin. God's curse on the woman deals exclusively with sexual roles. It establishes her submissive relationship to her husband, who "shall rule over [her]," yet she will nevertheless desire her husband, as a result participate in sexual intercourse, and, as punishment, experience pain in childbirth (Genesis 2:16). God's first act after cursing the couple is to make "garments of skin" to cover their no longer very good nakedness (Genesis 3:21).[14]

Uncovering Nakedness

> You shall not do as they do in the land of Egypt, where you dwelt, and you shall not do as they do in the land of Canaan, to which I am bringing you . . . . None of you shall approach any one near of kin to him to uncover nakedness.
>
> Leviticus 18:3–6[15]

The passage from Leviticus reveals that "uncover nakedness" is a figure for sexual intercourse. This charged language is implicated in a cryptic story about Noah. Following the Flood, as the story goes, "Noah was the first tiller of the soil. He planted a vineyard; and he drank of the wine, and became drunk, and lay uncovered in his tent." This is intriguing enough, but then something even more curious happens:

> And Ham, the father of Canaan, saw the nakedness of his father, and told his two brothers outside. Then Shem and Japheth took a garment, laid it upon both their shoulders, and walked backward and covered the nakedness of their father. Their faces were turned away, and they did not see their father's nakedness.
>
> Genesis 9:20–23

Canaan, Ham's son, will be "father" not only of the Egyptians but also the Canaanites, the peoples to which the Leviticus passage refers, and who in the future will be designated enemies of the invading Israelites. One of the accepted "truths" about the descendants of Canaan was that they engaged in forbidden sexual practices, including incest, bestiality, and homosexuality (Leviticus 18:22–23; 20:11–16). Thus, "When Noah awoke from his wine and knew what his youngest son had done to him," he uttered a curse *on Ham's son* that would echo through the centuries and take effect when the Israelites invaded Canaan: "Cursed be Canaan; a slave of slaves shall he be to his brothers" (Genesis 9:24–25).

What exactly has Ham done to Noah? How does Noah know that something has been done to him? Why curse Ham's son? One explanation is that Ham has taken sexual advantage of the drunken Noah,[16] and that somehow the forbidden sexual behavior is considered an inheritable trait that has been passed to Canaan and through him to his descendants. Thus, the story offers both an explanation of the Canaanites' supposed evil (sexual) nature and justification for wars of aggression and enslavement of Canaan's seed, who in the biblical view were habitual and indiscriminate uncoverers of nakedness.

The repeated admonition to the Israelites to avoid marriage with Canaanites lest they lead the Israelites astray is grounded on the notion of the evil nature of sexual behavior and its practice in worship. Hosea's marriage to the "harlot" Gomer builds on this theme, as does an equivocal account of Judah's marriage to the Canaanite woman Shua, and of Judah's son to the Canaanite woman Tamar. Shua had borne three sons to Judah (Er, Onan, and Shelah), at least two of whom seem to have been wicked. Judah then selects the Canaanite woman Tamar as wife for his eldest son Er, and although the nature of his evil is unstated, it is juxtaposed with his marriage to Tamar: "Er . . . was wicked in the sight of the Lord; and the Lord slew him." At this point the God-sanctioned convention of levirate marriage applies, and Judah orders his second son Onan to perform the levirate duty to "raise up offspring" for his brother. Onan becomes guilty of the "sin" of *coitus interruptus*, when he spills "the semen on the ground lest he should give offspring to his brother." The Lord, apparently watching the event, is displeased by Onan's refusal of his duty (and perhaps the wasted semen), considers it a capital offense, and kills him too. Tamar remains childless. Judah is understandably reluctant to send Shelah into what seems a dangerous situation. As the sexual saga continues, Tamar disguises herself as a prostitute (perhaps a "holy prostitute"), lies in wait for Judah, her father-in-law, and has sexual relations with him, resulting in pregnancy. Learning of her pregnancy, Judah orders her to be burned for playing the harlot. When she offers proof that the unborn twins are Judah's, he admits, "She is more righteous than I, inasmuch as I did not give her my son Shelah" (Genesis 38).

The tale is intriguing, but its premises concerning multiplying and sexual behavior are awkward: God is depicted as a sort of voyeur observing human sexual behavior; Canaanites are bad from the time of Noah; marriage with them might produce evil offspring (Er and Onan, whom God kills); the Canaanite Tamar can be killed for behavior (playing the harlot) in which Judah participates without censure. Despite all that, things proceed as God has written: Tamar's twins are born, one of whom will be a direct ancestor of the beloved King David.

THE UNCLEAN

> If a man lies with a woman and has an emission of semen, both of them shall bathe themselves in water, and be unclean until the evening.
> Leviticus 15:18

> When a woman has a discharge of blood . . . , she shall be in her impurity for seven days, and whoever touches her shall be unclean until the evening. And everything upon which she lies during her impurity shall be unclean; everything also upon which she sits shall be unclean. And whoever touches her bed shall wash his clothes, and bathe himself in water and be unclean until the evening.
> Leviticus 15:19–22

> On this day shall atonement be made for you, to cleanse you; from all your sins you shall be clean before the Lord.
> Leviticus 16:30

Again, an almost comical incongruity inheres in the Unknown's concern about and observation of natural processes connected with procreation. Such attitudes as Yahweh manifests toward "discharges" and "emissions" associate both evil and danger with desire. The general concept of uncleanliness (always associated with evil behavior) attaches to all sexual behavior, the women who become pregnant, and the babies born to them:

> The Lord said to Moses, " . . . If a woman conceives, and bears a male child, then she shall be unclean seven days; as at the time of her menstruation, she shall be unclean. And on the eighth day the flesh of his foreskin shall be circumcised. Then she shall continue for thirty-three days in the blood of her purifying; she shall not touch any hallowed thing, nor come into the sanctuary, until the days of her purifying are completed. . . . "

The birth of a female child produces twice the uncleanliness, the days of the mother's purifying doubled to fourteen plus sixty-six. After all her God-offending uncleanliness and purifying, she must bring a lamb and a young pigeon or turtledove to the priest for a "*sin* offering," and "he shall offer it before the Lord, and make atonement for her; then she shall be clean from the flow of her blood" (Leviticus 12:1–7). What is her sin? Apparently it is the fact that she became pregnant and gave birth. Uncovering nakedness leads to pregnancy; giving birth renders the mother unclean, sinful. Generation is evil; evil is passed to offspring—evil times two if the child is female.

Gods and Virgins

> Semele, daughter of Kadmos, lay in love with Zeus also
> and bore him a glorious son, Dionysus, giver of good things,
> she mortal, he immortal. . . .
>
> Hesiod, *Theogony* 940–42

> When his mother Mary had been betrothed to Joseph, before they came together she was found to be with child of the Holy Spirit.
>
> Matthew 1:18

Biblical morality is, then, figured in sexual terms. The reality of God's gender and the frankly sexual imagery used for Yahweh's relationship with his harlot/bride, combined with the many sexual tales of the patriarchs and other biblical characters, along with numerous laws governing sexual behavior and the resulting uncleanliness (sin), forge an identification of sex with evil and death that winds through God's Book from the moment Adam and Eve disobey God's command and become sexually aware to the triumphant destruction of the Whore of Babylon in Revelation. Considering the Bible's identification of sex with evil, of "original sin" somehow manifested as sexual generation, and Yahweh's distaste for, yet intense interest in, all things sexual, the story of his impregnating the human woman Mary is, to say the least, surprising, and yet it joins a number of similar tales among the world's mythological narratives.

The story of divine-human unions tells of the virgin who is loved by a god and is impregnated by him or the goddess who loves a man and is impregnated by him. The child born from the divine-human union is destined for greatness: he is a brave warrior, such as Achilles, Aeneas, or the biblical Nephilim; he performs superhuman labors on behalf of humankind, such as Gilgamesh or Heracles; he represents life, as does Dionysus or Perseus, and opposes the forces of death (embodied in terrible monsters—the Bull of Heaven, the Medusa, or the Hydra). Into this company comes the tale of Jesus.

The human model of the conjugal relationship is often modified in tales of divine-human mating. Zeus impregnates Danaë, for example, through a "shower of gold." He approaches Leda in the form of a swan and Europa in the form of a bull. He takes a human form in his conjugal relations with Dionysus' mother, Semele. The heroes of tradition are typically the sons of women whose virginity is intact at the time the god or a mysterious or distinguished father approaches her. Often the hero's conception is through unconventional means. As an appropriate consequence of the father's swan form, Leda lays one or two eggs, from which are hatched two sets of twins.[17] An important point of the story is that the mother of the half-divine child is a virgin when the deity inseminates her, perhaps to allay questions concerning the hero's divine paternity and miraculous destiny.[18] It follows that Mary's virginity is of particular importance, given the relentless biblical association of sexuality with evil. It is therefore necessary for Jesus to come into the world without the stain of original sin through "immaculate conception."[19]

Nevertheless, Mary finds this a difficult concept. When the angel Gabriel announces to Mary, "you will conceive in your womb and bear a son, and you shall call his name Jesus. He will be great, and will be called the Son of the Most High," Mary is skeptical: "How can this be, since I have no husband?" Gabriel's explanation is as mysterious as the conception itself: "The Holy Spirit will come upon you, / and the power of the Most High will overshadow you" (Luke 1:31–35). A subtle suggestion of *spiritual* or *metaphysical* intercourse is made problematic by the fact that Mary is a physical being in whose physical womb the divine child will be conceived.

MARRIAGE AND FAMILY IN THE NEW TESTAMENT

> Lord of the Universe! The celestials never die, and they do not reproduce their kind. Terrestrial beings die, but they are fruitful and multiply. Therefore I pray: Either make me immortal, or give me a son!
>
> Jewish Midrash, Hannah's Prayer at Shiloh[20]

> Jesus replied, "The people of this age marry and are given in marriage. But those who are considered worthy of taking part in that age and in the resurrection from the dead will neither marry nor be given in marriage, and they can no longer die; for they are like the angels."
>
> Luke 20:34–37

Nowhere is the New Testament's appropriation and revision of the Old Testament covenant—and what that covenant implies about human life, death, and immortality, or lack of it—more astonishing and problematic than in the realm of sexuality, marriage, and family. Hannah's prayer in the epigraph illustrates the Old Testament view that the covenant relationship assured Abraham and his descendants a sort of immortality through countless progeny, while accepting the finality of individual death.[21] It is only "the celestials" who do not die and, therefore, have no need to "be fruitful and multiply" as per God's command. In the epigraph from Luke, Jesus takes up this topic. He has been asked about a woman with seven husbands (all brothers):[22] "In the resurrection, therefore, whose wife will the woman be?" His response echoes and elaborates the idea of Hannah's prayer: there is no marriage in the resurrection, nor producing of children, for the resurrected are celestials—"like the angels"—who, enjoying immortality, have no need to live through children (cf. Mark 12:25).[23]

St. Paul's epistles, earliest of New Testament texts, confront the problem of what Herbert Marks calls "intertestamental continuity." The Old Testament as authoritative precursor text is a kind of elephant in the corner, impossible to ignore, even while one attempts to carry on one's own conversation. Such a situation, as Harold Bloom puts it, creates an "anxiety of influence"—arising from "the generic principle . . . that priority in the natural order is equivalent to authority in the spiritual order" (Marks, "Pauline Typology," 306). St. Paul, Marks argues, subordinates "the Jewish scriptures to their 'spiritual' understanding . . . , a paradigmatic instance of revisionary power realized in the process of overcoming a tyranny of predecession" (ibid.).

Indeed the concept of resurrection has the general effect of forcing a reinterpretation of all the predecessor texts. One effect of reinterpretation is to devalue not only marriage, but all family relationships. It is unsurprising that the marriage lyrics of the Song of Solomon, with their celebration of love, passion, and the pleasures of the body, find no echo in St. Paul's writings. In fact, Paul's discourse on marriage in 1 Corinthians might well be called an anti–Song of Songs:

> It is well for a man not to touch a woman. But because of the temptation to immorality, each man should have his own wife and each woman her own husband. The husband should give to his wife her conjugal rights, and likewise the wife to her husband . . . . Do not refuse one another except perhaps by agreement for a season, that you may devote yourselves to prayer; but then come together again, lest Satan tempt you through lack of self-control. I say this by way of concession, not of command. I wish that all were as I myself am [unmarried, celibate].
>
> 7:1–9

Paul associates sexual passion with vulnerability and sin. To his mind, self-control is a virtue; sexual passion, a weakness that Satan can use to tempt one to sin—sin equated with the pleasures of the flesh. In Paul's view, it is well to master the demands of the body so that one can devote oneself to the "affairs of the Lord." If one is unable to do so, marriage is the only not-altogether-satisfactory alternative: "He who marries his betrothed does well; and he who refrains from marriage will do better" (7:38).

JESUS, THE BRIDEGROOM

Generally speaking, a profound ambivalence marks the treatment of marriage, family, and family relations in the New Testament. On the one hand, Jesus will reprise Yahweh's role as husband, not to Israel, Judah, or Jerusalem, but to the community of believers—the Church, New Jerusalem, or even the wise virgins. In parables, either as bridegroom or wedding guest, he will be associated with wedding feasts and celebrations, but he will denigrate marriage in general: "[T]hose who are accounted worthy to attain to that age and to the resurrection from the dead neither marry nor are given in marriage" (Luke 20:34–35). Nevertheless, marriage recurs as a motif in New Testament parables.

Matthew offers an intriguing marriage parable, which begins with an unintelligible simile: "The kingdom of heaven may be compared to a king who gave a marriage feast for his son" (22:2). The subject is apparently the kingdom of heaven, the nature of which has been "hidden since the foundation of the world" (Matthew 13:35; 25:34). Is the kingdom like a king (powerful, anthropomorphic)? Like a feast? Like a feast for a son? Who is the son? Does it matter? Such questions lead to numerous others as the tale proceeds. When the king sends servants to issue invitations, the invited guests offer excuses and even kill the king's servants (22:3–6). As the tale progresses, responses of invited guests become increasingly surreal.

If the parable is intended to reveal the nature of the kingdom of heaven, what are the celestial referents for these figures? The angry king responds to the murder of his servants by sending his troops to destroy the murderers and burn their city (22:7). Is the city a part of the king's realm? Who/what are the troops? Finally, the king sends his servants to invite all whom they meet to the feast, "both bad and good," and "the wedding hall was filled with guests" (22:8–10). Who are these "bad and good" who were excluded from the first guest list? Why were they excluded? Why, now, are the "bad" welcomed?

After welcoming the multitude of "bad and good," the king notices a single guest who "had no wedding garment." This situation prompts the king to order his servants to "[b]ind him hand and foot, and cast him into the outer darkness; there men will weep and gnash their teeth" (22:13). Apparently the metaphor of the wedding garment is key, for its absence prompts the severest of punishments unvisited upon the "bad," who apparently have wedding garments. What is the celestial referent for this figure? Also, if the parable reveals something about the kingdom of heaven, down what winding street is the district of "outer darkness"? Who are the men there who weep and gnash their teeth? Do these also lack "wedding garments"? All these figurations are suggestive, while remaining indeterminate. Jesus provides what appears to be a "moral" at the end, yet that too presents difficulties: "For many are called, but few are chosen" (22:14). This summation resolves nothing, but rather adds a layer of confusion. In the context of the tale, might the man who lacks a wedding garment represent the "few" who are chosen, as opposed to the many "bad and good" who fill the wedding hall? The overarching metaphors of marriage and wedding hall are suggestive, but largely ignored in the narrative and its moral.[24] New Testament figuration associated with marriage and family leads away from the biological family and the blessing of descendants to a metaphorical "family" of those who reject marriage and their biological families. A Pauline tone permeates the parables in Matthew 22 and Luke 14, devaluing marriage and familial relationships in favor of otherworldly concerns.

Jesus is again figured as bridegroom in Matthew's parable of the wise and foolish virgins, which begins with a simile for the kingdom of heaven equally as strange as that which introduces the parable of the marriage feast: "Then the kingdom of heaven shall be compared to ten maidens who took their lamps and went to meet the bridegroom" (25:1). Do the virgins represent the population of earth or heaven? Why are they virgins, rather than men or women? What is their relationship to the bridegroom? Are they brides? Five of the maidens have oil for their lamps (is the oil a metaphor similar to the wedding garment?), and five do not. When the bridegroom comes, those who have no oil are excluded from the marriage feast, and the "Lord" (bridegroom?) tells them, "I do not know you" (25:1–12). Is exclusion akin to banishment to outer darkness? Again a sort of moral/admonition is provided: "Watch therefore, for you know neither the day nor the hour" (25:13).

Although Jesus asserts that there is no marriage in heaven, he provides an exception in his marriage to the virginal New Jerusalem. In Revelation, sexuality is a metaphor for all bad behavior and personified as the Whore of Babylon, whose destruction is Jesus' greatest victory:

> Fallen, fallen is Babylon the great!
> It has become a dwelling place of demons
> . . . .
> for all nations have drunk the wine of her impure passion,
> and the kings of the earth have committed fornication with her . . . .
> 18:2–3

Whereas the harlot has been separated from the blessed community, named Babylon, and consigned to the fiery pit, God's people have now been named the bride of the Lamb, a figure for Jesus (Revelation 5:6).

In John's vision, the Holy City, New Jerusalem, spotless, cured of the old Jerusalem's wanton ways, descends from heaven "prepared as a bride adorned for her husband." What is the nature of the marriage? It is, I think, far removed from the Old Testament's association of marriage with pleasure and family: "Enjoy life with the wife whom you love, all the days of your vain life . . . because that is your portion in life and in your toil at which you toil under the sun" (Ecclesiastes 9:9).

One can only speculate about the religious and theological consequences through the ages of the Bible's persistent association of sin with sex and the personification of evil as a harlot.[25] The figure of Jesus as bridegroom runs counter to his remaining unmarried and insisting that in the eternal realm there is no marriage. To paraphrase an old adage, he is always a bridegroom, never a husband.

Sex in Heaven?

But you were spiritual and immortal for all generations of the world. So I gave you no wives, for Heaven is your proper dwelling place.
2 Enoch, Barnstone 487

The Creator of the heavens and the earth! How could He have children, when He has no spouse, when He created all things, and has full knowledge of all things?
Qur'an 6:101–2

The human being, like the immortals, naturally places sexual intercourse far and away above all other joys—yet he has left it out of his heaven!
Mark Twain, *Letters from the Earth* 224

The Qur'an makes some notable revisions of the biblical visions of Heaven—whether as banquet hall, or marriage feast, throne room, or holy city. While the Qur'an's punishments of disbelievers (eternal suffering in the fires of hell) (67:5–10) and blessings for believers (immortality, joy, absence of pain) are similar to those in the Bible, the Muslim heaven is depicted as Gardens: "Those who are mindful of God are in Gardens and in bliss, rejoicing in their Lord's gifts: He has saved them from the torment of the Blaze":

> "Eat and drink with healthy enjoyment as a reward for what you have done." They are comfortably seated on couches arranged in rows; We pair them with beautiful-eyed maidens . . . ; We provide them with any fruit or meat they desire. They pass around a cup which does not lead to any idle talk or sin.
> 52:18–23

Lush foliage, springs of water, fruit and meat, maidens "restraining their glances untouched beforehand by man or jinn,"[26] kept in tents, reclining "on green cushions and fine carpets" (55:45–77)—these constitute rewards for believers in an extremely sensual heaven. (One wonders whether the mechanical dolls created expressly to serve as eternal sexual servants have minds, personalities, or aspirations.) Allah is concerned with fulfilling the desires (including sexual fantasies) of pious *men*. I find it hard to imagine that either St. Paul or Jesus would be blissful or even comfortable here. So, while the Qur'an insists that Allah has fathered no son and has no consort (that is, unlike Yahweh, he is not himself a sexual being [Qur'an 72:3]), his provisions for the blessed include virgins for sexual enjoyment.[27] Islamic resurrection to an immortal state seems not to result in that profound change from carnal to the unimaginable spiritual that St. Paul professed: "What no eye has seen, nor ear heard, / nor the heart of man conceived" (1 Corinthians 2:9), nor does it result in angelic celibacy which abjures all conjugal relations: "For in the resurrection they neither marry, nor are given in marriage, but are as the angels of God in heaven" (Matthew 22:30; cf. Mark 12:25, Luke 20:35).

Both the Christian and the Islamic heavenly mirrors reflect the strong patriarchal nature of the societies whose figurations and narratives attempt to represent the Unknown. The names *Yahweh* and *Allah* are predictably masculine. Biblical and Islamic angels are masculine, as are the Islamic Jinn. Patai, speaking of the gender of Allah and the angels in Islam, comments, "Islam, it can be stated outright, is the only one of the three monotheistic religions from whose divine realm the feminine was totally and definitely excluded" (*The Seed of Abraham* 194).[28]

The Christian heaven is, then, a sexless "spiritual" place, whereas the Islamic heaven is a sensual garden of "earthly" delights. The Christian mirror of heaven reflects the likeness of a cathedral or a church fellowship hall, with songs and prayers and constant adoration among one's figurative brothers and sisters. Rather than the mosque, the Islamic heaven reflects the likeness of a lush oasis, a welcoming haven providing for the physical needs and desires of the masculine believers who dwell in the harsh environment of Arabian deserts.

I turn next to one of the most complex of family relationships—that of fathers and sons—as it bears on "knowledge" of the Unknown, the figurative Father of Fathers.

CHAPTER 5

FATHERS AND SONS: VIOLENCE AND SACRIFICE

> It is your own son there
>   don't murder your son
> the wild and well born
>   son let him be. . . .
>
> Kinsella, *The Táin* 42

> We have a law, and by that law he ought to die, because he has made himself the Son of God.
>
> John 19:7

FREUD AND OTHERS—SACRED VIOLENCE AND SACRIFICE

The family offers one of the closest and yet most problematic of relationships in the father-son dyad, whether divine or human. Sigmund Freud thought that this relationship, with all its passions and strife, lay at the very core of Western culture and civilization and grew from the infantile, sexually driven competition of the son with the father for possession of the mother. He named the mindset of the son in such a situation the "Oedipus complex." The Oedipal phase of psychosexual development occurs normally, he thought, between the ages of three and five. He understood this phase as a *universal* human phenomenon that, if not "mastered," resulted in arrested psychic development, or "neurosis," in which one fails to evolve naturally through the stages of mental maturation and remains lodged in a mindset appropriate to a very young child.[1] Freud's idiosyncratically focused explanation does not help much as one seeks to understand the father-son relationship in religious/mythological narratives with their persistent echoing of sacred ritual, for it is indeed more rich and varied than Freud noticed. Freud recognized the Oedipus complex easily enough but failed to recognize what I call the "Laius attitude," manifested in the father's murderous intentions toward the son.[2]

René Girard offered another theory. He attributed father-son strife to what he called "mimetic elements" in the son's idealization of the father and identification with him in a "model-disciple" relationship. He finds that father-son strife is a common and focused manifestation of a *universal human tendency to violence* and of society's need to deflect and defuse that violence through ritual—especially blood sacrifice. Gerard acknowledges a form of Oedipal conflict, but for him the engine that powers that machine originates in hero worship involving the son's identification with the father model:

> The identification is a desire *to be* the model that seeks fulfillment, naturally enough, *by means of appropriation*; that is by taking over the things that belong to his father. As Freud says, the son *seeks to take the father's place everywhere*; he thus seeks to assume his desires, to desire what the father desires [including the mother].
> *Violence and the Sacred* 170; emphasis supplied

Girard's claim is that "mimetic rivalry" must end in *reciprocal* violence, which is initiated by the father's interpretation of the son's actions "in terms of usurpation" (*Violence and the Sacred* 174)—the father's response describable (in my terms) as the "Laius attitude." Girard believes that society, unable to contain such violence and continue to function, provides means for its safe dispersal, often redirecting and containing it as "sacred" violence through sacrificial rituals. As Girard puts it, "When unappeased, violence seeks and always finds a surrogate victim." The sacrifice thus has a dual nature—as both sacred act and at times "as a sort of criminal activity": "If sacrifice resembles criminal violence, we may say that *there is ... hardly any form of violence that cannot be described in terms of sacrifice. ...*" (*Violence and the Sacred* 1; emphasis supplied).

Ritual sacrifice, Girard says, is controlled, directed, approved violence: "The sacrifice serves to protect the entire community from *its own violence*; it prompts the entire community to choose victims outside itself" (*Violence and the Sacred* 8),[3] that is, to direct its natural violence toward objects outside the social unit. Animal victims are "sacrificeable," as are certain humans: "prisoners of war, slaves, small children, unmarried adolescents, and the handicapped" (ibid. 12). In the case of Oedipus' father, Laius has incurred divine wrath by violating the sacred ties of guest and host. When he consults the Delphic oracle, Apollo tells him,

"I will give you a son, but you are destined to die at his hands" (Morford and Lenardon 380). Seeking to evade this divinely imposed destiny, Laius directs that his infant son be exposed[4] to die on a mountaintop, a spike driven through his ankles.[5] The narrative thus takes the potentially incendiary relationship of father and son, and adds elements of guilt, fate, divinity, and violence. Laius initiates Girard's "reciprocal violence" between father and son upon his recognition that the child poses the threat of usurpation. The child is "sacrificeable" because it is not yet integrated into the society.

For Freud, and, with a different emphasis, Girard, psychological and cultural components of human sexuality and potential for "sacred" violence through sacrifice are epitomized in the narrative of Oedipus, the son fated to kill and usurp his father and marry his mother. This story, Freud asserted, is *the* psychosexual key to Western civilization. However, even if one grants that infantile sexuality may play a part, it is only one key, and, as Girard suggests, other keys, psychological, social, and cultural, are required to open the door to understanding: sometimes "Oedipus" kills "Laius"; but more frequently "Laius" kills "Oedipus," and the mirror of heaven inevitably reflects the human psychology and culture implicit in the father-son relationship. Uranus tries to deny birth (and hence life) to Kronus and his siblings; after castrating Uranus and displacing him, Kronus devours his own sons and daughters as they are born; after Zeus, Kronus' son, defeats Kronus in a great battle, Zeus appropriates his power, but later swallows his pregnant wife Metis to prevent the birth of a son. In each case, the father acts in response to a prophecy—a sacred message—that his son will appropriate his power and property and displace him.

Like the Greek, Old Testament texts examine the troubled father-son relationship, and its heavens reflect the violence-riddled relationship between the Father, Yahweh, and Israel, his disobedient firstborn "son" whom Yahweh thinks at times to destroy. The human narrative of son Absalom's rebellion against David relates that one of Absalom's first aggressive acts against King David consisted of the decidedly Oedipal act of appropriating David's harem (2 Samuel 20–21). His rebellion is resolved when David's forces kill Absalom. The New Testament makes the story of the violent death ("sacrifice") of the son (or Son)—at the will of the Father—its signature narrative.

Augmenting the potentially incendiary relationship of fathers and sons is the fact that, in the natural way of the world, sons bury fathers. The theme rises to particular prominence in societies with patrilineal descent and the poignant human situation that dictates that fathers yield their positions, power, wealth, and even their lives to the necessities of time and generation. Often there is a gradual, ritual yielding of power to the son. The biblical father's impending death is occasion for blessing and yielding of power—including the covenant relationship with Yahweh. It is intriguing to notice that whereas in the Greek tradition the son tends to prevail over the father or father figure (e.g., Kronus over Uranus, Zeus over Kronus, Oedipus over Laius, Pelops over Oenomaüs, Perseus over Acrissius), resulting in the father's death or deposition, in crucial biblical accounts, father-son relationships (biological or figurative) are fulfilled in the death of the son.

SACRIFICE—FOOD FOR THE GODS

> Then [Abraham] took curds, and milk, and the calf which he had prepared and set it before [Yahweh and his divine companions]; and he stood by them under the tree while they ate.
>
> Genesis 18:8

From a modern perspective it is difficult to understand the logic behind the practice of animal or human sacrifice. One might wonder, what in the world the Unknown, or indeed any local deity, would do with the burned carcass of a human or an animal. Why would sacrifices be pleasing to the gods? One common rather unsatisfactory explanation is that sacrifice was meant to show fealty or to appease or propitiate the gods for human failings. However, the ancient and original purpose was a practical one: to feed the gods, whose physical needs reflected those of their worshipers (Jaynes 243). The slaughtered victim (often accompanied by libations) furnished, in effect, a meal to be shared by men and gods: the receiver of all gifts (humankind) returns to the giver of all gifts (the deity) the sustenance the god requires—in a divinely mandated reciprocity—*das ut dem*.[6] In ancient worship, every meal was a sacred meal, and each required donation of the god's portion. Hesiod tells the story of Prometheus' trick of Zeus that explains why the thighbones and fat constituted the gods' portion of the sacrificial animal (Hesiod, *Theogony* 556–57).

The practice of burning food for the resident god on his altar or placing it in his "house" or temple was widespread. The god was often an elaborately carved, jewel-encrusted, sumptuously dressed effigy or statue "dwelling" within his temple. The statue did not merely represent the god, but was the "living" god himself. In Mesopotamia, numerous cuneiform texts describe the special care given to the resident gods. Jaynes describes the lengths to which the priests would go to serve the deity: "The gods . . . liked eating and drinking, music and dancing; they required beds to sleep in and for enjoying sex with other god-statues on connubial visits from time to time; they had to be washed and dressed, and appeased with pleasant odors . . ." (Jaynes 178–79). Biblical authors commonly viewed these gods of neighboring people as lifeless artifacts; they were not "living" as was the Israelites' unrepresentable Yahweh. The psalmist responds to criticism by neighboring people, who question the reality of the invisible deity and ask, "Where is their God?" "Our God is in the heavens," the psalmist replies. He is unlike the idols of silver and gold—the "work of men's hands":

> They have mouths, but do not speak; eyes, but do not see.
> They have ears, but do not hear; noses, but do not smell.
> They have hands, but do not feel; feet, but do not walk;
> And they do not make a sound in their throat.
>
> Psalm 115:2–8

Yet from their worshipers' perspective, the idols did possess human senses and appetites; they needed to eat, and so the priests brought them food. After a time during which the god was left to enjoy his meal, the steward or priest would, no doubt, consume what the god had left (Jaynes 180). The continued worship of such "other" gods by the Israelites as well as the Canaanites and others in the Promised Land furnishes the background for the prophetic texts. Ezekiel's Yahweh accuses Jerusalem of receiving Yahweh's bounty and rather than returning a portion to Yahweh, giving it to the images that have mouths but do not speak (Ezekiel 16:16–21).

Like other gods, Yahweh was thought to dwell in his temple, to descend in a cloud into the House of Yahweh. Also like other gods, Yahweh received food sacrifices, which the Aaronic priests shared as "wave offerings," or "priests' portion" (Exodus 29:26–28).[7] The food consisted of both animal and cereal offerings, along with libations of wine offered twice daily. Feeding the God is graphically depicted in the story of Abraham's preparing the meal consumed by Yahweh at Mamre (Genesis 18:6–8; epigraph).[8] In the late apocryphal story of Bel and the Dragon, a dispute arises between the prophet Daniel and the king of Babylon over who is the "living" god—Yahweh or Bel. King Astyages claims that Bel is a living god because he consumes the food left for him in his temple: "Do you not see how much he eats and drinks every day?" (Oxford Annotated Bible, "Bel and the Dragon" 1:6). Through a clever trick, Daniel reveals that it is the seventy priests of Bel and their families who consume the food, whereupon the angry king orders the priests and their families killed (1:22). An implication is that a living god would eat the sacrifice, whereas a lifeless idol could not.

At the end of the Flood, Noah builds an altar and offers Yahweh a great sacrifice of "every clean animal and of every clean bird"; the Lord (unlike the idols) has a nose and can smell, and he responds to the odor of the cooking/burning meat: "And when the *Lord smelled the pleasing odor,* the Lord said in his heart, 'I will never again curse the ground because of man'" (Genesis 8:20–21; emphasis supplied; cf. Exodus 29:38–43). A similar scene had occurred in the Epic of Gilgamesh. Following the universal Flood, Utnapishtim offers a sacrifice, to which the gods, responding to the "sweet savor," are drawn and "crowd like flies about the sacrificer"; as will Yahweh, the collective gods accept the food offering and agree that the deluge was a bad idea (Pritchard 70–71).[9]

BORN FOR GOD—SACRIFICE OF THE FIRSTBORN AND SLAUGHTER OF THE INNOCENTS

The first-born of your sons you shall give to me. You shall do likewise with your oxen and your sheep; seven days it shall be with its dam; on the eighth day you shall give it to me.

Exodus 22:29

About midnight I will go forth in the midst of Egypt; and all the first-born in the land of Egypt shall die.

Exodus 11:4–5

Sacrifice is primarily an act of violence without risk of vengeance.

Girard 13

Intricacies of the father-son relationship are woven together with the notion of feeding the gods. The practice of animal sacrifice takes on darker connotations when one considers that human sacrifice belongs to the same mindset. Do the gods smell the sweet savor of burning human flesh? Human sacrifice is, like animal sacrifice, God-sanctioned and validated violence. Girard does not comment on the motives or role of the gods in such narratives. If, as Girard claims, violence and the sacred are an inextricable pair—the figurative assignment to the Unknown of the human tendency to violence not only diverts the actual violence to an acceptable object (the victim), but also the impulse to violence is diverted to the divine. That is, if the eruption of violence can be directed to a sacrificial victim, it is also true that "guilty" motive can be cleansed by assigning it to the will of the gods. It is Apollo, for example, who requires Orestes to kill his mother and who prompts Laius to initiate violence against his son. The narrative motif associated with the deaths is that the gods must eat; they require the violence; humans merely carry out divine orders.

The enigmatic tale of "The Binding of Isaac" or Akedah (Genesis 22:1–13)—often explicated, seldom illuminated[10]—brings into focus the figurative complexities of the father-son relationship as enacted in the ritual of child sacrifice, as well as the relative responsibilities of divine and human participants. I agree with Eric Auerbach that the inexplicability of the tale arises as much from what is not said as from what is,[11] from the casual demand by Yahweh that Abraham sacrifice his son, from the equally casual manner in which Abraham proceeds to do so, to the fact that almost every aspect of the tale is not only illogical and paradoxical, but shockingly devoid of human feeling. God and Abraham proceed as dispassionately as laboratory scientists: Abraham is God's subject; Isaac is Abraham's. Nineteenth-century philosopher Sören Kierkegaard acknowledged the textual difficulties when he commented that understanding Hegel was relatively easy compared with understanding Abraham: "I strain every muscle to get a view of it—that very instant I am paralyzed" (*Fear and Trembling* 23).

Perhaps the abrupt nature of Yahweh's command and the prompt, unquestioning nature of Abraham's response simply reflect a generally accepted precept concerning sacrifice of the firstborn: "The first-born of your sons you shall give to me" (Exodus 22:29). In Israelite law, the boy child becomes a member of the covenant community on his eighth day, when he is circumcised; hence the sacrifice on the seventh day. In the case of David's first son by Bathsheba, that child lives seven days and dies—by Yahweh's command. After David admits his guilt (adultery and murder), the prophet Nathan tells him, "The Lord also has put away your sin; you shall not die. Nevertheless, because by this deed you have utterly scorned the Lord, the child that is born to you shall die" (2 Samuel 12:13–14). The child is clearly a guilt offering, "sacrificeable" (in Girard's term), required by Yahweh on behalf of the offending father. In this fascinating case, David's "Laius attitude," his desire to be rid of the potentially usurping child, and the associated guilt are ascribed to the heavenly Father, who then exacts the human sacrifice to expiate both deed and desire. In a series of refractions, the father's human violence (which has been wrongly exercised within the community against Uriah) is projected onto the Sky Father and redirected to the child: David kills Uriah; Yahweh kills the child.

The case of Isaac is similar in that here, too, it is Yahweh who would exact a particular child sacrifice: "Take your son . . . whom you love . . . and offer him . . . as a burnt offering upon one of the mountains of which I shall tell you" (Genesis 22:2; see 22:1–13). Abraham has apparently not sinned, but his love for God and unquestioning obedience are nevertheless to be "tested." Such testing is inexplicable in view of Abraham's life-long acquiescence to Yahweh's every demand. It would likewise be inexplicable if Yahweh were "omniscient"—as is often claimed.[12] If he were omniscient, such "testing" could only be considered sadistic cruelty. Isaac is the son long promised, the means by which Yahweh would fulfill his covenant agreement to make Abraham a "great nation" with countless descendents. Although the narrative claims that Abraham loves Isaac, there is nevertheless an almost robotic quality to Abraham's response to the authoritative command. Perhaps the jealous Yahweh wonders whom Abraham loves more, himself or Isaac. Either way, it makes no sense. Abraham's prompt obedience to the demand stands in stark contrast to his earlier concern for his nephew Lot, citizen of Sodom. On hearing Yahweh's plan to destroy the city, Abraham stands blocking the way and offers Yahweh a lesson in divine justice: "Far be it from thee to do such a thing, to slay the righteous with the wicked so that the righteous fare as the wicked! . . . Shall not the Judge of all the earth do right?" (Genesis 18:25). Abraham's silent complicity in the intended killing of Isaac is impossible to reconcile with his earlier passionate questioning.[13]

In another way, however, perhaps the story indicates that the sacrifice of the firstborn was so common a practice that it raised no ethical questions for Abraham, as it would for Kierkegaard. After all, Yahweh has commanded the Israelites to give him their firstborn sons (Exodus 22:29). Although Kierkegaard assumes that human sacrifice is unacceptable, neither Abraham nor his God appears to have made such an assumption. Kierkegaard then inquires whether faith and duty to obey God supersede the ethical.[14] It is one of the ironies of our language-made, human-mirroring deities that they are often unconcerned with the ethical, which philosopher Kierkegaard considered a universal standard. Kierkegaard's inquiry whether faith and duty to obey obviate ethical considerations and his tentative answer in the affirmative are disappointing. Today, those whose faith prompts them to murder their children are considered monstrous—perhaps insane, but nevertheless guilty of criminal acts.

Another tale of child sacrifice concerns one of the judges, Jephthah, a "mighty warrior," who promises Yahweh that if he prevails in an ensuing battle, he will sacrifice to Yahweh whoever "comes forth from the doors" of his house to meet him. As Stephen L. Harris points out, "The Judges author presents Jephthah's vow to sacrifice a human being as if it were not unusual" (112). Yahweh apparently acquiesces in the arrangement by giving the enemy "into his hand." When Jephthah returns home, the one to greet him is his only child, a virgin daughter, who is subsequently sacrificed to Yahweh (Judges 11). Jephthah does not "redeem" his child, nor does Yahweh provide a surrogate victim. What can the sacrifice mean to the deity? Does it please him? Does it provide sustenance? Does the victim matter?

Part of what remains unsaid in the Akedah—and, in truth, in all tales of human sacrifice—is what, if anything, it will mean—to the deity, to the sacrificer, and to the victim. This sacrifice, especially, but indeed all sacrifice, presents what has been called an "irreducible enigma," the sense that here is a sign, "the explanation of which has been lost" (Robbins 286).

Like Kierkegaard, the prophets Jeremiah and Ezekiel (writing in the late seventh and sixth centuries BCE) were concerned with the ethics of child sacrifice, but nevertheless had to consider the authority of the Torah and Yahweh's specific law. Jeremiah resolves the problem by ascribing the practice of child sacrifice to Judah's and Jerusalem's worship of Baal. The people, Yahweh says, have "filled this place with the blood of innocents, and have built the high places . . . to burn their sons in fire as burnt offerings to Baal. . . . " Having ascribed child sacrifice to Baal worship, a practice with which Yahweh disclaims any connection, he says, ignoring (or forgetting) his command in Exodus, "I did not command or decree [child sacrifice], nor did it come into my mind" (Jeremiah 19:4–5). In other words, he would never have even thought such a thing. By contrast, Ezekiel, acknowledging the authority of the ancient texts, presents another solution. Yahweh claims that he did in fact decree the practice of child sacrifice, but deflects blame to the Israelites themselves. Yahweh explains that, angry at the generation of Israelites who had made the golden calf, he refrained from destroying them for the sake of his reputation among the nations, but he punished them, nevertheless, by giving them "statutes that were not good and ordinances by which they could not have life; and *I defiled them through their very gifts in making them offer by fire all their first-born, that I might horrify them;* I did it that they might know that I am the Lord" (Ezekiel 20:21–26; emphasis supplied). It would be difficult to claim that Ezekiel enhances Yahweh's ethical stature here, but at least he has Yahweh denounce child sacrifice, even as he insists on its being performed.

SMOKE AND BLOOD

In its origins, the practice of sacrifice grew out of certain assumptions made by two distinct mythic systems. Herders and hunters, on the one hand, and farmers, on the other, brought their typical notions about the relationships of divine and human beings to the ritual of sacrifice, organized around two different metaphors—cooking and planting. The hunter/warrior sky Father of herders and hunters required sustenance, which was offered by way of a cooking metaphor—the burnt offering "cooked up" into its smoke and "sweet savor" as food for the sky gods. Farmers were dependent upon the fertile earth Mother, with her regenerative potential, who required sustenance too—the offering consisting of virtually all her "offspring," vegetal, animal, human, that were returned to her, the womb and tomb of everything that lives, to be reborn with the renewal of nature in its cycles. One mythic type tended, therefore, to offer burnt offerings, the smoke ascending into the heavens; the other to the "planting" of sacrifices—blood and libations poured into the ground, or dismembered bodies and seed scattered in the fields, to foster the life not only of nature, but of all Earth's children. Over time, the two types of sacrifice merged in a ceremony that revealed accommodation of both systems. Homer's description of a sacrifice to Athena has this dual nature. A heifer (a virgin cow representing Athena), its horns gilded, is slain, while barley and lustral water are sprinkled on the ground for the earth goddess. As the "heifer's spirit failed . . . all the women gave a wail of joy." For a while the men held the victim, finally permitting the carcass to sink down, catching the blood in a bowl, and burning the fat and thighbones to the sky gods (*Odyssey* 3:48). Earth and sky gods have been nourished. The humans share the meal by consuming the remainder of the animal.

Whether as smoke or blood, the sacrificial victim originally served as food for the gods, either through cremation or burial, practices that tend to be reflected today in care for the dead. The feeding of the gods and the sharing of the sacred meal remain elements in the purported purpose of sacrifice throughout the ages of its practice. One can only wonder at all that food burned on altars, poured into the ground, or left on the tables of the gods' "houses" to be consumed by the deities and shared by priests or members of the community.

Other purposes gradually accrued to sacrificial rituals—the primary one being to appease the gods for whatever might anger or disappoint them (for example, inadequate acknowledgement of the role of gods in victories—the cause of the Greeks' misfortunes after the Trojan War) or violate their codes of conduct, religious or secular (for example, the Israelites' worship of the golden calf—the cause of Yahweh's wrath and punishment). Hence sacrificial rituals became opportunities to expiate sin or guilt.

It may seem curious today that ancient people would, through metaphor, have created gods who then required feeding or appeasement. Did no one in those long-ago times raise the questions, "What would sustain the voracious gods if humans did not feed them?" or "How can a dead animal or human quiet divine wrath?" The latter question becomes pertinent when considering the sacrifice of the "Lamb of God." Today the burned corpse may seem analogous to the Christmas fruitcake. What in the world does one do with it? The author of Job has God raise the issue: "Who has given to me that I should repay him? Whatever is under the whole heaven is mine" (41:11).

The Lamb of God

> With this money, then, you shall with due diligence buy bulls, rams, and lambs, with their cereal offerings and their drink offerings, and you shall offer them upon the altar of the house of your God which is in Jerusalem.
>
> Ezra 7:17

> The next day John saw Jesus coming toward him and said, "Look, the Lamb of God, who takes away the sin of the world!"
>
> John 1:29

The crucifixion is the New Testament's paradoxical center and, one might say, its raison d'être—the sacrifice of God to God,[15] and the illogic or "mystery" implicit in the *slaughter* of an *immortal* whose existence spans and exceeds the limits of time: "I am the Alpha and the Omega, the first and the last, the beginning and the end" (Revelation 22:13).[16] The ritual of the Eucharist, which commemorates and endlessly repeats the sacrifice of Jesus' flesh (bread) and blood (wine), draws into the sacrifice the ancient implications of consumption of the sacrificial victim by gods and mortals. Jan Kott has described the Eucharist as "a re-creation of the death and resurrection of a god," in which "[t]he Surrogate and the One who has been substituted, the Sacrificed and the Sacrificer, God-man and God the Creator, the Son of God and God the Father are figures, opposites and situations of one Person" (208–9). The Eucharist, in effect, endlessly repeats the crucifixion, a ritual of child sacrifice, and is validated by a deity who has in the past both insisted upon the rite and rejected it as unthinkable. Furthermore, the crucifixion is performed in accordance with the will of a supposedly omnipotent God, one who has created a universe merely by speaking it into existence, but who can conceive of no other means of annulling *his own decree* of death. Finally, the crucifixion foregrounds and nearly reconciles father-son violence and mimesis in its image of sadomasochistic, mutually engaged acts of torture, humiliation, and murder/suicide.[17] And, to repeat, "How can a dead animal or human (or a god) appease divine hunger or quiet divine wrath?"

While the account of a dying and reviving god would have been familiar in the early years of the Common Era when the New Testament texts were produced, it had not been given legitimacy in Old Testament texts (for example, the adamant rejection of Baal worship), so its centrality in the New Testament presents at the outset seemingly insurmountable difficulties for the writers who appropriate the Old Testament's authority as context for their own narratives. Nevertheless alive in the times were the stories of Baal and Osiris, for example, along with Dionysus, Adonis, and Persephone—all gods who personified the "life" of nature, dying and reviving with the turning of the seasons. Some (Osiris, Dionysus, Persephone), like Jesus, had become archetypes for their worshipers, offering through their own deaths and rebirths a model and promise of continuing life for the individual initiate. What makes the story of Jesus' crucifixion and resurrection remarkable is not the narrative type itself, but its place in what has been called "biblical theology"—"the exposition of biblical texts (both O.T. and N.T.), based on the *presupposition that there is a common biblical way of thinking which informs the Bible as a whole*" (*OED* at *theology*). Beginning with some of the epistles of Paul and continuing through the centuries, a chorus of contradictory, yet "authoritative," voices has retold, revised, analyzed, and interpreted the narrative, while attempting to contend not only with the many inconsistencies among New Testament texts, but the glaring incongruities between the mysteries implicit in Jesus' story and the worldview and assumptions manifest in the Old Testament, whose texts are nevertheless called upon to "validate" Jesus' life and career.[18] The result is to create complexity and contradiction, endless debate, and, in short, *biblical theology*—that "common biblical way of thinking."

In any case, accounts of vegetation gods by neighboring peoples have prepared the way for Jesus' form of divinity, one quite different from that of divine sky fathers like Zeus, Jupiter, Odin, and Yahweh. Among the Christian Jews, the account of a dying and reviving god who offers eternal life to his followers is joined with the Old Testament anticipation of the restoration of God's kingdom under the rule of a "Messiah," anointed king, in the line of David. As the Old Testament texts enter the New Testament through citation and allusion, they bring their sacrificial spirit, manifested in the common practice of animal and human sacrifice, including tales of genocidal slaughter of innocents (by Yahweh as well as the Egyptian Pharaoh, and mimicked by Herod); the portrait of a usually wrathful Father as supreme deity who calls Israel his firstborn son and demands blood sacrifice of his worshipers' firstborn sons and livestock; notions of the "promised land" and "holy city," inscribed (even scribbled over) with sacred history and littered with altars, shrines, synagogues, and dedicated "high places" for the worship of Yahweh and other gods; and, dominating the place and time, as center of religious observance, the Solomonic and Second Temples (God's houses), with their elaborate priesthood, and Mosaic-law-dictated rituals.

It is fair to say that this culture took the idea of sacrifice for granted, the bloody ritual having through long practice grown incapable of arousing wonder or dismay or eliciting interrogation. The New Testament authors were, of course, of their time and place, shaped by their history and culture. Their deity was Yahweh; their religious authorities were the Sadducees and Pharisees; their place of worship, the Jerusalem temple; their sacred texts, those of the Old Testament, related commentary, apocryphal works, and oral tradition. New Testament writers faced the daunting task of recording the peaceful passage of Yahweh, God the Father (angry, jealous, vengeful, partial, capricious, violent deity of the Old Testament), into the story of his "beloved son," forgiveness, and the rescision of his own universal sentence of death.

The metaphor of Jesus as the "Lamb of God" illustrates this point. One of the background texts is the Old Testament narrative of the tenth plague of Egypt as recounted in Exodus. The tenth plague was the grand finale of a series of devastations sent by Yahweh to establish his name as the most powerful deity (e.g., Exodus 7:4–5). Yahweh informs Moses that he is about to kill "all the first-born in the land of Egypt"—an ironic Egyptian sacrifice to the foreign Yahweh. This son-slaughtering deity instructs Moses that on the appointed day each Israelite household should slaughter a yearling lamb and place its blood on the lintels and doorposts of its house as a sign: "[W]hen I see the blood, I will pass over you, and no plague shall fall upon you to destroy you, when I smite the land of Egypt" (Exodus 11:4; 12:1–13). The lamb, figurative for the endangered son, is killed, its sacrificial blood becoming a metaphor for the blood of the firstborn in each household, and deflecting from that child the divine plague. So, to call Jesus the "Lamb of God" incorporates by allusion the "sacrifice" and protective blood of the Passover lamb. Emphasizing the connection, Jesus' last supper and crucifixion are said to have occurred during the celebration of Passover.

The Akedah, too, stands behind the New Testament's "Lamb of God" metaphor, the narrative claimed to be an antetype of Yahweh's sacrifice. Abraham, on the verge of sacrificing his son is given the surrogate ram, to be killed in place of Isaac. The ritual substitute of one life for another is implicit in the instruction that "the firstling of an ass" may be redeemed with a lamb, and also the rather problematic command, "the first-born of your sons you shall redeem" (Exodus 34:20). Echoing God's observation that Abraham loves Isaac, is Yahweh's reference to Jesus as "my beloved son" (Mark 1:11); both the "unclean spirits" and the Roman centurion recognize Jesus as "the Son of God" (Mark 3:11; 15:39). Whereas Jesus frequently refers to himself as the "Son of man," John calls him the "Son of God," and Jesus declares, "For this is the will of my Father, that every one who sees the Son and believes in him should have eternal life" (John 6:40).

Looking backward through time, one finds in the mirror of heaven the ancient image of manlike gods. If gods are like men, it follows that they need nourishment, an idea manifest in the ritual practice of the shared feast of the sacrifice (of cereal, wine, and human and animal victims). The New Testament substitutes Jesus for the Old Testament's sacrificial victim, a figurative variation of the Passover's ritual wherein a lamb redeems a son, allowing him to live. In his figurative role as "Lamb of God," Jesus is both son and sacrificial animal. A meal for both God and man, his "death" seen as redemptive of his followers, allowing them to evade the divine sentence of death, to "live"—not necessarily in the world, but in "the resurrection." And so the ancient conflict, love, fear, and violence inherent in the patriarchal father-son relationship are gathered in a pernicious relationship that merges father and son into a single murderous/suicidal entity. "Believe me that I am in the Father and the Father in me" (John 14:11):

THE EATING OF THE GODS[19]

> Now as they were eating, Jesus took bread, and blessed, and broke it, and gave it to the disciples and said, "Take, eat; this is my body." And he took a cup, and when he had given thanks he gave it to them, saying, "Drink of it, all of you; for this is my blood of the covenant, which is poured out for many for the forgiveness of sins...."
>
> Matthew 26:26–29

On the occasion of the first Passover, Yahweh instructed that each household select as surrogate for the firstborn a perfect lamb, of either sheep or goat, slaughter it in the evening, roast it—"its head with its legs and its inner parts"—and consume it entirely in that one night (Exodus 12:8–10), a figurative sort of cannibalism. But the matter is complex, for the sacrificial animal was frequently understood to be the god him- or herself in theriomorphic form. In the *Odyssey*, the Greeks at Pylos offer Poseidon a bull sacrifice, but to the virgin goddess Athena they present a heifer (47), the animals corresponding to the sexual nature of the gods. Baal was worshipped as a bull, and Yahweh as a bull or bull calf (Exodus 32:1–6; 1 Kings 12:26–28), and sacrifices in those forms were offered and consumed. In Euripides' *Bacchae*, Dionysus appears as a bull, and Pentheus, who is "sacrificed" to the god, assumes another of Dionysus' forms—that of a lion, in which illusory shape he is killed, dismembered, and partially eaten by Dionysos' worshipers (Morford and Lenardon 288–29). Dionysus himself was said to have been killed, dismembered, and eaten by the Titans. After Zeus destroyed the Titans with a lightning bolt, human beings are said to have been crafted from their ashes. In this way, humans acquired a dual nature, inasmuch as the ashes contained both the Titanic cannibals and divine matter of the god they had ingested. To consume the god meant to "become one" with the deity.

Sacrificial rituals tend to imbricate these concepts—food and the need for man and deity to eat; the shared feast of the sacrificial victim, cereal, and wine; identification of the victim (human or animal) with the deity. Ritualized, sacred violence becomes productive of communion, community, and cannibalistic identification. Those who consume the victim become one with the victim: "Take eat; this is my body."

The ritual of the Christian Eucharist is "a re-creation of the death and resurrection of a god" (Kott 208). In other words, worshipers at the communion can consume Jesus, the Lamb of God, in the mysteriously literal/figurative[20] forms of bread (flesh) and wine (blood). The scene in Euripides' *Bacchae*, in which Pentheus is offered as a sacrifice to Dionysos, involves his dismemberment by communicants, who strip his flesh and consume it in a sacred frenzy. In leading Pentheus to the ritual and placing him in view in a pine tree, Dionysus has perhaps said, in effect, "Take, eat; this is my body." Certainly, the victim reenacts the passion of the god who has himself been dismembered and eaten. In ceremonies involving theophagy, an elaborate system of metaphors and figurative acts has been reified to create, through ritual and its accoutrements, an endlessly repeatable miracle, validated in its mere recurrences, stripped of wonder or horror. Citizens of the modern world, who would reject as barbaric the theophagy of Osiris or Dionysus worship, may find a Sunday communion unremarkable. The paradox-ridden metaphor of the Son, the Lamb of God, crucified by the will of a supreme, omnipotent deity, the Father—as, apparently, his best or only means of annulling his own sentence of death to "immortal" souls—has for two millennia constituted for untold millions "knowledge" of the Unknown.

Several forces combine in the familial figure of the father god, his sons, and the stories told about him: human psychology associated with the complex father-son relationship (the Oedipus complex, the son's identification with the father model, the Laius attitude); perhaps a human need for a safe outlet of violent tendencies; an ancient theory of sacrifice as food for the manlike gods who enjoy the savor of cooking meat; and an embarrassing tendency toward symbolic theophagy in attempts to become one with the incomprehensible Unknown and live forever.

CHAPTER 6

LOOK WHO'S TALKING—AND WRITING: THE LANGUAGE OF HEAVEN

> And God said, "Let there be light. . . ."
>
> Genesis 1:3

> This is how God creates what He will: when He has ordained something, He only says, "Be", and it is.
>
> Qur'an 3:47

> Praise be to God, who sent down the Scripture to His servant and made it unerringly straight. . . .
>
> Qur'an 18:1

MY THESIS IS THAT HUMANS have characterized the Unknown and created gods and heavens with words—figures, linguistic maneuvers of various sorts, and narratives. Prominent in the process of that creation is an implicit denial of human creativity. One finds instead the story of deities who imagine humankind, the natural world, and the things of the world, and speak them into being. Having done so, they then write the story of human history. Everything depends upon god-language.

IN THE BEGINNING WAS THE WORD

> In the beginning was the Word, and the Word was with God, and the Word was God.
>
> John 1:1–3

In Genesis 1, the Unknown speaks. One by one his words take form in the world as things—*light, firmament, sun, moon, stars, night, day*. Then, in Genesis 2, Yahweh initiates "communication" when he speaks to the first human (a clay man inspirited with divine breath), assuming that the man, his clay, or the breath would understand God-speak: "You may freely eat of every tree of the garden; but of the tree of the knowledge of good and evil you shall not eat, for in the day that you eat of it you shall die" (Genesis 2:15–17). The message must sound strange to new ears, and the import of these few words far from transparent, for they serve both to grant permission and deny it, as well as to introduce rather specific verbs and nouns (*eat, tree,* and *garden*), along with abstract concepts (*good* and *evil*) and, at least from some theological perspectives, the impossible-to-define *death*.[1] Furthermore, as the narrative develops Yahweh appears guilty of misrepresentation, for Adam does not die "in the day" he eats the fruit, but some nine hundred years later.

What language did God speak? What about the serpent? Was it ancient Hebrew, as many believed? Was it Phrygian, as an experiment reported by Herodotus suggested (Histories 2:3)? Was it Arabic, supposedly the language spoken to Muhammad by Gabriel and written in the Book Allah commanded Muhammad to read: "Read! In the name of your Lord who created.... Read! Your Lord is the Most Bountiful One who taught by ... the pen, who taught man what he did not know" (Qur'an 96:1–5).

Such questions notwithstanding, the Abrahamic religions represent God as the originator of language, one who creates by speaking, calls Jesus the incarnate "Word," writes the Mosaic Code (Exodus 32:16), the design for the temple (1 Chronicles 28:19), the "book of truth" (Daniel 10:21), the "Book of Life," and the Qur'an, documents that contain not only God's plot of history, but the predetermined fate of everyone "from the foundation of the world" (Revelation 17:8) to the grand climax of history at End Times inscribed on Revelation's seven scrolls of the apocalypse. Islam understands that Allah is not only Author of the Mother of Books and the sacred Qur'an, but that he has taught speech and writing to mankind (55:3; 96:5). Both Bible and Qur'an purport to be God's language (Yahweh's or Allah's)[2] dictated to and recorded verbatim by prophets from Adam to Abraham and Ishmael to Moses, Ezekiel, Jesus, and Muhammad (Jeremiah 1:9; Qur'an 3:84).

As the announcement to Adam illustrates, God's language is not free from ambiguity, for like human language, the archetypal language must be figurative—figurative in the sense that all language is figurative (the word is not the thing), figurative again in its use of symbol and trope (personification, metaphor, analogy, irony), and figurative yet again in the sense described by a theory of accommodation (in Robert Lowth's explanation, *a divine attempt in language to "accommodate" things beyond the reach of human knowledge to human understanding*). The theory of accommodation reverses my argument, which claims, rather, a human attempt in language to accommodate human understanding to things beyond the reach of minds and words. Supposedly, God's language, whatever language that may be, and discounting all problems of transcription, translation, and redaction, is recorded verbatim in sacred texts; it is "inerrant" or "unerringly straight." And yet the very nature of language renders that record irremediably figurative and, thus, equivocal, so that multiple and conflicting meanings arise across time and space in interpretations by untold numbers of readers.[3]

Given that no characteristic so clearly distinguishes human beings from the rest of earth's creatures as the ability to use language, accounts of the divine origins of language are curious. This powerful tool is the major source of human creativity—the formation of human societies and cultures (speech communities); the formulation of theories (scientific, historical, philosophical); the recording of history; the telling of stories; and, not least, the establishment of the world's religions, from the first myth and ritual forward, and all their heavenly realms, the beings who inhabit them, and their horses.

People use language to educate the young. Each generation receives inherited "wisdom." Much of theological "knowledge" originated with the ancient, the fearful, the biased, and the ignorant; it comes in the form of sacred texts. Jewish children hear one version; Christian children, another; Muslim children, yet another. They all, no doubt, learn about God's admiration of the unicorn (Job 39:9–10). Effortlessly the thing-that-never-was takes its place in the "knowledge" realm of children. It exists today as a word for a reality "called into life" through a word, lacking only a referent.[4]

DIVINE NOMOTHETES—NAME-GIVERS, LAW-GIVERS

> Then I, Lipit-Ishtar . . . king of Sumer and Akkad . . . established justice in Sumer and Akkad in accordance with the word of Enlil.[5]

A speaking, writing human observer must find, reflected in the depths of the heavenly mirror, hugely magnified and perfected, a speaking, writing deity who is Creator, Poet, Author, Word, Nomothete. The Sumerians, inventors of writing, found in their mirror one of the first written law codes. The Lipit-Ishtar Code, c. 1868 BCE, is purportedly a system of laws given to King Lipit-Ishtar "in accordance with the word of Enlil," head of the Sumerian pantheon. The laws enable the king to "establish justice in the land, to banish complaints, to turn back enmity and rebellion by force of arms, and to bring well-being to the Sumerians and

Akkadians."[6] Babylonian king Hammurabi claims to have received the famous code named for him from the gods—"Anu, the Sublime, and Bel, lord of Heaven and earth" (Prologue, Code of Hammurabi)[7] or the sun god Shamash (Stephen L. Harris 55). The code is inscribed on the Stele of Hammurabi, bearing the legend that it is intended "to bring about the rule of righteousness in the land, to destroy the wicked and the evil-doers; so that the strong should not harm the weak; so that . . . [Hammurabi] should rule over the black-headed people like Shamash, and enlighten the land, to further the well-being of mankind." At the top of the stele, an artist has depicted the king in a submissive posture receiving the law from an enthroned deity (Stephen L. Harris 51–55). It may seem odd, however, that in composing the Babylonian law the god has "borrowed" extensively from the Sumerian Enlil, practicing a sort of divine plagiarism. In any case the deities of both kings gave particular and nearly identical divine attention to the fairly unlikely crime of secret tree destruction: Law 2 of the Sumerian code states, "If a man cut down a tree in the garden of another man, he shall pay one-half mina of silver," which is echoed in Law 59 of Hammurabi's code: "If any man, without the knowledge of the owner of a garden, fell a tree in a garden he shall pay half a mina in money."

Several hundred years later, Moses ascended Mount Sinai (or Mount Horeb) where he received the Mosaic Code from Yahweh. God not only spoke/dictated the law, but actually inscribed it on tablets of stone: "And he gave to Moses, when he had made an end of speaking . . . the two tables of stone, written with the finger of God" (Exodus 31:18). Again, however, the law-giving God has appropriated parts of an earlier code and assumed similar principles to lie behind the laws. Chief among these principles is that of revenge. *Lex talionis*, the law of strict retaliation, characterizes both the Hammurabi and Mosaic laws, and encodes a cruel, if not unusual, form of justice:

> He who blasphemes the name of the Lord shall be put to death; all the congregation shall stone him. . . . When a man causes a disfigurement in his neighbor, as he has done it shall be done to him, fracture for fracture, eye for eye, tooth for tooth; as he has disfigured a man, he shall be disfigured.
> Numbers 24:16–20

Community members carried out the death sentence by stoning those who had blasphemed or murdered. Yet the law does not specify who will be bone-breakers, eye-gougers, or tooth-knockers.

Whereas most such early codes tended to concern themselves with punishments for crimes against civil, economic, or domestic order, the Mosaic Code, in addition, stressed crimes against Yahweh, and imposed the death penalty not only for civil crimes (adultery, cursing one's parents [Leviticus 20:9]), but also for religious infractions (e.g., blasphemy and idolatry [Deuteronomy 17–2–7]). That Yahweh "favored" the death penalty is everywhere apparent. Not only does God write laws that require it, he personally acts as judge and executioner for a variety of failures. Indeed his very first law to humankind forbidding the eating of the fruit of the tree of knowledge of good and evil provides the death penalty, to be imposed not only on the first couple, but also on all their descendants, forever. In another instance, God kills nearly all of humanity with a flood, the populace of cities with fire and brimstone, and the Egyptian first-born with a plague. While Moses is on the mountain receiving the law from Yahweh, his anxious followers in the valley below construct an image of God that they can worship. This religious crime provokes Yahweh to such anger that he resolves to destroy the entire nation. It is only when Moses reminds Yahweh of the damage such action would cause to his international reputation, that Yahweh relents, settling instead for the slaughter of a mere three thousand (Exodus 32:7–14, 25–29). Such almost casual destruction carries over into international relations. God's laws grant approval of what civilized nations consider heinous war crimes—rape, pillage, enslavement, and genocide (Deuteronomy 7:1–2; 20:12–14). Both Yahweh and Allah glory in the slaughter of Egyptians; Yahweh repeats again and again—almost as a form of self-identification—that it was he who defeated the Egyptian slavemasters and led the Israelites out of bondage. Allah identifies himself as this same deity and points with pride to his victory (Qur'an 17:103).

The law codes of heaven—spoken or written by the gods—obviously mirror the attitudes, societal structures, economic, and domestic concerns of the people whose deities are said to have composed them. Societies that practice slavery tell of gods who write laws for buying and selling slaves and their "just" management: "When a man strikes his slave, male or female, with a rod and the slave dies under his hand, he shall be punished. But if the slave survives a day or two, he is not to be punished; for the slave is his money" (Exodus 21:20–21). The system of divine justice also reflects the social strata of ancient societies. Hence, various Mesopotamian law codes as well as the Mosaic code, although matter-of-factly accepting the principle that law is grounded on revenge and requires strict retaliation, adjust the nature or severity of the punishment to the social status of the wrongdoer and recipient of the wrong. From the Code of Hammurabi:

> If a man put out the eye of another man [of the upper social stratum], his eye shall be put out. If a man break another man's bone, his bone shall be broken.

> If he put out the eye of a freed man, or break the bone of a freed man, he shall pay one gold mina.
>
> If he put out the eye of a man's slave, or break the bone of a man's slave, he shall pay one-half of its value.
>
> If a man knock out the teeth of his equal, his teeth shall be knocked out. If he knock out the teeth of a freed man, he shall pay one-third of a gold mina.
>
> If any one strike the body of a man higher in rank than he, he shall receive sixty blows with an ox-whip in public.
>
> 196–202

Hammurabi's code thus overtly distinguishes among social classes, requiring more severe penalties for injury to one in the upper class. The Mosaic Code echoes such laws: "When a man causes a disfigurement in his neighbor [another Israelite], as he has done it shall be done to him, fracture for fracture, eye for eye, tooth for tooth" (Leviticus 24:19–20). Although Israelites tended to eliminate social strata among themselves, they created such strata among cultures: Israelites were of the privileged class, God's chosen; people of "other nations" were of lower status and lesser breed:

> Your male and female slaves are to come from the nations around you; from them you may buy slaves. You may also buy from among the strangers who sojourn with you and their families that are with you who have been born in your land [ethnic minorities]; and they may be your property.... But over your brethren the people of Israel you shall not rule.
>
> Leviticus 44–46

The Qur'an, too, provides laws for the handling of slaves, even for the breeding of slaves: "Marry off the single among you and those of your male and female slaves who are fit [for marriage]" (24:32). Islam conflates attitudes toward social strata, slavery, and retaliation, but allows for monetary retribution:

> You who believe, fair retribution is prescribed for you in cases of murder: the free man for the free man, the slave for the slave, the female for the female.
>
> 2:178[8]

In the Mesopotamian and biblical texts, divine lawgivers mirror all the flaws and biases—all the inhumanity—of the humans who "receive" the laws. Later codes perpetuate the example of Ur-Nammu's code, which established the principle that laws exist primarily to designate punishment for offenses, couched in casuistic pattern—if (crime), then (punishment).[9]

It is only to be expected that an ancient society would "legitimize" its attitudes about appropriate behavior by ascribing the language of its codes, commandments, and advice to its gods. It is reassuring that among those attitudes in all places and times is discernible a human concern for the helpless, the infirm, and the aged, a concern that speaks of a common (as opposed to ethnic) core of human morality (e.g., Hammarubi's "rule of righteousness in the land . . . so that the strong should not harm the weak"). This too is ascribed to the gods. The assumption is that modern law has evolved from such ancient codes and the attitudes they legitimize: echoes of the words of Enlil sound in the law code of Hammurabi; the Mosaic Code borrows from Hammurabi's; and Roman law, with its Etruscan religious origin, merges with Mosaic law in the codes of modern nations. Through the ages, humans have recognized certain principles and behaviors that foster a peaceful society, and these form the foundation of many ancient and modern law codes. It is when ancient law perpetuates ethnic prejudices, attitudes, ignorance, and barbaric practices legitimized by the voice of the divine figure that one has cause for alarm. Such have been the causes of historical horrors (e.g., seemingly endless religious wars, the slave trade and institutionalized slavery practiced in Europe and America for several hundred years, and the witch trials of the early modern period, which continue in parts of the world even now—"Thou shalt not suffer a witch to live" [Exodus 22:18]).[10]

Then there are today's debates about the desirability of posting the Decalogue in parks, schools, and courthouses. Is it appropriate today to admonish a man (for the commandments are clearly directed to men) not to "covet [his] neighbor's house; . . . [his] neighbor's wife, or his manservant, or his maidservant, or his ox, or his ass, or anything that is [his] neighbor's" (Exodus 20:17)? The commandment makes the wife a part of the neighbor's chattels, along with his slaves and his ass. The earlier admonition against stealing might have covered this ground, except for the fact that in biblical law the rule does not apply universally, for in the conduct of "holy war" waged against non-Israelites, the divine directive is to pillage (steal from defeated enemies) as well as to murder (negating the sixth commandment) and enslave (Deuteronomy 20:10–15). Especially hollow is the sixth commandment, "Thou shalt not kill" (Exodus 20:13), when it is uttered by Yahweh, known for his murderous inclinations, and followed in the next chapter of Exodus by this and similar laws: "Whoever curses his father or his mother shall be put to death" (Exodus 21:17). Why not inscribe that commandment on stone and display it on courthouse grounds as the eleventh commandment? No doubt a person could follow exactly the ten rules of the Decalogue and nevertheless remain a selfish, evil-minded, filthy-talking, arrogant, vindictive, unfriendly, wife-beating, child-abusing, dog-kicking, thoroughly unpleasant (although "pious"!) individual.[11]

An incident in the career of Elisha, God's chosen prophet, who inherits the mantle of Elijah, illustrates the silliness of arguing over the modern relevance of the ancient law. Elisha is on his way to Bethel when some "small boys" jeer at him and call him "baldhead" (a misdemeanor not mentioned specifically in the voluminous Mosaic code): "And [Elisha] turned around, and when he saw them, he cursed them in the name of the Lord. And two she-bears came out of the woods and tore forty-two of the boys. From there he went on to Mount Carmel. . . . (2 Kings 2:23–25). For these small sinners, it might have been well to include a twelfth commandment or an addendum to the sixth: Thou shalt not call a prophet baldhead; or whoever calls a prophet baldhead shall be torn by a she-bear.

LANGUAGE—DIVINE AND HUMAN

If it had been possible to build the tower of Babel without ascending it, the work would have been permitted.

Franz Kafka

The Bible tells of a time when postdiluvian descendents of Noah spoke a single language—full, complete, and true—with which they achieved perfect communication. Those ancient people decided to use their language to bridge the gap between human and divine, earth and heaven, mortal and immortal. And so, on the plains of Shinar, they begin to build a magnificent tower that would extend into heaven. However, when God notices the building project, he is taken aback, perhaps even frightened. Seeming to acknowledge an unlimited power in perfect communication, he exhorts his divine companions, "Behold, they are one people, and they have all one language; and this is only the beginning of what they will do; and nothing that they propose to do will now be impossible for them" (Genesis 11:6). God implies that with this "one language" people can imagine, speak, and accomplish simultaneously—recalling the divine creation in Genesis 1: "'Let there be light,' and there was light." God sees this as a problem, perhaps an encroachment on his power and majesty.[12] His solution is simple—to spoil the perfection of this first human language: "Come, let us go down, and there confuse their language, that they may not understand one another's speech" (Genesis 11:7). God proceeds to confuse the language "of all the earth" and scatters the people, now babbling incomprehensibly to each other. The ruined tower—Babel—is left as a monument to fallen language, its very name illustrating the failure and confusion, for whereas *Babel* in Babylonian is a noun meaning "gate of God," in ancient Hebrew it is similar to and interpreted by the verb for "to confuse" (Editor's note, Genesis 11).

The story of the tower is an example of a motif that runs through ancient narratives, expressing a general sense that there must sometime, somewhere have been a language created by the gods, universally understood, unambiguous, and complete. Islam, for example, embraces the notion of an ultimate book, a hidden, heavenly Book of Books, known as the *Umm al-Kitab*, or "Mother of Books," from whose language "*all* revealed scriptures are derived" (Aslan 99). Jorge Luis Borges fancifully embraces a similar concept in his depiction of the universe as a divinely constructed, eternal Library and man an "imperfect librarian":

> Man, the imperfect librarian, may be the work of chance or of malevolent demiurges; the universe with its elegant endowment of shelves, of enigmatic volumes, of indefatigable ladders for the voyager, and of privies for the seated librarian, can only be the work of a god.
> *Ficciones*, "The Library of Babel" 81

Borges' Library is a version of the idea behind the "Mother of Books," for it "comprise[s] all books"; "Everything is there," including the "minute history of the future, the autobiographies of the archangels, the faithful catalogue of the Library," countless false catalogues along with demonstrations of their falsity, commentary, and commentary upon commentary, "the veridical account of your death," and "a version of each book in all languages, the interpolations of every book in all books" (*Ficciones* 83). Borges' narrator relates a "superstition" about someone called the "Man of the Book": "In some shelf of some hexagon, men reasoned, there must exist a book which is the cipher and perfect compendium of all the rest: some librarian has perused it, and it is analogous to a god" (*Ficciones* 85). The idea of the Book, God's ultimate book, even the Book identified with and as the god, the "Word," is the graphic version of human longing for a single, perfect, creative language like that spoken by all before the fall of language at Babel.

As the Book or a book relates a narrative of meaningful time, with a beginning, a middle and an end, isolated from the unimaginable and insignificant sweep of cosmic time, and as its language spins the plot, a frail time shelter telling a story of the world or the individual, flawed, figurative, and equivocal human language struggles to make sense of it all, even telling of a time of perfect communication soon lost, but still, clothed in metaphor and mystery, speaking in sacred texts as the "inerrant" language of God. These elements—book, time, and language—converge in a single stream, and the stream falls into a bottomless cistern: the Book ends, time ends, language is silenced: "All streams run to the sea, but the sea is not full" (Ecclesiastes 1:7).

The Language of End Times

> When the Lamb opened the seventh seal, there was silence in heaven for about half an hour.
>
> Revelation 8:1

Apocalyptic traditions eagerly anticipate the last syllable of recorded time, the simultaneous end of human history and the Book, along with destruction of the confused language of Babel spoken by "peoples and multitudes and nations and tongues" (Revelation 17:15), and the restoration at End Times of the original perfect language. Steven Goldsmith has argued cogently that apocalypse as a genre only emerges with the establishment of the book—in particular, the canon of sacred texts. As he puts it, "Between prophecy and apocalypse falls canonization, the largely undocumented process by which a collection of binding sacred texts . . . emerged sometime between the exile in Babylon . . . and the beginning of the second century B.C.E." (30). Prophecy, Goldsmith explains, understands history as the means by which God accomplishes his plans for the world; it is largely an *oral* genre addressed to the moment. By contrast, apocalypse is a *written* genre. Its authors encounter a history so degraded by sin and evil that "it cannot possibly function as the medium of divine activity" (Goldsmith 31) and thus records an account of the imminent end of history (ibid. 35). There is, no doubt, something in the written account of history, the sacred texts—the tone, themes, recorded events—that contributes to the apocalyptic despair and longing. Divine intervention is required to end history and redeem humanity from the limping, diseased progress of time: "[R]edemption can only be imagined as the abrupt end of history brought about by a thoroughly transcendental agent, a messiah who introduces a new and otherworldly order typically distinguished by its atemporality" (ibid. 32).

When history is conceived as the Book, its beginning and end are contemporaries, coexisting within the same space; every event, including the catastrophic end, must inevitably occur according to the telos—the goal and the *inscription*—of the divine Author. Whatever freedom or flexibility might be ascribed to the prophets' God of history is lacking in apocalypse. In apocalypse, the spatial (the Book and the city New Jerusalem) supersedes the temporal: "The transformation of prophecy into apocalypse is complete when Revelation merges its own linguistic order with the sacred space of the New Jerusalem and makes both sites, verbal and architectural, antithetical to history" (Goldsmith 44). As the Book ends, so ends time.

The most interesting of Goldsmith's points concerns a radical transformation of language. He notices that the textualizing of history in the process of canonization is brought to an abrupt end by apocalypse—evident particularly in the most influential of such works, Revelation, which "describes a fundamental change in the nature of language" growing from the fact that "the representation of the end of history must in a convincing way seem already to participate in a language beyond history" (56). At the transformative moment, which Goldsmith calls the "sublime rupture that occurs when time becomes space" (56), the natures of both time and language are said to change fundamentally, as time becomes stalled in/as space, and the confused languages of Babel are silenced. Goldsmith describes one such moment:

> The first time Revelation achieves an eschatological climax . . . the odd result is the text's quietest moment: "When the Lamb opened the seventh seal, there was silence in heaven for about half an hour" (8:1). . . . The fourth book of Ezra [2 Esdras] . . . describes an interlude between the temporary millennial kingdom and the definitive Last Judgment: "And the world shall be turned back to primeval silence for seven days, as it was at the first beginnings; so that no one shall be left."
> 2 Esdras 7:30–32; Goldsmith 57

The terror and fascination of the apocalyptic silence vividly signal a change so final and complete that not only are language and time altered irrevocably, but also universal de-creation and recreation result in "a new heaven and a new earth" (21:1). In order for the new creation to emerge, the degraded space of fallen language, personified as both fallen woman (whore) and corrupt city (Babylon) with its tower of confusion (Babel), is destroyed to make way for perfect language, personified as pure woman (Bride) and inviolate city (New Jerusalem).[13] John's whore of Babylon represents all evil and corruption—language and time spoiled by confusion, polyglot dissention rampant among peoples and nations, worship reduced to idolatry and sensual indulgence. Therefore, Revelation lavishes attention on descriptions of her destruction and eternal punishment. The text comments several times on the swiftness of her destruction, which will come "in one hour," after which she will become "a dwelling place of demons, a haunt of every foul spirit . . . for all nations have drunk the wine of her impure passion, and the kings of the earth have committed fornication with her" (Revelation 18:2–3). Once the "great harlot [who] has corrupted the earth with her fornication" has been silenced and cast into the sea or the fiery pit, the way is clear for the reemergence of God's original, prelapsarian language. Fornication has come to represent not just illicit sexual behavior, but all evil, including the fallen languages of the world.

The reinstatement of perfect language is central to the transformation: "This change in language brought about by the end of history is no auxiliary matter, no mere side effect of the general transformation, for *the only human activity left after history ends is a distinctly linguistic one—the worship of God in prayer and song.* . . . 'His servants shall worship [God]; they shall see his face, and his name shall be on their foreheads' (22:3–4)" (Goldsmith 57; emphasis supplied). Post-apocalyptic human activity will be linguistic, but it will entail language use unmarked by personality, originality, or creativity, for speech in eternity will be limited to ritualized language, the songs and prayers spoken in unison by the community of heavenly beings and the redeemed, repeated continually, day and night, in perpetuity (4:8–11; 5:11–14; 11:16–18; 15:2–4).

This song-singing eternity (however blissful and untroubled the redeemed) fails to provide all readers cause for celebration. Mark Twain captures what for some must be the horror of the imagined existence. His Satan writes from earth concerning what he considers the odd religious beliefs of humans, remarking that although few humans enjoy worship services and equally few are musically inclined, yet in man's heaven all existence is a worship service and *"everybody sings"*:

> This universal singing is not casual, not occasional, not relieved by intervals of quiet, it goes on, all day long, and every day. . . . And *everybody stays*; whereas in the earth the place would be empty in two hours. The singing is of hymns alone. Nay it is of one hymn alone. The words are always the same, in number they are only about a dozen, there is no rhyme, there is no poetry: "Hosannaah, hosannah, hosannah, Lord God of Sabaoth, 'rah! 'rah! 'rah!—ssht!—boom...a-a-ah!"

Twain's Satan is further astonished to consider that humans actually believe that God enjoys "this insane compliment" and *"commands* it" (*The Bible According to Mark Twain, Letters from the Earth* 225).

In apocalyptic thought, the transformation of language at End Times, must therefore signal a profound change in what it means to be human. One recalls the rather chilling assertion of St. Paul:

> Lo! I tell you a mystery. We shall not all sleep, but we shall all be changed, in a moment, in the twinkling of an eye, at the last trumpet. For . . . this perishable nature must put on the imperishable, and this mortal nature must put on immortality.
>
> 1 Corinthians 15:51–53

I am reminded here of William Butler Yeats's "Sailing to Byzantium," in which the poet leaves the world ("no country for old men") and embraces a dehumanized existence: "Once out of nature I shall never take / My bodily form from any natural thing, / But such a form as Grecian goldsmiths make / Of hammered gold and gold enamelling. . . ." The songs and prayers recited in unison as imagined by John of Patmos suggest that in his view humans will, in fact, be stripped of one of their defining characteristics. Speaking man will become reciting man, like mechanical birds, a congregation mindlessly prattling for an unimaginable forever the same words over and over. The human voice will be indistinguishable from that of angel or clam or rat or earthworm: "And I heard every creature in heaven and on earth and under the earth and in the sea, and all therein, saying, 'To him who sits on the throne and to the Lamb be blessing and honor and glory and might for ever and ever!'" (Revelation 5:11–13).

It might be possible to hear in the language of End Times an ironic allusion to that of the tower builders who, as God observes, had "one language and few words." Post-apocalyptic humans as depicted in Revelation likewise have one language and few words. The irony lies in the fact that language spoken on the plains of Shinar permitted perfect communication, imagination, innovation, and cooperative achievement. In Revelation, however, although redeemed humans are said to have reached that earlier inaccessible heaven, their transformed language has been disengaged from their defining humanity as creatures who speak, who exist in time, who build cities and towers, whose story inevitably ends. In Revelation, the world of time, figured as the whore/city of Babylon, and all her many human voices are silenced, along with her "harpers and minstrels . . . flute players and trumpeters" (18:22).

Insofar as heaven is a mirror in which appears the human image hugely inflated, sacred texts also appear, enlarged, perfected, inerrant, written by the finger of God. Depending on culture, upbringing, or inclinations, one may see there the Pentateuch, the Book of Books, the Qur'an, or the Mother of Books. One might hear, echoing from that glass a voice of Authority, whose word is creative and power unlimited. Many embrace the vision of John of Patmos, who projects the power of God-write and God-speak into End Times, where a heavenly linguistics reduces the "redeemed" to mindless, immortal mechanical dolls.

A problem in any imagined End Times (or transition into eternity) is that discussed in Chapter 1. There is really no way for creatures of time to define or even imagine nontime. It is incomprehensible. Mark Twain thought that most humans would grow weary of singing hymns after two hours, but the prospect of engaging in any human activity—singing hymns, or dining, or having sex—*ad infinitum* is unbearable. Islam, for example, provides the redeemed an eternal pleasure garden, with food and drink, leisure, and multiple sexual partners. According to Homer, Odysseus on Kalypso's Ogygia endured a similar situation for seven years. He could not leave fast enough.

CHAPTER 7

THE GREAT FIGURES OF LIFE AND DEATH: DUALISM AND DIVINE JUDGMENT

> He has created man to govern the world, and has appointed for him two spirits in which to walk until the time of His visitation: the spirits of truth and injustice.
> Vermes, *The Dead Sea Scrolls*, "Community Rule" 101

DEFINING DUALISM

Some would limit "religious dualism" to systems that conceive of two eternal, creative principles—one Good and one Evil, Life and Death[1]—in universal conflict. As so limited, religious dualism is to be distinguished, on the one hand, from "religious monism," which recognizes only one original and creative principle (Mazda, Yahweh, Allah), and on the other from ethicoreligious forms of dualism that permeate both philosophy and common religious understanding.[2]

My concern is with dualism and the metaphor of the Two as it affects religious thought and behavior from early times to the present, aligning evil with death and good with life, and embodying these in opposing figures. Reality presents conscious, forward-looking humans with these two fundamental states—life and death. To be alive is good; to be dead is bad. William James thought that recognition of death fosters dualistic religious thought in many. There are the "healthy-minded," the "once-born," and the "sick souls," the "twice-born." These "twice-born," confront a dualism of nature and spirit: "Natural good is not simply insufficient in amount and transient, there lurks a falsity in its very being . . . and renunciation and despair of it [natural good] are our first step in the direction of the truth." "Sick souls" are faced with a choice: "There are two lives, the natural and the spiritual, and we must lose the one [natural life] before we can participate in the other" (155). "Sick souls" or the "twice-born" are psychologically predisposed to a dualist stance.

James would see St. Paul, for example, as one of the "twice-born." St. Paul's lament reveals the ethicoreligious dualist's vision of himself and his universe:

> I delight in the law of God, in my inmost self, but I see in my members another law at war with the law of my mind and making me captive to the law of sin which dwells in my members. Wretched man that I am! Who will deliver me from this body of death?
>
> Romans 7:22–25

Speaking of the Pauline epistles and the "Pauline tradition" as found in the letter to the Ephesians (2:1–3), Forsyth observes that "[t]he separation of the two powers, of darkness and light, of evil and good, is confirmed both spatially and temporally by the Resurrection. Thus . . . the Pauline tradition solidified the dualistic idea of a world divided between opposing forces. And the split was both cosmic and personal" (282).

St. Paul had not always been a dualist, for he began his religious career with another name (Saul) as a zealous Jew intent on eliminating a heretical sect of Judaism—the people of "the Way." One day, carrying authorization from the high priest, he set out for Damascus to arrest the Christians he found there and bring them to Jerusalem for trial:

> Now as he journeyed he approached Damascus, and suddenly a light from heaven flashed about him. And he fell to the ground and heard a voice saying to him, "Saul, Saul, why do you persecute me?" And he said, "Who are you, Lord?" And he said, "I am Jesus, whom you are persecuting. . . . "
>
> Acts 9:3–5

Gaining "spiritual illumination"—the vision of Jesus as light—Saul undergoes a debilitating spiritual crisis. He is physically blinded, the blind/seeing motif fitting nicely with the figurative split of darkness and light, death and life. After several days, he is "filled with the Holy Spirit," the scales fall from his eyes, and he regains his physical sight. Soon he will be known by his Roman name, Paul, and become not only an avid spokesman for Jesus but also the virtual creator of the nascent Christian Church.[3] With his sight restored and mysteriously altered, Saul is a different man in a different world; what was one has become two; a monistic

Gestalt has given way to the dualist's vision. No longer is there one law (of God), but two—the law of God and the law of sin; an "inmost self" opposes its "members"; the mind or spirit (of Life) despises the flesh or body ("of death"). Each pair of opposites wages a war—God and sin, good and evil, mind and body, life and death. In Galatians, Paul elaborates: "But I say, walk by the Spirit and do not gratify the desires of the flesh. . . . [F]or these are opposed to each other. . . . " (5:16–17). Life and death, too, have undergone a transformation in the new vision: life (in the world) is really death; death of the body is the entry into Life in eternity.

THE ONE—RELIGIOUS MONISM

And [King] Saul's servants said to him, "Behold now, an evil spirit from God is tormenting you."
1 Samuel 16:15

Cosmic monism is the view generally expressed in Old Testament texts; it is based on the figure of the One, in which, despite appearances of multiplicity and opposition, the universe is understood as a single whole, the work of one creator—one god, one source of power, one law. Apparent opposites are simply extreme points on the scale of a single principle: light and darkness, for example, are not at odds with each other, but each a gradation on a scale of visible light. Moreover, the word *evil* (both moral and natural) in Old Testament usage by no means suggests what it will signify in the New Testament. Rather, moral evil consists of disobedience to the law; natural evil is that which harms or opposes human wellbeing. The One (Yahweh) is the source of all natural or physical "evils" (plagues, droughts, floods, wars), tools with which he administers justice to the disobedient, often on a national level. Yahweh also creates and controls "evil" or opposing spirits for his uses (e.g., the "Evil spirit from God" that rushes upon King Saul, driving him mad [1 Samuel 18:10]). This view of evil, controlled by Yahweh, might be called "evil in the service of justice." The first and most dramatic example of such justice is the universal sentence of death imposed on Adam and all his descendants: "In the sweat of your face you shall eat bread till you return to the ground, for out of it you were taken; you are dust, and to dust you shall return" (Genesis 3:17–19). Adam's disobedience (moral evil) requires the exercise of divine justice, resulting in the imposition of the now natural "evils"—thorns, thistles, and death. Natural evil is Yahweh's response to moral evil, human *disobedience* of an increasingly elaborate code of divine law. Moral evil is humanity's responsibility and therefore might seem to be subject to control by humans. Only the notion of *willful* disobedience seems able to account for God's punishment and the wrath that persists as an almost constant divine state throughout the Old Testament. But the matter is uncertain.

Cosmic monism is dominant in the long biblical tradition, especially so in the Old Testament and the Qur'an, but becomes problematic[4] in the New Testament: God (Yahweh/Allah) is one and indivisible, creator of all and source of all power. In neither the Old Testament or the Qur'an is there an Evil hypostasis capable of offering real opposition, and although Islam recognizes a sort of trickster figure—Iblis or Satan (Shaitan)—he is not the powerful embodied wickedness of the New Testament's Satan or Devil, who is given presence in Christianity. According to the Qur'an, Iblis was an angel or Jinn who refused to adore the beings Allah had made out of clay or blood. As a result, Allah sent him forth under a curse until the "Day [of Judgment]." Granted "respite" by Allah, Iblis vows to "lie in wait" for the first humans and seduce them. Iblis has a sort of divine commission, serving by Allah's "respite," for Allah vows to "fill hell" with Iblis and those who follow him (Qur'an 7:9–18). God-empowered, Iblis is rather more like the Satan or Adversary of the book of Job than the Devil of the New Testament. He opposes humans as their "sworn enemy" (7:22), yet Allah is in control and uses the acts of Iblis for his own purposes (22:51–54).

Despite differences in the conception of Satan in Islamic and Christian thought, strong strains of ethicoreligious dualism are present. In each case a single criterion is used to sort the good from the evil in "eternity"—the test of *faith*, a subject to which I shall return in the next chapter. For now, it is enough to notice that the Christian heaven and the Islamic Gardens of Paradise are places of reward for believers. Yet in both instances, faith is bestowed, not achieved. In both systems, hell is a place of eternal punishment *for those who disbelieve*. Although *faith* at times implies certain sorts of approved behavior, it need not; nor is such behavior necessarily humane, generous, or tolerant, as biblical law and the history of faith attest.

DUALISM—FROM EAST AND WEST

Dualistic thought and its forms of figurative expression in Christianity, and later in Islam, emerge from a caldron of ideas stewing in middle and near eastern lands in the post-exilic (after 538 BCE), intertestamental, and early Christian periods, and in Arabia even up to the time of Muhammad (early seventh century CE).[5] During the Babylonian captivity (587–538 BCE), the Jewish intelligentsia had for nearly fifty years been exposed to Babylonian culture, science, and theology—all of which left their marks on biblical texts as they underwent a process of editing and compilation during and following the captivity. Then, in 539, Cyrus of Persia conquered Babylon, permitting the captives to return to Judah. Persia remained the ruling power[6] throughout the area for the next two hundred years, during which Persian thought, including its evolving, syncretic religious ideas, infused the area with a dualism characteristic of Zoroastrianism (Stoyanov 35–37). Thus, during the exilic and post-exilic periods, both Babylonian and Persian metaphysics left their marks on Judaism, as its sacred texts continued to be gathered, edited, and augmented with post-exilic writings. Persian and Mesopotamian influences include eschatological anticipation, warring hosts of angels and demons, and named angels (Gabriel, Michael, Raphael, Uriel) with particular stations and duties in the divine hierarchy (Stoyanov 54–55).[7] The book of Daniel, written in the post-exilic period of the second century (167–164 BCE) is a demonstration of the influence exerted by eastern ideas, as the book anachronistically brings together an Israelite prophet from the sixth century BCE, who serves under Babylonian kings of the period of captivity, and combines these with a version of Persian dualism and apocalyptic anticipation—"the final conflict between cosmic good and evil" (Stephen L. Harris 43).

Also apparent in the book of Daniel is a strain of Hellenic Platonism underlying the expectation of resurrection. Hellenic forms of dualism swept into the area from the west after the defeat of the Persian Dynasty by Alexander the Great. This wave brought with it the metaphors of *soul* and *body*—two distinct entities said to coexist in the individual and, with these, notions of an afterlife, either through resurrection or reincarnation. Greek tradition attributes the dualistic figure of an immortal soul distinct from a mortal body to the theological philosopher, Pythagoras, and various related Orphic cults of the sixth century BCE.[8] Orphism, whose founder was said to be the poet Orpheus, directed its worship to the deities (called "saviors") of Greek mystery religions—most prominent of whom were Dionysus and Persephone, evolved forms of ancient vegetation gods.[9] Such figures were thought to demonstrate through their deaths and resurrections the coexistence of a mortal body and an immortal soul. As objects of devotion such deities exhibited the dual nature of their worshipers and became exemplars for the individual's own expected resurrection and/or reincarnation. The Greek mysteries parallel in several ways the underlying figures and narratives of early Christianity (Bultmann 156–61; Davies 124–30[10]).

THE MYSTERY RELIGIONS

> Happy is one of mortals on earth who has seen these things. But those who are uninitiated into the holy rites and have no part never are destined to a similar joy when they are dead in the gloomy realm below.
>
> Morford and Lenardon, "Hymn to Demeter" 317

> Unless a grain of wheat falls into the earth and dies, it remains alone; but if it dies, it bears much fruit. He who loves his life loses it, and he who hates his life in this world will keep it for eternal life.
>
> John 12:24–25

The Greek mysteries evolved later than the state religion evident in Homer and Hesiod's epics, with their acceptance of universal death. Each of the mystery religions represents a "variation of a fundamental and recurring theme—the death and rebirth of vegetation as a metaphor or allegory for spiritual resurrection" (Morford and Lenardon 318). The idea of the resurrected god was by no means new. However, as it was reintroduced from the East and retrieved from remnants of agricultural religions, it would now emphasize the mystery of the god's resurrection as a model of existence for worshipers.

Worshipers embraced the idea that through initiation into the "secrets," performance of ritual, and observance of ritual purity, they like the god could avoid the terrifying prospect of death. Bultmann describes the mysteries as originally national or tribal cults, transported from the soil in which they were born, but flourishing alongside city-state religions (157). The "official" religions were aristocratic and propitiatory, glorifying the great fighting men and their warrior gods. These had offered communal ritual practice, but for most, little comfort. The mystery cults, in contrast, were classless communities headed by a priest or mystagogue as "father of the community" and promised initiates "salvation."

While the mystery rites were "secret," membership was not exclusive. They included aristocrat, commoner, slave, native and foreigner, man and woman. One might join any number of cults, while still observing the official city-state religion. Typically included in the mystery religions were a secret rite of initiation preceded by rites of purification ("fastings, lustrations and baptisms, and occasionally castigation"); separation of the members from the unconsecrated; and presentation of the sacred formula, "culminating in the vision of the deity":

> In this vision union with the deity was attained, the initiate being thus endowed with immortality.... The general sense of the mysteries may be defined as the imparting of "salvation".... Hence the deities are called "saviors".... This salvation includes ... above all ... salvation of the soul and immortality....
>
> Bultmann 157–58

Focus of worship was a "youthful god who dies and rises again." The believer's union with such a figure permits him or her to share not only the death of the god but his "rising again to immortal life"—a process said to result in "rebirth" or being "'born again', 'changed', 'deified', and 'enlightened'" (Bultmann 159). The promise of immortality is linked inextricably with the cult member's "union" with the god. The believing and performing "insiders" will avoid the common way of all flesh.

A Platonic Archetype

Heir to Pythagorean and Orphic ideas, Plato elaborated and merged those ideas with influences from Zoroastrianism to create a system in which immortality was linked to reincarnation.[11] Platonic and Neo-Platonic texts assert that the cosmos and the individual consist of a material body (perceivable by the senses) and an ideal soul. The material world is understood as one of appearances, and all that it contains is a delusive system of passing forms,[12] an imperfect representation of the timeless, immaterial, ideal forms in the mind of the creator. An individual's body belongs to the world of appearances, a form that is born, lives, dies, and is no more. The soul as essence of the individual is ideal and immortal, born in a series of forms or incarnations until it is released through successive purifications from the cycle of corruption and becomes incorruptible. The object of religious and philosophical practice is for the individual, through learning, rational behavior, and ritual observance, to obtain the wisdom and virtue necessary for the soul to escape from incarnation into eternity.[13]

Platonic dualism is elaborated in the *Dialogues*, especially *The Phaedo*, and given graphic representation in Book 10 of *The Republic*, where Plato recounts "The Myth of Er" (350–59). Er is a warrior who has a "near-death" experience. Having apparently died on the battlefield, he is given a tour of the afterlife, where he observes the progress of individuals through the process of reincarnation. He sees two openings in the earth and, opposite these, two openings "in the sky above" (351). Between these sit gods who judge the dead, finding them either just or unjust, and who then direct the unjust downward into the earth and the just upward into the sky. At the heart of this system, as in the "Last Judgment," is the premise that the variety of beings (human and animal) can be sorted into two kinds—they are either good or bad. As Er's story continues, he offers a Platonic version of divine justice, involving thousand-year periods of rewards for virtue and punishments for sin (351–52). Er finishes his story of the afterlife by detailing the process by which the returned souls choose their new bodies and "lives" (fates), forget their former lives, and are reborn, "like shooting stars" (Plato 359).

Many aspects of Platonic dualism will echo in the halls of Christianity and Islam—the duality of soul and body; the immortality of the soul; the vertical dimension of the afterlife; the association of the good or just with light, joy, and cleanliness, and the bad or unjust with darkness, suffering, and soil; a system of rewards and punishments in an afterlife; the sorting of souls into two groups; and even the notion of a geocentric universe with which, many centuries later, Christianity would part reluctantly. Notable differences include the role of individual responsibility. Plato insists that while there "is an element of necessity or chance," souls are the authors of their lives; they control their fates and are thus responsible "for the good and evil" (Plato 350). In Plato's system there is no Author whose comprehensive divine plot determines the course of lives, events, beginnings, and ends. Hence another interesting difference concerns the "bad" or "unjust," or "evil." In Plato's ideal realm there is no "soul of evil," no figure intent on disrupting a divine plan. The material realm is undesirable in that it is an imperfect and delusive representation of the ideal, but it has no animate, willful existence. That is, there is no Devil in the Platonic universe.

The Devil, You Say! Monism and the Problem of Evil

> I am the Lord, and there is no other.
> I form light and create darkness,
> I make peace and create evil,
> I am the Lord who do all these things.
> (Isaiah 45:6–7)[14]

> Shall there be evil in a city, and the Lord hath not done it?
> (Amos 3:6)

In its beginnings, the Bible brings together a cluster of ideas that will remain thematically interrelated in the biblical understanding of the ways of God to man. These ideas include moral evil (Adam's and Eve's disobedience), divine justice (God's imposition of the universal sentence of death), natural evil (death), and, in the grassy ground of Eden, the enigmatic talking snake, a creature subject to reinterpretation through the millennia. Also of interest is the fact that the earliest narratives reveal a thematic edginess about sexuality and gender relations that will endure throughout biblical history and long after, even into the present. The two trees at the center of the garden are, in effect, a graphic image and metaphoric restatement of all these themes. They are the Tree of Life (obedience, honor, and immortality) and the Tree of the Knowledge of Good and Evil (disobedience, shame, and death), in Christian dualism a representation of the opposition of Jesus and Satan. God's command not to eat of the tree of knowledge suggested that the first humans, so long as they obeyed, might enjoy an innocent immortality through the miraculous tree of life. Before eating the forbidden fruit, Adam and Eve are almost asexual—"naked and not ashamed." Afterward, they recognize their nakedness and are ashamed, thus associating sin (disobedience) with sexuality. Gender relations are foregrounded in God's curse on the man that begins, "Because you have listened to the voice of your wife," implying another commandment never until this moment made explicit. Eve's secondary status and greater culpability are implied in the curse on her: "[Y]our desire shall be for your husband, and he shall rule over you" (Genesis 2–3). Life, obedience, sexual innocence, and male domination are good; death, disobedience, sexual awareness, and female domination are evil. However ancient the roots of these ideas, biblical divine justice abides in the dualistic alignment of obedience, good, and life, on the one hand, and disobedience, evil, and death, on the other, an order established from the opening narratives. Thus, in Old Testament narratives, collective and individual obedience to divine law reaps rewards—peace, prosperity, long life, and progeny. Disobedience, collective and individual, calls down a host of evils administered by Yahweh as punishment—war, poverty, illness, childlessness, and early death.

No Devil is required. God is One and all-powerful. Given this background, Satan's subsequent evolution and rise to prominence in the New Testament require investigation. Although Christianity embraces a form of cosmic monism—professed belief in one omniscient, omnipotent, and omni-benevolent creator—it cannot get by without a Devil. It blurs the monistic vision by including in its universe a trope for evil—Satan or the Devil, a figure who owes something to the Zoroastrian evil twin and his evolved persona as the destroyer, Ahriman. The New Testament's Satan is a malevolent, embodied evil and enemy of God. Whereas in his Old Testament beginnings he is said to be God's creature (a son of God), as the centuries pass it seems either that God cannot control him (in which case Yahweh would not be omnipotent), does control him, or actually directs the fiend's behavior in the world (in which case Yahweh would not be omni-benevolent[15] (González 48, 169).

Aside from his Zoroastrian models, the New Testament's Satan has numerous precursors to whom he is actually more similar than to the Satan of the Old Testament, who through all but the late texts is clearly Yahweh's minion (cf. Numbers 22–23; Job 1–2). Stoyanov says of the Old Testament's *The Satan* or Adversary (a title, not a proper name) that he "serves as an accusing and punishing angel under the supreme authority of Yahweh" (56). To illustrate, Stoyanov cites the early story of David's census (2 Samuel 24), in which *God* (for incomprehensible reasons) orders David to take a *divinely forbidden* census and then sends *as punishment* a pestilence that destroys seventy thousand Israelite men. David's predicament is one from which he cannot emerge unscathed: faced with the illogic of the situation, he must disobey one commandment (against taking a census) in order to obey another (to take a census). God's justice is indeed inscrutable. The story's later retelling in 1 Chronicles 21, composed in the late Persian period, bears marks of the revisionist's impulse. Now the tale reflects Zoroastrian dualist influence and evolving Hebrew ideas about The Satan and his relationship to Yahweh, for in this version *Satan, rather than Yahweh,* incites David to take the unlawful census. In the later account, Satan supposedly acts on his own authority and emerges "as an individual and independent force," his name now a "proper name of the spirit of evil" (Stoyanov 57–58).

The transformation of Satan will continue in the "silence" between the testaments (a silence that was not silent at all, merely not productive of canonical texts). Gradually ideas stirring in late Old Testament period evolved and gained acceptance. A reader feels the effect of such flowering of ideas as one moves across more than two centuries from the Old Testament to the New. Almost immediately, one senses that, in the interim, evil has metamorphosed and proliferated and now infests the entire creation in new and malignant forms. Satan has evolved to become a powerful, at least superficially autonomous, enemy of Yahweh.

The importance of this figure cannot be overestimated, for his mere presence focuses not only on the dual character of the Christian Gestalt, but actually makes the Christian narrative and its climactic resolution possible. Without him, there would be no story. He is the enemy required by the hero, having proven indispensable throughout history in endless retellings of the most ancient and universal of narrative types, the combat myth. This story-type pits a hero who battles on behalf of the life and welfare of his community against an enemy who threatens that life. In a moment of crisis, everything hangs in the balance; an enemy (often serpent- or dragon-like) threatens; a hero steps forward. Thus Marduk volunteers to wage war against the ancient dragon, Tiamat; Zeus accepts the challenge of the hundred-snake-headed Typhoeus; Apollo defeats the great python at Delphi; Yahweh overpowers and controls Leviathan; and Michael opposes and defeats the seven-headed, ten-horned "great red dragon, that ancient serpent,"[16] who is called the Devil and Satan" (Revelation 12:3–9). Without heroic opposition, the old enemy would impose his will and all would be lost.

The form of this timeless tale of hero and enemy is explicitly taken up and refashioned by Christian interpreters. For example, in his *Divine Institutes*, the early Christian apologist, Lactantius, invokes the story-type along with the motif of brother strife[17] to "explain" the origin of the Christian Satan and his opposition to God and Jesus, "his elder brother"[18]:

> Before creating the world, God the Father produced a spirit similar to himself and filled with his virtues. He then made another on whom the mark of divine origin did not remain. For he was tainted with the poison of jealousy and thus passed from good to evil by his own will. . . . He is a black fount of all evils. For he was jealous of his elder brother who, remaining attached to God the Father, obtained his affection. This being who, from the good which he was, became evil, is called Devil by the Greeks.
>
> Cited in Forsyth 14[19]

In retelling as an origin myth the narrative of brother strife (a variation on the Zoroastrian tale of primordial twins), Lactantius places Jesus and Satan in the ancient tradition, yet noticeably he does not comment on the origin of the "poison of jealousy."

The biblical Enemy has a number of titles—he may be given the name of the Old Testament adversary (Satan) or the Greek form, translated "Devil"; he may be called murderer (John 8:44), oppressor (Acts 10:38), one who has the power of death (Hebrews 2:14), Prince of the power of the air (Ephesians 2:2), great red dragon, and ancient serpent (Revelation 12:3–9). The New Testament's Jesus is the hero who opposes Satan. Jesus is called the "Author of life" (Acts 3:15)—life and light itself; Satan is death and darkness. It is the oldest story, made new in every hero tale in every age, whether Death is given a name like Tiamat, Typhoeus, or Satan, or as in St. Paul's invocation of the Resurrection of Jesus, identified plainly: "Death is swallowed up in victory" (1 Corinthians 15:54).[20]

Monism and Divine Justice

> Moreover I saw under the sun that in the place of justice, even there was wickedness, and in the place of righteousness, even there was wickedness."
>
> Ecclesiastes 3:16

Many people who embraced various forms of the Near Eastern and Greek mystery religions and their divine figures of life (beginning in the sixth century BCE) as well as those who joined the Christian movement in the early years of the Common Era needed a new kind of divine being, a hero for the common man. The Christian movement began amid a troubled people whose covenant relationship with their God appeared to have faltered. The destruction of the Second Temple in 70 CE was a devastating blow, as it effectively banished Yahweh from Jerusalem. Many sought reassurance that divine justice would prevail.[21]

As discussed in Chapter 2, a growing concern with divine justice is apparent in the latter part of the Old Testament period. As the books of Job (exilic) and Ecclesiastes (post-exilic) demonstrate, writers were increasingly concerned with what appeared to be the failure of both collective and individual justice. God's chosen people suffered more than her enemies; evil individuals prospered, while the righteous suffered and died; even worse, there was no discernible pattern, and no one seemed to be in charge. People seemed subject to time and chance (Ecclesiastes 9:11), whose rule produces an absurdity that cannot be reconciled with Old Testament notions of the Covenant, the power of Yahweh, and his administration of divine justice: "Like fish which are taken in an evil net, so men are snared at an evil time when it suddenly falls upon them" (Ecclesiastes 9:12). Death is the common fate of all: "For the fate of the sons of men and the fate of beasts is the same; as one dies, so dies the other. They all have the same breath, and man has no advantage over the beasts; for all is vanity" (Ecclesiastes 3:19).

It became even more difficult in the intertestamental period to retain confidence in divine justice. The apocryphal book of 2 Esdras raises the Joban dilemma to a national level. Why, Ezra asks his angelic guide, has Babylon, a nation that does not serve Yahweh, prevailed over the chosen people? He wonders, "Are the deeds of those who inhabit Babylon any better? Is that why she has gained dominion over Zion?" Ezra is mystified: "I have seen how thou [Yahweh] dost endure those who sin, and has spared those who act wickedly, and hast destroyed thy people, and hast preserved thy enemies, and *hast not shown to any one how thy way may be comprehended*" (2 Esdras 3:28–31; emphasis supplied).

Ezra's angel informant offers two reasons for the apparent breakdown of God's justice, both of which will become thematic in New Testament texts. First, Uriel explains, Yahweh's creation has been corrupted from the beginning: "For a grain of evil seed was sown in Adam's heart from the beginning, and how much ungodliness it has produced until now and will produce until the time of threshing comes!" (2 Esdras 4:30). This "evil seed" seems to account for Adam's original sin of disobedience, although, as in Lactantius' attribution of evil to the "poison of jealousy," no source for the seed is mentioned, nor any sower of the seed. At one point, in despair for the sad lot of humanity, Ezra cries, "O Adam, what have you done?" (2 Esdras 7:118). The second reason offered is that the failure of justice is only *apparent*. For, in fact, the scene of justice has shifted from the confines of the corrupt world to incorruptible realms of eternity. Ezra learns that a few righteous dead will awaken in eternity to a new "paradise of delight" and the rest of the dead will awaken to a "furnace of hell." At the time of the awakening, God will take the "seat of judgment," and "compassion shall pass away" (2 Esdras 7). The book of 2 Esdras provides a strong link between the last-written books of the Old Testament and those of the New. In response to a perceived failure of divine justice, Ezra anticipates many New Testament developments: dualism of body and spirit, the immortal soul, a Messiah, the Two Ages, the Resurrection, End Times, and Last Judgment.

He includes, however, no figure equivalent to Satan. Instead, evil infests humanity as a whole (the evil seed) and takes human, historico-political forms—a series of beasts representing, in succession, the dominant powers of the area, enemies of Yahweh and his elect. The fourth and last is a monstrous eagle representative of Rome, to whom a Messiah figure in the form of a lion speaks, announcing its end:

> Therefore you will surely disappear, you eagle . . . so that the whole earth, freed from your violence, may be refreshed and relieved, and may hope for the judgment and mercy of him who made it.
> 2 Esdras 11:43–46

Ezra's solutions to the problem of evil raise as many questions as they answer. Most important is the problem that Christianity will attempt to solve—the unspecified origin of the "evil seed" that has flourished through all of time and the identity of its sower.

DIVINE JUSTICE AND THE DEVIL

Forsyth makes the case that "Christianity began as one more Jewish apocalyptic sect with a peculiar messianic belief" that developed in two ways—Gnostic Christianity and Catholic Christianity. Each approached Ezra's unresolved problem of the origin of evil: "[W]as it human or angel, the sin of a broken covenant or the evil of a cosmic power . . . ?" (221). New Testament texts (Catholic Christianity) answer those questions by assuming an autonomous, malevolent figure who has from the beginning sought to impede God's purposes, hence the identification of Eden's serpent with Satan. He is the sower of the "evil seed"; he is a figure like that who emerges in the retelling of the story of David's census. Stoyanov shows that as "ethical religiosity" took its place at the center of attention, along with the perceived cosmic and personal conflict between the forces of good and evil, "trends emerged that sought and approached dualist solutions to the riddle of the origin of evil." In this process, Satan was promoted from just another of the servants of God to the "superhuman agency that was opposed to God and man and had brought sin and death into the world to thwart divine purposes" (58–59). Satan's "elevated" role is apparent, for example, in an apocryphal book, The Wisdom of Solomon, which claims, as will Lactantius and other apologists, that the assault on God's purposes is prompted by the devil's envy and identifies him unequivocally with death: "[F]or God created man for incorruption, and made him in the image of his own eternity, but through the devil's envy death entered the world, and those who belong to his party experience it" (2:23–24).

Satan became a key metaphor, a trope for and identical with Death and Evil—they are all one. New Testament texts display not only the personification of evil, but also its proliferation among a fearful people in chaotic times. In the synoptic gospels, especially, demons (servants of the evil one) willy-nilly infest those whom they wish.[22] In a particularly graphic tale of "possession," versions of which appear in all three of the synoptic gospels, a "Legion" of evil spirits inhabits an unfortunate fellow, whose dwelling, appropriately enough, is a graveyard. Isolated, mad, self-battering, the demoniac inexplicably runs to Jesus and "worships" him:

> Crying out with a loud voice, he said, "What have you to do with me, Jesus, Son of the Most High God? I adjure you by God, do not torment me." For he [Jesus] had said to him, "Come out of the man, you unclean spirit!" And Jesus asked him, "What is your name?" He replied, "My name is Legion; for we are many."
>
> Mark 5:6–9; cf. Matthew 8:28–34 and Luke 8:26–39

The demoniac's humble supplication and entreaty suggest that this meeting poses no threat to Jesus. Even more remarkable are the curious need of the spirits for bodies and the transportability of "spirit" from body to body, for the Legion begs to be sent into a nearby herd of swine. Jesus grants permission, after which the demon-possessed swine ("about two thousand") run like lemmings into the sea and drown. Appropriately and ironically, Jesus has sent the unclean spirits into unclean animals. What prompts the pigs' mass suicide? The demons? Jesus? Does the death of the pigs imply destruction of the unclean spirits? Is water lethal to demons? Are unclean spirits immortal, or can they be killed? Jesus' victory over the spirits seems almost effortless, while the demons appear weak and submissive, and yet, as a passage from Matthew would indicate, the demons can and perhaps will return, which raises a question about the efficacy or even advisability of exorcism:

> When an unclean spirit has gone out of a man, he [the spirit] passes through waterless places seeking rest, but he finds none. Then he says, "I will return to my house from which I came." And when he comes he

> finds it empty, swept, and put in order. Then he goes and brings with him seven other spirits more evil than himself, and they enter and dwell there; and the last state of that man becomes worse than the first.
>
> 12:43–45

The easy return of the demons is like a reinfestation of cockroaches.

One effect of body-soul dualism is apparent, as it makes possible the sort of metaphor in which the relationship of body to soul is understood as that of container to contained. The container is devalued in relationship to the contained, as St. Paul indicates when he cries, "Who will deliver *me* from this body of death?" (Romans 7:24; emphasis supplied). That which is contained (the immortal "me") can be "delivered" from its no-account, temporary, mortal, disposable body. In Matthew's tale of the returning demons, the "contained" includes alien spirits; the container is a body (house) into which the spirits have come uninvited. The metaphor reifies the body as a dwelling place (swept or unswept), for spirits, clean or unclean—the "me" and the uninvited guests. A similar metaphor works in the notion of body as the "temple" of the soul, or Holy Spirit (John 2:21, 1 Corinthians 3:16, 6:19).

The gospel of John offers no similar accounts of demonic possession but does record a sort of possession that presents even greater problems of interpretation. This tale concerns a moment during the last supper when Jesus announces that one among the disciples will betray him. When asked who this is, Jesus replies, "It is he to whom I shall give this morsel [of bread] when I have dipped it": "So, when he had dipped the morsel, he gave it to Judas. . . . *Then after the morsel, Satan entered into him.* Jesus said to him, 'What you are going to do, do quickly'" (John 13:21–27; emphasis supplied). Here Judas becomes "inhabited" by both Jesus (in the form of the sacramental wine-soaked bread) and Satan, prince of demons, who "moves in" after seemingly being invited, or at least granted permission. To whom is Jesus statement, "What you are going to do, do quickly," addressed? Judas or Satan? In the tales of the Gerasene demoniac, Jesus addresses the demon, as in Mark 5:8. Does Jesus have the same sort of authority over this prince of demons? In this instance, rather than casting out demons, he seems to invite Satan to take possession of Judas. The death and resurrection of Jesus is figured in the bread and wine of the Eucharist—repeated in the wine-soaked morsel of bread. Having partaken of an ironic sacrament, Judas will then "betray" Jesus as an apparently necessary part of Yahweh's divine plan.[23] Without betrayal, there would be no crucifixion, without crucifixion, no resurrection, without resurrection no heroic victory over Death, and without that victory, no Church and no story.

THE UNDISCOVERED COUNTRY: IMMORTALITY AND THE TWO

> Bitterly Gilgamesh wept for his friend.... "What my brother is now, that shall I be when I am dead. Because I am afraid of death I will go as best I can to find Utnapishtim ... for he has entered the assembly of the gods."
>
> Sandars 94

Absorbing both eastern and western dualistic influences, Christianity found means—often problematic—of accommodating its monistic and monotheistic inheritance from the Old Testament to dualistic features characteristic of Zoroastrianism, Greek mysteries, and Platonism. While Christianity ostensibly maintains a monotheistic stance, it nevertheless incorporates forms of ethical or ethicoreligious dualism based on the metaphor of the Two. Good and Evil are hypostasized as Yahweh/Jesus and Satan. These opponents are elegantly and simply figurative for Life and Death, for implied in dualistic thinking is the idea that death is not merely the natural end of all that live; rather it is an embodied malevolent power eager to do battle with and overcome the figures of life.

Moreover, whereas Christianity made Satan an autonomous or semi-autonomous figure for death, Islam, in its later emergence, retained God's curse of death from the story in Genesis, but revised it. In the Qur'an, the curses on Adam and Eve are combined; the first humans are cast out of Eden and placed in contention, one with the other; but their sentence of death is mitigated at this early moment by the promise of deliverance or resurrection: "He [Allah] said, 'All of you get out of Eden! You are each other's enemies. On earth you will have a place to stay and livelihood—for a time.' He said, 'There you will live; there you will die; from there you will be brought out'" (7:24–25). Thus Allah is equally author of life and death, and no separate divine "savior" who undergoes incarnation, death, and resurrection, is required to restore immortality, for Allah has spoken a blessing as part of the curse: "[F]rom there you will be brought out." The Qur'an presents Jesus as a creature of Allah, a great prophet, but not divine. Allah speaks to Jesus and announces, "O Jesus! I will make Thee die and take Thee up again to me and will clear thee of those who misbelieve, and will make those who follow thee above those who misbelieve, at the day of judgment, then to me is your return" (3: 47–50).

The metaphoric creation of the Unknown is ongoing work that extends as far as human ignorance. Quite obviously, primary nodes of life and death dominate the network of Unknowns. This centrality is paradoxical, for in a purely natural sense, death takes its place among things well known. As Sam Harris puts it, "Our felt sense of what is real seems not to include our own death. We doubt the one thing that is not open to any doubt at all" (38). Logically, Shakespeare's Caesar finds death the "necessary end" of all that live (*Julius Caesar* 2.2.33–38). The author of Ecclesiastes commonsensically comments, "[T]he fate of the sons of men and the fate of the beasts is the same; as one dies, so dies the other" (3:19).

Their experience of death as conscious creatures sets human beings apart. We observe with grief and fear the inanimation and transformation that accompany it—a crushed spider, a dead dog by a roadside, a breathless parent, spouse, child, or friend. We have seen the rotting remains.[24] We anticipate with fear our own "ceasing to be." Ezra regretted the curse of the conscious mind: "[L]et all who have been born lament, but let the four-footed beasts and the flocks rejoice! For it is much better with them than with us; for they do not look for a judgment, nor do they know of any torment or salvation promised to them after death" (2 Esdras 7:65–66).

Unable to bear the consciousness of inevitable death, we can attempt to transform it through language. We can create a word—*afterlife*. We can create by naming gods who live forever in a perfect place, a home to which at least some humans may be invited. We can speak of it as a country, however unknown, as does Shakespeare's Hamlet (3.1.77–79). However pessimistic, Hamlet's metaphor of a country of the dead opens up a space for the possible continuation of life's journey whose "necessary" end concerns us. We can let our desire and our imaginations run wild and create a walled, twelve-gated garden-city with streets of gold, a place without darkness or time, through which the "river of the water of life" flows, where the lost Tree of Life flourishes and nourishes and heals the immortal blessed, a city of God, where the unknowable creator of everything sits on a throne and lights the city with his shining (Revelation 21:15–22:5). Or we can create Gardens of sensual delight. Referred to as *Jannah* (Garden), this Islamic place, like the New Jerusalem, is walled, with eight gates. Here the blessed will enjoy an existence lush with riches, food, drink, and multiple immortal sexual consorts.[25] In both cases, whatever seems good in mortal existence is transposed into a higher key to become part of the undiscovered country of eternity. At the same time, whatever harms or frightens is figured in the inexhaustible fires of hell where the damned will suffer forever.

In many lands through much of history, figurative work has suggested that life will continue. Our narratives create places for the "afterlife" and provisions for its enjoyment. This has not always and everywhere been the case. Gilgamesh's quest for immortality led to the terrible knowledge that only the gods are immortal (Pritchard, *The Ancient Near East* 64). Likewise Odysseus learned in the underworld the unpleasant fate of humanity—to become the insubstantial, wraithlike, "dimwitted dead," mere "after images of used-up men" (Homer, *The Odyssey* 200). Given human antipathy to death, there can be no mystery in a willingness to embrace duality, the concept of a soul separate from the body that dies, and the promise of afterlife in a Holy City or the Gardens of Paradise. Only one thing is required: one must believe. This necessity raises the notion of faith and its relationship to will. Can one "will to believe?" In the next chapter I turn my attention to the criterion of belief for "salvation" and the relationship of belief to will or "free will."

CHAPTER 8

THE WAYS OF GOD TO MEN: BELIEF, PREORDINATION, PREDESTINATION, REWARDS AND PUNISHMENTS, SPIRITUAL ECONOMICS

> Indeed, belief... seems to have been the pivot around which Christians have told their own history.
> Lopez 21

> Their [those who believe] reward with their Lord is everlasting Gardens graced with flowing streams, where they will stay forever.
> Qur'an 98:7–8

> Now faith is the substance of things hoped for, the evidence of things not seen.... Through faith we understand that the worlds were framed by the word of God, so that things which are seen were not made of things which do appear.
> King James, Hebrews 11:1–3

> Faith, n. Belief without evidence in what is told by one who speaks without knowledge, of things without parallel.
> Ambrose Bierce, *Devil's Dictionary*

EVIDENCE OF THINGS NOT SEEN

Hamlet was right. No traveler returns from the undiscovered country of death. We have no empirical evidence[1] that the "country" exists anywhere outside the graveyard. What might constitute "evidence of things not seen"? St. Paul does not elaborate; he merely leaves the paradox in place. One sort of answer, however, is the one I have offered: the "evidence" is linguistic—figure and narrative, trope and story. Bringing linguistic tools to bear on the Unknown, *things seen* easily invoke *things not seen*. To approach and allay the abhorrent prospect of mortality, we have merely to add the negative morpheme to create a *thing unseen*, never seen, unseeable: *immortality*. If bodies grow old and die and rot in time, again a negative morpheme produces *eternal*; *corruptible* becomes *incorruptible*; *death* in time becomes *Life* in eternity. We create a narrative in which death is not an end, but a beginning, an entry into a time*less* abode. A story may present that "country" as an ideal place—a blessed island, a golden city, a paradisiacal garden, a snow-white mansion—from which the vicissitudes of mortal life are absent; it may be a dark land of insubstantial shades or eternal suffering—sheol, hades, the fiery pit. With a quick "slight of language"—a spatial metaphor, a few negative morphemes, and a story—death takes on dimension and extension, transforms into life; we claim the *un*discovered country for our eternal habitation; we create for ourselves divine models—beings who die yet live forever: we ourselves become *im*mortal.

For some, to profess belief in the tropes and narratives seems prudent, and so Kierkegaard offers a philosophical version of the child's "Let's pretend." He speaks of a blind "leap into faith" or "leap of faith," involving the spontaneous assent to something despite a lack of empirical evidence and whatever irresolvable paradoxes may be implicated. Then there is Pascal's wager, applying game theory to the self-interested choice to wager that God exists. If the choice proves incorrect, one loses nothing; if it proves true, one stands to gain "infinite happiness."[2] Lopez explains, "[A]ccepting Pascal's premise that God is ultimately unknowable, some philosophers and theologians have argued that religious belief is qualitatively different from other forms of belief because it is an assent to that which can never be justified by conventional means." He cites Tertullian's paradox: *"Credo quia absurdum"* (I believe because it is absurd) (23). Well . . .

THE ECONOMICS OF BELIEF

Belief . . . occurs between the recognition of an alterity and the establishment of a contract.

Certeau 192

> To believe, [Benveniste] says, is to "give something away with the certainty of getting it back."
>
> Certeau 192

> Then Jacob made a vow, saying, "If God will be with me, and will keep me in this way that I go, and will give me bread to eat and clothing to wear, so that I come again to my father's house in peace, then the Lord shall be my God . . . and of all that thou givest me I will give the tenth to thee."
>
> Genesis 28:20–22

Pascal's unabashed inclusion of a quid pro quo aspect of belief (or what Certeau calls an "ethics of a *dos ut des*" [192]) only makes explicit what has from the beginning been a part of it, for an economic metaphor has always rested at the center of the religious concept of belief.[3] Belief is a special sort of contractual or covenantal affair entered into by two parties, one of whom is superior and divine, the other, inferior and human. Usually, in such an agreement, the human party promises something (belief, loyalty, sacrifice, tithe, ritual observance) in exchange for a *future* return from the divine party or spiritual guarantor (victory, prosperity, immortality).

When in a dream God appears to Jacob at Bethel, he reveals himself as the God of Abraham and Isaac, establishes with Jacob the contract (or covenant)—a reiteration of the Abrahamic covenant—and promises, as his part of it, to give to Jacob and his descendents the land on which he lies. Moreover, God promises to "keep" Jacob wherever he goes and to return him safely to this Promised Land. The ever-cautious Jacob replies (epigraph) in a conditional mode, indicating clearly the mutual expectations of the parties to the contract, "If God . . . " In this interesting instance, both parties make future promises. Jacob takes a wait-and-see attitude, expecting God to perform some of his contractual duties before Jacob performs his. Jacob will not return to Canaan for twenty years. It is only then that, as Jacob agrees, "the Lord shall be [his] God."

An early, paradigmatic example of the economic metaphor appears in the covenant with Jacob's grandfather, Abraham. Abraham, at that time seventy-five years old, is living with his clan in Haran when the Lord speaks to him, telling him to leave Haran for "a land that I will show you" (Canaan), offering as inducement a promise to make the childless Abraham "a great nation" (Genesis 12:1–2). Two main versions of the covenant between God and Abraham are recorded, one in Genesis 15 (the Elohist's account) and another in Genesis 17 (from the Priestly tradition). In both, God initiates the making of the contract by his "choice" or "election" of Abraham, promising that Abraham will father the multitudes of God's worshipers, to whom he will give the land of Canaan and from whom he will require fealty and, in the Priestly account, a curiously unlikely (even grotesque) "textual notation" of the covenant: circumcision. As a "written" sign and record of the covenant, circumcision is endlessly repeatable through successive generations in the flesh of the male members of the community, a semiotic reiteration of the contractual obligations between God and his chosen people:

> And God said to Abraham, "As for you, you shall keep my covenant, you and your descendants after you: Every male among you shall be circumcised. *You shall be circumcised in the flesh of your foreskins, and it shall be a sign of the covenant between me and you.* He that is eight days old among you shall be circumcised; every male throughout your generations. . . . So shall my covenant be in your flesh an everlasting covenant. Any uncircumcised male . . . shall be cut off from his people; he has broken my covenant."
> Genesis 17:9–14; emphasis supplied[4]

In return for God's future performance of the contract terms—the granting of the land and descendents—Abraham agrees to make Yahweh his God and to record the transaction in his own flesh and that of all the males when they reach the age of eight days: "So shall my covenant be in your flesh an everlasting covenant" (17:13).[5]

The mark of circumcision has been and remains problematic, for despite theological ponderings, it persists as a largely indecipherable notation, a mark manifesting all the sign's abilities to hide meaning, to deceive, and to create the illusion of a of a hidden reality. All the difficulties of figurative language are implicated in the sign. It is both linguistic sign and physical representation of another thing or several other things. Although signs point to "signifieds," as Marshall Blonsky points out, "concepts, themes, signifieds might be undone"; those whose work is the study and analysis of signs must take notice of the fact that "within the obvious or unobvious statements made by an utterance are murmured meanings from 'between the words', words under words" (xvii), or an "invisible wound" behind the visible wound.[6] Approaching the sign naively, one asks, why is this the chosen sign? Is the sign appropriate? What are its implications? One looks for meaning, some gesture toward a truth or reality, but, again, as Blonsky puts it, "signs lie, make no responsible pronouncements, but they *act on people*" (xxi). To focus for a time on this particular figure, one might ask, what are the murmured meanings? Are there words under the words?

As a beginning, one can follow the sign to other, perhaps related signs. In connection with his covenant obligation to provide Abraham a "multitude" of descendants, God promises Abraham (at that time 100 years old) a son by his well-past-menopausal wife, Sarah. On hearing the claim, each laughs at what seems a divine jest (Genesis 17:17; 18:12). Sarah asks a pertinent question, "After I have grown old and my husband is old, shall I have pleasure?" (Genesis 18:12), implicating sexual enjoyment and physical "potency" in the rite and in God's manipulation of events and behaviors (18:14). Associating himself with the way of the penis, God seems to establish himself as the manipulator/initiator of sexual activity as well as master of fertility, a role reprised from his initial creation when he blessed the living creatures and admonished them to be "fruitful and multiply."

One might inquire how circumcision, a visible sign of covenant obligations, is different from the circumcision rituals practiced by neighboring peoples. Is Yahweh revising an ancient, widespread practice to serve these needs and this moment? What ancient meanings does the sign bring with it? A brief, inexplicable tale in Exodus offers a hint of murmured meanings between the words. The narrative is inserted into the story of Moses as he (finally persuaded to accept Yahweh's commission and approach the Pharaoh) is traveling from Midian to Egypt:

> At a lodging place on the way the Lord met him [Moses] and sought to kill him. Then Zipporah [Moses' Midianite wife] took a flint and cut off her son's foreskin and touched Moses' feet [a euphemism for genitals] with it, and said, "Surely you are a bridegroom of blood to me!" So he [Yahweh] let him [Moses] alone. Then it was that she said, "You are a bridegroom of blood," because of the circumcision.
>
> Exodus 4:24–26

Although anachronistic in the marriage of Moses, here the "surrogate" circumcision is associated with marriage ritual—the groom, newly circumcised, is a "bridegroom of blood." Some ancient cultures (here, apparently, the Midianite) considered marriage a time when the bridegroom became vulnerable to attack by supernatural beings who wished to enjoy the bride sexually. They established rituals, often circumcision, as a means of warding off such attacks.[7]

Another biblical narrative likewise associates circumcision with marriage, sex, and violence—in this case involving not divine, but human attack. The tale concerns the marriage of Dinah, Jacob's daughter. Shechem, a prince of a Canaanite city, seeks to marry Dinah. (Apparently he has "taken her" without the proper marriage negotiations.) When he does seek formal agreement to the "marriage," the sons of Jacob reply "deceitfully," claiming that they cannot "give [their] sister to one who is uncircumcised." They pretend to consent to the marriage and establish as a condition that Shechem and all the males of his city be circumcised (inscribing in their flesh the sacred sign and in effect "converting" to Yahwism). Shechem agrees to the condition, and the circumcision takes place:

> On the third day, when they were sore, two of the sons of Jacob . . . took their swords and came upon the city unawares, and killed all the males.

They slew Hamor and his son Shechem with the sword, and took Dinah out of Shechem's house, and went away. And the sons of Jacob came upon the slain, and plundered the city . . . ; they took their flocks and their herds, their asses, and whatever was in the city and in the field; all their wealth, all their little ones and their wives, all that was in the houses, they captured and made their prey.

Genesis 35:25–31

A cluster of motifs—penis, sword, marriage, violence, power and impotence (sexual and military)—is carried along in the narrative. Dinah's brothers counter Shechem's sexual potency (his "taking" of Dinah) by the requirement of circumcision, which renders him and his men not only sexually impotent, but also militarily powerless—the sword and the penis are both disempowered. Shechem is a "bridegroom of blood." At the same time, the covenant empowers Dinah's brothers—both militarily (two of them defeat an entire population with their swords) and sexually (they seize the women of the Shechemites, along with their property). Behind the requirement imposed on Shechem by Dinah's brothers is ironically the primary agreement, the covenant between them and Yahweh, their divine guarantor of ultimate success over the Canaanites.

The mass circumcision of the Shechemites and the required recovery period will be mirrored in similar events in the Israelite camp as the people prepare to invade the Promised Land. The generation born in the wilderness has not been circumcised, so a communal ritual is required and performed at a place with an appropriate, but ludicrous name—Gibeath-haaraloth, "the hill of the foreskins" (Joshua 5:3). Once circumcised and therefore party to the covenant, the Israelites are empowered by Yahweh to begin the genocidal conquest of the land of the covenant, promised to Abraham by God hundreds of years before. Their first conquest is the ancient Canaanite city of Jericho: "they utterly destroyed all in the city, both men and women, young and old, oxen, sheep, and asses, with the edge of the sword" (Joshua 6:21). In the land of the covenant, the sign of the covenant in the penises of the Israelites is again associated with divinely sanctioned military power, as the city is *utterly* destroyed.

Many associations—divine, sexual, military weakness and potency, sword and penis, fertility and sterility, covenant and marriage contract, sacred and profane wounding, and violence (self-inflicted and other-inflicted)—create complexity by their convergence in circumcision, sign of the covenant. What sort of worldview emerges from such defining (dis)figuration, each man's constant reminder of identity and purpose? A disconcerting aspect of this sign is the persistent reminder that sex and violence are parties to and characteristic of God's "contract" with the Israelites and the suggestion that Yahweh is keenly interested in conquest, sex, reproduction, and masculine power.

DIVINE SELF-MANIFESTATION AND THE INITIAL WOUND

God's approach to Abraham marks the beginning of the contractual relationship with his chosen people specified in mutual agreements and sealed in blood. Speaking of the primacy of beginnings, Edward W. Said remarks that "[t]he beginning . . . is the first step in the *intentional production of meaning*," the point from which follows all that subsequently unfolds in a text (*Beginnings* 5; emphasis supplied). Reb Alcé adds another dimension to the consequence of beginnings. The text begins with a "wound": "Mark," he says, "the first page of the book with a red marker. For in the beginning, the wound is invisible," but somehow present nevertheless (Quoted in Jabes 13). Does a hidden wound exist beneath the blood of circumcision? In this case one must also ask, what meanings inhere in and proceed from the initial wound? What does its imposition reveal about the divine party to the covenant? David Tracy analyzes the reciprocity and exchange between God and believer as consisting of God's "gift" of self-manifestation and, on the human's part, "re-cognition": "the category often employed as a counterpart on the side of human reception to the event/gift/grace of revelation as divine self-manifestation is the gift, grace, happening (never work) of 'faith' as reorientation of trust in and loyalty to the God presencing Godself. . . ." ("Writing" 387). God reveals himself; humans believe. What, if anything, do the contract terms disclose about the Godself? Specifically, what does God self-reveal through the covenant requirement of circumcision? When and how is the invisible wound revealed to have been there always on the "first page"?

To begin, one can say that God reveals himself as a contract-maker with an interest in divine economics, in that he approaches Abraham and makes certain promises in exchange for Abraham's agreements. According to the terms, God owes Abraham's descendants a land. Not now, however, and not for a long time. God tells Abraham that only after *400 years*, once the "iniquity of the Amorites" is complete, will Abraham's "countless" descendents enter and inhabit the land long-promised (15:16). According to tradition, for the next roughly half a millennium, the Abrahamic, future-looking contract with its deferred maturity date and pay-out will pass from father to son, until becoming enormously elaborated in the Mosaic code. The parties to the contract are the Israelite clans, and the powerful initiator and surety, God. God's being the "other" party to the give-and-take of the contract of belief, as Certeau observes, "poses a problem":

> We have to presume a guarantee from . . . an [absent] other . . . endowed with power, will and knowledge that can mete out "retribution". . . . The interrogation born from the possibility that he might default essentially bears on two points: that he recognizes himself as *obligated* and that he

is *capable* of *paying up*. . . . The guarantor is seen as the reflection of the characteristic features of the believer. He functions as his mirror.

199

The believer, as one who can both make the verbal commitment and perform the promised duties, must see himself in the divine mirror. The contract of belief focuses most closely the question of how to know "*if there is a surety*" (Certeau 199). The displacement of the guarantor to some "elsewhere" and the indefinite deferment of fulfillment of the contract to some "*further on*" raise the question, "How can we be sure that the partner will act as obligated, that he will be 'faithful' to what is expected of him, or 'straight'...?" (ibid. 199–200). Certeau proposes as a "first verification" the presumption on the part of the believer that "the other, in a certain sense, also 'believes' and that he considers himself obligated by the gift given to him": "It is a *belief in the belief of the other* or in what he/one makes believe that he believes, etc. . . . [I]t must presume that some Real will stand surety" (ibid. 200).

The metaphor shaping the contract of religious belief, then, starts with an *a priori* presumption of a reality or "the real" toward which the metaphor gestures: God exists. To this initial "truth" it adds the further presumption that the powerful God can and does make contracts with whom he chooses—contracts that obligate the parties, human and divine, to perform certain acts or present certain goods. A further presumption is that God will be "straight" and "faithful" to his contractual obligations; that he will "stand surety." The displacement of fulfillment of the contract into a distant future (400 years in the case of Abraham, End Times in Christianity and Islam, imminent or unimaginably far away—who knows?) saves the present from any shadow of default. The metaphor ignores the niggling general question, given the first presumption, "Why/how would divine economics benefit the absent supernatural party to the contract?" God's question to Job responds ironically to almost every claim of the economics of belief: "Who has given to me that I should repay him? Whatever is under the whole heaven is mine" (Job 41:11).

The contractual relationship entered into between God and the Israelites has continued in effect through the millennia, a legacy in one or another form in all three Abrahamic religions. Throughout Old Testament times, the relationship is stormy, cycling through periods of compliance and default, obedience and sin, reward and punishment. The people apparently are never quite willing or able to sustain their covenant obligations, and God is perpetually angry, punishing, and then fiercely forgiving. The repeated refrain of the prophets through pre-exilic, exilic, and post-exilic times is that in response to the Israelites' default, God will destroy the people, keeping alive a "remnant" who will remain party to the contract when God at some point will at last return to them the land promised so long ago to Abraham.

The Evolving Contract

Real circumcision is a matter of the heart. . . .

Romans 2:29

The nature of the contract of belief evolves in the intertestamental period, undergoing transformations that become readily apparent in the New Testament, as the covenant relationship emerges with ever more ethereal promises while imposing transcendent, empirically unverifiable obligations on the parts of participants. The focus of the old covenant was, one might say, rather mundane: the geographically locatable land, Canaan, with its heart and temple in the city of Jerusalem, even Jacob's very practical "bread to eat and clothing to wear"; the proliferation of offspring as heirs to the Promised Land; obedience to divine law as recorded in the Mosaic Code; and the very physical and visible inscribing of the contract in the wound of circumcision. During its sea change, all aspects of the covenant are purged of their earthy odors and rarified in anticipation of a new heaven and a new earth. The "land" of the new covenant is a city-bride descending to a "new earth" from a "new heaven." Gone is the emphasis on family and "immortality" through descendants, for those who will be among the immortal redeemed have no need of offspring, and, indeed, offspring can prove a detriment, drawing an individual toward the corrupt world and away from his contemplation of spiritual matters (1 Corinthians 7:8–9).

As to the covenant obligation to obey the laws of the Mosaic Code, the new covenant equivocates. Jesus reiterates the validity of each smallest portion of the law: "For truly, I say to you, till heaven and earth pass away, not an iota, not a dot, will pass from the law until all is accomplished" (Matthew 5:17–18). This seems clear enough, yet he is berated in the temple for violating the law by "working" on the Sabbath. He has healed the demon-possessed woman (Luke 13:14–16), an activity he justifies *figuratively*—by analogy with animal husbandry. As the covenant is read "spiritually," the important obligation of circumcision undergoes reinterpretation. Paul makes a figurative argument, contrasting physical with "true" or "inward" circumcision:

> Circumcision indeed is of value if you obey the law; but if you break the law, your circumcision becomes uncircumcision. . . . For he is not a real Jew who is one outwardly, nor is true circumcision something external and

physical. He is a Jew who is one inwardly, and real circumcision is a matter of the heart, spiritual and not literal.

Romans 2:25–29[8]

The tendency, in brief, is to read the recorded law not literally, but metaphorically or "spiritually." In the new covenant, the legalistic, written materiality of the Mosaic code is reinterpreted for an immateriality that has sprung into existence and flowered during the interstice between Daniel and Paul. Gauzy, ethereal, imperceptible (with its land not of this world, its spiritual interpretation of the law, its perhaps infinitely deferred promise of immortality, the figurative, inward wound of circumcision and bleeding in the heart)—it is this covenant to which a Christian populace is asked to agree.

THE CONTRACT FOR IMMORTALITY

And many of those who sleep in the dust of the earth shall awake, some to everlasting life, and some to shame and everlasting contempt.

Daniel 12:2

The smoke of their torment goes up for ever and ever; and they have no rest, day or night. . . .

Revelation 14:11

Woe on that [Judgment] Day to those who deny the Truth . . . : on that Day they will be thrust into the Fire of Hell. This is the Fire you used to deny. . . . Burn in it. . . .

Qur'an 52:11–16

From late Old Testament times forward, those who believe and in so doing embrace the doctrine of immortality find that one of the flies in the soup is the necessity to accept as his part of the agreement that God will impose *eternal* suffering. Some sacred texts suggest that those excluded from eternal life will simply cease to be (a notion implied in Daniel and the mystery religions and tacitly accepted, for example, by those who deny the reality of hell or the immortality of *all* souls). More commonly, texts assert that (merciful) death for an unbeliever is not an option, and that those excluded from Life must suffer through eternity.[9] Who will be blessed? Who damned? With less at stake (through the notion of reincarnation) and without the necessity for "belief," Plato was able to treat the sorting of *immortal* souls for blessedness or suffering rather casually. By contrast, intertestamental writer Ezra examined the problem with great sorrow when he was shown that the "paths of perdition" are intended for "not just a few of us but *almost all who have been created*" and that "the world to come will bring delight to few, but torments to many"—forever (2 Esdras 7:47–48; emphasis supplied). It is safe to say that a majority of people might want to live forever, but that the idea loses appeal in the prospect of eternal suffering.

How does one qualify for membership in the society of the blessed? As mentioned, unless they are divine, semi-divine, or among the orders of *super*natural beings, those few who find the heavenly abode are those who *believe*.[10] The doctrine of belief is, however, odder than at first appears and more ambiguous. Can one simply will to believe—whatever system he or she encounters? Members of mystery religions earned immortality through what seems a religious version of Coleridgean poetic faith, the "willing suspension of disbelief."[11] Embracing the notion of immortality involved joining the cult, performing its ritual, and gaining knowledge of the "secret" signs or language needed to assure immortality in an afterlife. The resurrected Jesus perhaps requires a similar suspension of disbelief as he tells his skeptical disciples, "He who believes and is baptized will be saved; but he who does not believe will be condemned" (Mark 16:16). Predicting his own crucifixion, Jesus announces, "No one has ascended into heaven but he who descended from heaven, the Son of man. . . . So must the Son of man be lifted up, that whoever believes in him may have eternal life" (John 3:13–15). In Christianity, belief by itself is said to be sufficient to exempt one from the Final Judgment: "[H]e who hears my word and believes him who sent me, has eternal life; he does not come into judgment, but has passed from death to life" (John 5:24).[12] Allah, addressing Jesus, speaks of the criterion of belief. After promising to give special status to those who believe, he announces, "I will make the disbelievers suffer severely in this world and the next; no one will help them." The text continues, identifying belief with justice or righteousness: as for those "who believe and do what is right," God "will pay . . . their reward in full" (3:56–57). Are the "unjust" merely those who misbelieve? In another passage, Allah is said to be "the ally of those who believe: He brings them out of the depths of darkness and into the light. As for the disbelievers, their allies are false gods who take them from the light into the depths of darkness, they are the inhabitants of the Fire, and there they will remain" (2:257). This raises another question—especially in Christian and Islamic thought: Not who does believe, but who *can* believe?

WHO CAN BELIEVE?

> For those whom he foreknew he also predestined to be conformed to the image of his Son. . . . And those whom he predestined he also called; and those whom he called he also justified, and those whom he justified he also glorified.
>
> Romans 8:29–30

The Old Testament book of Isaiah introduces an idea that will echo and reecho in the New Testament and the Qur'an—the premise that the individual has little or no part in deciding whether or not to believe. When Yahweh calls Isaiah to prophesy, he instructs him to say to the people, "Hear and hear, but do not understand; see and see, but do not perceive." Yahweh further instructs Isaiah to "[m]ake the heart of this people [the Israelites] fat, and their ears heavy, and shut their eyes; lest they see with their eyes, and hear with their ears, and understand with their hearts, and turn and be healed" (Isaiah 6:9–10).[13] Preparing to devastate the Promised Land and its people, Yahweh issues the command that will prevent their "turning" and "healing." A "remainder," less than a tenth of the holy seed will survive—all sinners, selected from among sinners (6:13).

The import and echoes of this language recur in all four of the gospels, in Acts, and in the Qur'an, along with the idea that, regardless of human desire or intent, God actually bars belief for the many and selects, or "elects," for salvation only a few. Mark tells of Jesus' teaching a gathered multitude "many things in parables." Having narrated the parable of the sower, Jesus concludes, echoing and revising God's instructions to Isaiah, with the admonition, "He who has ears to hear, let him hear." When the disciples ask him about the parables, he responds mysteriously, again recalling the instructions to Isaiah: "To you has been given the secret of the kingdom of God, but for those outside everything is in parables; so that they may indeed see but not perceive, and may indeed hear but not understand; lest they should turn again and be forgiven" (Mark 4:1–12). The disciples, chosen ones in the company of Jesus, have been given "the secret of the Kingdom of God." The others—the multitude "outside"—mystified by the parables, quite literally do not stand a chance of believing or of turning and being forgiven. (The fact that the disciples, who supposedly know the secret, must have the parables explained to them adds to the muddle [Luke 8:9–15; cf. Matthew 13:10–15].)

The gospel of John echoes similar language, but changes the context. Here Jesus has shown miraculous "signs" to a crowd, who nevertheless do not *believe*. According to John, this failure of belief is a direct result and verification of the "word spoken by the prophet Isaiah": "Therefore *they could not believe*" (John 12:20–40; emphasis supplied). The situation calls into consideration such notions as "free will," predestination, and faith: the unbelief of the crowd is somehow controlled by ancient divine words spoken by a long-dead prophet: "Therefore they could not believe." And, lacking belief, they are damned.

Centuries later, Allah, speaking to Muhammad, will reprise Yahweh's message to Isaiah, and Jesus' message to the disciples: "Among them are some who [appear to] listen to you, but we have placed covers over their hearts—so they do not understand the Qur'an—and deafness in their ears. Even if they saw every sign they would not believe in them. So when they come to you, they argue . . . [saying], 'These are nothing but ancient fables' . . . " (Qur'an 6:25).[14] There is an almost playful irony in God's self-quotation and the allusion *by disbelievers* to "ancient fables" about disbelievers! The criterion of belief is stressed again somewhat later: "God leaves whoever He will to stray, and sets whoever He will on a straight path" (6:39).

Even the patriarch Ibrahim (Abraham), epitome of faith in all three traditions, has questions about a difficult-to-imagine resurrection and the immortality in which the blessed must believe, a resurrection Allah describes in some detail as "put[ting] his bones back together" and "reshap[ing] his very finger tips" (Qur'an 75:3–4). The Qur'an tells of a moment when Ibrahim, addressing Allah, makes an intriguing request: "My Lord, show me how You give life to the dead." Allah replies, "Do you not believe, then?" Abraham replies, "Yes, but just to put my heart at rest." Allah in response offers an allegory: 'Take four birds and train them to come back to you. Then place them on separate hill-tops, call them back, and they will come flying to you . . . " (2:260). This charming allegory shares with the biblical parables a demand for interpretation. The tale suggests that the trained birds are to Ibrahim as believers are to Allah. Distinguished by their pre-selection and training, though they are scattered (In time? In space? Dead?), they obey ("flying"!) the summons to life, resurrection—the already-bestowed blessing of immortality.

The allegory of the trained birds presents in miniature some of the perpetually debated questions in Jewish, Christian, and Muslim theology—preordination, predestination, free will, and reward and punishment.

THE BELIEF IN BELIEF

And straightway . . . [he] cried out, and said with tears, Lord, I believe; help thou mine unbelief.
Mark 9:24

Jesus said to her, "I am the resurrection and the life; he who believes in me, though he die, yet shall he live. . . . "
John 11:25

So also will be the judgment which I have promised; for I will rejoice over the few who shall be saved . . . . And I will not grieve over the multitude of those who perish. . . .
2 Esdras 7:60–61

A belief in belief as the key to blessedness in an afterlife seems straightforward enough: as St. Paul states it, "He who through faith is righteous shall live" (Romans 1:17).[15] However, as this discussion has shown, both the

Bible and the Qur'an provide numerous suggestions that God grants the *condition of belief* as he will; those who believe, like Ibrahim's birds, have been pre-selected for belief and, therefore, for "life" or salvation. Given this logic, those to whom God grants faith are by definition righteous and will be redeemed: "Abraham *believed* God, and it was reckoned to him as righteousness" (James 2:23). God's criteria are never mentioned, but judging from his selection of Abraham and, through him, the Israelites—a "stubborn people"[16]—the divine choice may perhaps be whimsical, erratic, or arbitrary. In the main line of Christian thought from St. Paul, to St. Augustine, through Aquinas, Luther, and Calvin, all humans springing from the evil seed of Adam are sinners and therefore, on the face of it, unworthy of salvation.[17] God's response to the individual human being's inevitable "sin" is a matter of divine will, rather than human merit or lack of it. This argument asserts that God "has determined beforehand who is destined for eternal life"—the "elect," as opposed to the "reprobate," those predestined for eternal damnation. Human "free will" to choose behaviors is limited to choices among sinful options: "It requires a divine intervention to make it possible for a sinner to accept God's offer of salvation and new life. This intervention cannot be due to anything the sinner does or desires, but simply and solely to divine initiative" (González 136).

Free Will?

> Predestination, n. The doctrine that all things occur according to programme. This doctrine should not be confused with that of foreordination, which means that all things are programmed, but does not affirm their occurrence, that being only an implication from other doctrines by which this is entailed. The difference is great enough to have deluged Christendom with ink, to say nothing of the gore. With the distinction of the two doctrines kept well in mind, and a reverent belief in both, one may hope to escape perdition if spared.
>
> Ambrose Bierce, *Devil's Dictionary*

The popular assumption among believers of whatever sort is that the admonition to believe carries with it the element of free will: one is free to believe or not, making belief a matter about which one makes a conscious decision. But the sacred texts (explicated by a long line of theologians) announce that all decisions have always (or *nearly always*) already been made.[18] God chooses. As discussed in chapters 2 and 6, the metaphor "God is Author," whose major opus is the Bible (the story of humankind), implies the imposition of a plot on human history. The notion of a divine plan toward a predetermined end (telos), and the recording of the plan in a book from beginning to end, entail the inevitability of each smallest event or act, for example, the fall of a sparrow (Matthew 10:29). In other words, God does not leave things to chance as he, in Philosophy's words, "constraineth all things to order" (Boethius, 174). What God's narrative, like human-crafted narratives, permits is the *appearance of choice* or chance. Seen in retrospect and figuratively (which is the only way the "beginning" can be seen), God's plot for the story of human history only seems to allow for choice or chance, but in reality requires Adam's disobedience. To use a sporting metaphor, the game is fixed. This notion appears in various forms in theological discussions of ideas named *original sin, preordination, predestination, soteriology, omniscience,* and *teleology.*

THE BEGINNING—ORIGINAL CONTRACT, INFRACTION, PENALTY

My earlier discussion of the covenant highlights the inception of the contract between Yahweh and Abraham, a contract inscribed in blood in the genitals of Abraham and his descendants. I spoke of the sign of circumcision as a wound and suggested another, invisible wound beneath, behind, or before this grotesque inscription and the meanings inhering in it. Traveling back in the biblical narrative from the beginning of the covenant to the beginning of the world and the Yahwist's story of Adam, one finds a place for the red mark that highlights the wound behind the wound, the invisible injury from which follows every single thing and event in God's story of human history; the first violation of the first covenant, a violation required by God's "plot" for human history and its necessary components of guilt, sexuality, procreation, and death.

The Yahwist's darkly comic tale of beginnings and of the original contract (Genesis 2–3) supplies the exposition from which everything will follow. The Yahwist's God places his newly crafted first man and woman in a garden-orchard of his own design and planting. Smack-dab in the center of that design is a tree of the knowledge of good and evil—the subject of the first covenant and the one tree whose fruit the first humans are forbidden to eat, lest they die. As this story goes, death, an altogether natural and inevitable event in the world, is said to be divine punishment for human failure to perform the one requirement of the original covenant. They do (as expected? planned? plotted?) the one forbidden thing.

The Yahwist tells the needed story to explain his world. The nature of that world and the human relationship with the divine are suggested in the series of curses and punishments God imposes, first on the serpent, then on the woman, and finally on the man. For his part in the affair, the rhetorically adroit serpent (one of God's "wild creatures" with the unusual ability to talk) is condemned to go on its belly and to exchange wounds with the "seed" of the woman. The woman is cursed to suffer pain in childbearing, to desire her husband, and to be ruled by him. The man is condemned to farm the now cursed, thorn- and thistle-infested ground, to eat bread "in the sweat of [his] face," and to die. In a few words the narrative has explained facts of life in the Yahwist's world, including its uniquely biblical sense of shame and guilt, the danger to the covenant people implicit in "other" religions,[19] the patriarchal organization of society, the human common lot of life-long labor, and mortality.

Although God has told the man that "in the day" he eats of the fruit he "shall surely die," the serpent has "truthfully" told the woman that she would not die, but become as gods, knowing good and evil. (God later verifies that as a result of eating the fruit "the man has become as one of us.") The ironic comedy emerges from several facts: neither God nor the serpent tells the entire truth; creatures supposedly without knowledge of good and evil are expected to make a moral judgment whose contractual consequences will extend to the entire human race; nobody knows what death means;[20] the misnamed fruit of knowledge of good and evil turns out to be the fruit of sexuality and death; the God-like wisdom it provides is sexual knowledge; and the transgression of the covenant has the effect of linking inextricably the concepts of death, sin, evil, sex, marriage, procreation, and pain. The red mark on "the first page" of the text, then, is a record of the first violation of God's covenant, and introduces themes that will inhere in the later covenant obligation of circumcision.

The covenant narratives and divine economics described therein have, for many, long constituted the images seen in the mirror of heaven. The story of beginnings adds to the difficulty of making sense of the religion-forming biblical narrative. Adam often takes the blame for transgressing the first covenant and bringing death to humanity. One recalls Ezra's anguished, "O, Adam, what have you done?" Hosea's God, too, thinks of Adam when he thinks of the broken covenant: "Like Adam, they have broken the covenant—they were unfaithful to me there" (Hosea 6:7). And St. Paul makes Adam the death-bringing counterpart of Jesus, who brings life: "Therefore as sin came into the world through one man and death through sin, so death spread to all men because all men sinned. . . ." (Romans 5:12–14). Historically, a popular position with a measure of biblical authority[21] is to ascribe to the woman responsibility for the guilt of humanity and the stark fact of death: "I permit no woman to teach or to have authority over men; she is to keep silent. For Adam was formed first, then Eve; and Adam was not deceived, but the woman was deceived and became a transgressor" (1 Timothy 2:12–14). This position treats Eve as a first sinner and a metaphor for all individual women.

However, behind the theological doctrines of salvation, predestination, and preordination is a more ancient, if more disquieting, position: that God "plotted" the whole affair. In the Second Book of Enoch, God tells Enoch that he used the woman for the express purpose of bringing death to Adam: "I took a rib from him, and *created a wife for him that death should come to him by his wife,* and I took his last word and called her name mother, that is, Eva" (2 Enoch, Barnstone 6; emphasis supplied). Here God says in effect that it was not the woman who brought sin and death into the world, but God himself, who has planned the whole affair. The Jewish apocalyptic sect known as the Dead Sea Community likewise ascribed all events to divine will: "From the God of Knowledge comes all that is and shall be. Before ever they existed He established their whole design, and when, as ordained for them, they come into being, it is in accord with His glorious design that they accomplish their task without change" (Vermes, *The Dead Sea Scrolls*, 101). An echo of this claim can be heard in the writings of St. Paul: "But we speak the wisdom of God in a mystery, even the hidden wisdom, which *God ordained before the world* unto our glory. . . . " (1 Corinthians 2:7; emphasis supplied). Before the world, God produces the plot, the design, of the human story. In the beginning, on the very first page, Yahweh inflicts the wound that will drive the plot, and the wound is invisible.

THE COVENANT AND THE PLOT

If readers were to assume for a moment that the first couple faithfully obeyed the divine injunction, they might ask, what then? The answer: no guilt, no strife, no work, no birth, no death, no time, indeed no life: in short, no (his)story. Homer narrates the tale of Odysseus as he travels homeward, offering accounts of his adventures at sea and on the various islands that he visits. Odysseus' journey takes ten years. Readers learn the story of three of those years, and yet the great Homer falls silent during the seven years Odysseus spends on the paradisiacal, timeless island of Ogygia in the company of the goddess Kalypso. All they know is that there he is provided food, sexual companionship, and immortality. As in Paradise before the Fall, nothing happens on Ogygia, and so there is no story. The hero responds to his confinement in this "perfect place" with grief and despair, longing for "home" in the world of action, time, and death.

The view that God plans and controls all events, including the Fall, but also all making and transgressing of human-divine covenants is supported by the very practical demands of narrative; the "chance" that Adam and Eve might have chosen to obey the injunction against eating the fruit of the tree of the knowledge of good and evil was always only apparent. Thinking about this possibility, T. S. Eliot finds that the first couple's choices included one for the world and human history ("what has been") and one for a world that never was nor could be ("What might have been," a "world of speculation"):

> What might have been and what has been
> Point to one end, which is always present.
> Footfalls echo in the memory
> Down the passage which we did not take
> Towards the door we never opened
> Into the rose-garden.
> "Burnt Norton," 6–13

SUMMING UP

> [Our chosen servants] will enter lasting Gardens where they will be adorned with bracelets of gold and pearls, where they will wear silk garments. They will say, "Praise be to God, who has separated us from all sorrow. . . . He has, in His bounty, settled us in the everlasting Home where no toil or fatigue will touch us."
> Qur'an 35:31–35

At the center of the three major Abrahamic religions, one finds a Book, a story of human history whose prevailing themes are mortality/immortality and the economics of belief, a quid pro quo, an ethics of *dos ut des*, of contracts and covenants, sorting the characters, directing their behavior, and shaping both the divine-human relationship and the plot of their interaction. In return for the Israelites' faith, obedience, and circumcision, the Old Testament God agreed to give them a land, prosperity, and the sort of immortality one can obtain through innumerable descendants. Breaches of the contract by the human parties drive the action. In the New Testament and the Qur'an, Jesus and Allah agree to grant their followers in return for belief an individual immortality in an eternal land of promise.

The Book is, however, God's book. As Author of the sacred texts, God supposedly inscribes the reality of history and of everyone and everything of which it is constituted—belief and disbelief, the countless breaches of the contract, the resulting penalties, salvation and damnation. He writes the prophecies, composes the confrontations, and foreshadows the anxiety-ridden dénouement—the Last Judgment. A good plot requires a measure of action and conflict, protagonists and antagonists, and the sacred texts—the two testaments and the Qur'an—offer good, even archetypal, plots. In the next chapter, I will turn my attention to the notions of action and conflict, protagonists and antagonists, and the rather complex role the prophets play in God's narrative.

CHAPTER 9

PROPHECY AND PLOT: THE MAKING OF THE HERO AND THE VILLAIN

> You [Apollo] know the appointed end
> of each thing and the ways they are brought to pass;
> and the number of the spring leaves earth blossoms with. . . .
> Pindar, Ninth Pythian Ode 44–46

WHAT THE GODS KNOW AND WHEN THEY KNOW IT

Prophecy is one manifestation of the ancient and universal human impulse to communicate with the Unknown. It is a category of divination defined as "[t]he action or practice of divining; the foretelling of future events or discovery of what is hidden or obscure by supernatural or magical means; soothsaying, augury, prophecy" (*OED*).[1] Behind it is the idea that the gods see time stretched out like a tapestry with all its smallest, incidental details, patterns, acts, and events in full view. Apollo knows, for example, just how many leaves the earth unfolds in spring. Similar, but more problematic, is the notion of supernatural authorship of the progress of time, with the corollary that the future is *designed* to unfold in a predetermined way, including the fall of each sparrow. The Greek Morai, the Roman Parcae, and the Norse Norns are said to be determiners of the future—for individuals and Nations. Hesiod says of the Morai, for example, that they "at their birth / bestow upon mortals their portion of good and evil, / and these control the transgressions of both men and divinities" (*Theogony* 218–20). In this respect, they are like God (Yahweh or Allah), who (as discussed) determines the destinies of both blessed and damned and the date of final judgment and resurrection. Thus, the god himself or his prophet can convey knowledge of this already written future to people: "I will give you a son, but you are destined to die at his hand."

PROPHECY AND THE HERO

> Come, tell me: if, by an oracle of the gods,
> some doom were hanging over my father's head
> that he should die at the hands of his own son,
> how, with any justice, could you blame me?
> I wasn't born yet . . .
>   Sophocles, *Oedipus at Colonus* 1106–12

> Now the word of the Lord came to me saying, "Before I formed you in the womb I knew you, and before you were born I consecrated you; I appointed you a prophet to the nations."
>   Jeremiah 1:4–5

At one point in Sophocles' *Oedipus the King*, Oedipus, most fated of heroes, ignorant of his tragic situation, ironically calls himself the "son of Chance, / the great goddess, giver of all good things" (1188–89). Jocasta, his mother-wife, likewise insists that it is chance, not fate, that directs human lives and that the prophets are opportunistic liars. She ironically tells him not to be afraid, for "[i]t's all chance, / chance rules our lives" and counsels, "Live . . . as if there's no tomorrow!" (Sophocles, *Oedipus the King* 1069–78). Yet there is no chance at all in Oedipus' career nor, for that matter, in hers; all has been determined in the distant past. Bernard Knox describes Oedipus' final recognition of his situation:

> He recognizes . . . that the prophecies given to his father and to him by Apollo were true prophecies, that they had been fulfilled long ago, that every step taken to evade them, from the exposure of the child to the decision never to go back to Corinth, was part of the pattern of their fulfillment . . . . And this does pose, for the modern reader as for the ancient spectator, the question of fate and . . . of free will and human freedom.
>   143

In such thinking, the figure of the human author who determines details, acts of characters, events, and outcomes in his or her narrative is projected into the heavens as a supernatural author whose story is human history. In the Greek narratives both heroes and gods are subject to a primordial plot created by the Fates. They hear the dreadful prophecies and take evasive action, in the process moving relentlessly toward the predicted act or catastrophe.[2] What appears to be freedom of action actually serves the end of fulfilling the prophecy.

Related to questions of free will and freedom of action is that of human responsibility. In a system where all is determined, can one take credit for achievements or blame for bad behavior? In a key episode in Book 9 of *The Odyssey*, Odysseus has apparently used his keen intelligence to extricate himself and his men from the cave of Polyphemos, the Cyclopes intent on eating the Greek sailors. Odysseus has tricked the giant by telling him his name is Nobody. Once he is free, however, he ironically takes full credit for his victory: "[I]f ever mortal man inquire / how you were put to shame and blinded, tell him / Odysseus, raider of cities took your eye . . . ." Then, however, readers learn that what has seemed Odysseus' ingenious maneuver to defeat the cannibal had always been fated to occur; he could have done nothing else. Polyphemos, on hearing Odysseus' name, remembers an old prophecy. "Now comes the weird upon me, spoken of old," he says. A wizard had "foretold for time to come: my great eye lost, and at Odysseus' hands" (Homer, *Odyssey* 160).

In fact, nothing in Odysseus' career is a matter of choice or chance. Like Oedipus, he and his shipmates are set on a predetermined course from which they cannot swerve. At the very outset of the long ordeal, the prophet Halitherses had "seen" it all: "My forecast was that after nineteen years, / many blows weathered, all his shipmates lost, / himself unrecognized by anyone, he would come home" (Homer, *Odyssey* 24). Odysseus, like Oedipus, seems at last to realize how little his actions are his own when, after he has killed the intruders in his hall, he stifles Eurykleia's cries of triumph, refusing to take either credit or responsibility for their deaths. "Rejoice inwardly," he tells her. "To glory over slain men is no piety. / Destiny and the gods' will vanquished these . . . " (ibid. 422).

Biblical heroes are likewise players performing their parts in a divine script. In the case of Jacob, Yahweh himself is not only author but also prophet of the course of Jacob's life. While Jacob is still in the womb, the strife that will mark his existence and be figured in his renaming (Israel—for he has "striven with God and with men") emerges as part of his destiny. When Yahweh causes the previously barren Rebekah to conceive twins, he explains his design: "Two nations are in your womb, and two peoples, born of you shall be divided; / the one shall be stronger than the other, the elder shall serve the younger" (Genesis 25:23). The younger emerges from the womb holding the heel of the firstborn and is named Jacob, "He takes by the heel or He supplants." Jacob's destiny will be to supplant his twin brother Esau, his father-in-law Laban, and his brothers-in-law. He takes Esau's birthright as firstborn (a double share of Isaac's property); he tricks Isaac into giving him the blessing intended for the firstborn, including the covenant relationship with Yahweh; through magic he tricks Laban out of property; and, through Rachel's theft of Laban's household gods, he seizes the inheritance of his brothers-in-law.[3] As a final, glorious act of supplanting, he prevails in the wrestling match with Yahweh, and when his divine antagonist asks Jacob to release him,

Jacob astonishingly replies, "I will not let you go, unless you bless me" (Genesis 32:26). Jacob's life was one of taking, seizing, lying, supplanting, and tricking—all in accordance with the divine plot. He had no choice, no chance that he might, for example, have pitied his famished brother and simply given him something to eat rather than forcing him to trade his birthright for a "mess of pottage," or that he might have refused to participate in the heartless trick of the blind Isaac to gain the blessing, for that would have changed God's story—and all of subsequent history.

The lives of Jacob's sons are similarly determined and repeat the theme of brother strife so beloved by the divine author. In the story of Joseph and his brothers, God transmits his prophecies through dreams that will determine the Israelites' course for several hundred years. The dreams come in pairs, and the "doubling" of the dreams means "that the thing is fixed by God" (Genesis 41:32). The first pair of dreams occurs when Joseph is seventeen and reveals through agricultural and celestial symbols (sheaves of grain and sun, moon and stars) that Joseph is destined to rise to a position of power over his brothers (Genesis 37:5–11). Their resulting jealousy leads them to sell Joseph into slavery (hence furthering fulfillment of the prophecy), and he ends up in Egypt. God sends a second pair of dreams to the Pharaoh's imprisoned butler and baker. Joseph correctly interprets the dreams, and is brought to the Pharaoh's attention later when the Pharaoh receives the third pair of dreams. Upon interpreting the Pharaoh's dreams as predicting a seven-year period of plenty followed by a seven-year period of famine, the Pharaoh, recognizing God's hand in such matters, places Joseph in charge "over all the land of Egypt" (Genesis 41:41). Years later, during the lean period, when the brothers and Jacob have journeyed to Egypt for grain, Joseph welcomes them and reassures them that they are not at fault, telling them, "God sent me before you to preserve for you a remnant on earth .... *So it was not you who sent me here, but God* ..." (Genesis 45: 5–8; emphasis supplied). Joseph's comments indicate that the brothers had no choice. From their God-inspired jealousy to their act of treachery, they were playing their parts in the divine script: it was not they who sent Joseph into slavery, but God. And, this lack of responsibility for bad acts raises a question about the notorious wife of Potiphar. For the script to play itself out, Joseph must be sent to prison (as he is, at her instigation) where he will interpret the dreams of the Pharaoh's butler and baker. Might Joseph have said to her also, "[I]t was not you who sent me here, but God"?

The authorship of God, the all-encompassing nature of his narrative, and the revelation of the progress of the plot through prophecy—all produce a world without space for the contingent or fortuitous and without human freedom, imposing constraints upon human action that extend (as discussed in Chapter 8) even to the act of "belief." In the divine plot, Jacob is born to supplant and inevitably does so. As Joseph's life unfolds, the brothers must sell Joseph into slavery, for this is necessary to advance God's design. Odysseus cannot take credit for besting Polyphemos nor be held responsible for the deaths of the suitors. Oedipus cannot be blamed for the long-plotted killing of his father: "[H]ow, with any justice, could you blame me?"

PROPHECY, THE HERO, AND THE VILLAIN

Before Abraham was, I am.

John 8:58

[E]verything written about me in the law of Moses and the prophets and the psalms must be fulfilled.... Thus it is written, that the Christ should suffer and on the third day rise from the dead....

Luke 24:44–45; emphasis supplied

The examples of Odysseus, Oedipus, Jacob, and Joseph lead to questions: can one be a hero, can one be a villain, or can one take credit or blame when one's actions are "written" in the divine plot? As Jesus says, it is necessary that "everything written" about him in the Old Testament—the law, the prophets, and the psalms—be fulfilled. Jesus is the apparent hero of the Christian Bible, but is he? God's book consists of both Old and New Testaments, the older canon having been appropriated and reinterpreted essentially as antecedent action, often as coded prophecies of the life of Jesus. He, like his predecessors in the heroic tradition, is made subject to a plot whose shape the Old Testament prophets have "revealed." Like other heroes, therefore, he lives within the scope of a divine narrative that determines not only the course of his life but constrains his freedom to do anything other than what "is written."

In the universal catalogue of pre-birth prophecies, none is more compelling or momentous than those concerning Jesus' life and death. In the Christian reinterpretation and revision of the Old Testament, the weight of ages—even from the realms of eternity—bears down on him, determining the details of his birth, ministry, and crucifixion. Matthew, placed first among the gospel writers, is particularly cognizant of a sacred tradition of texts by old authorities with which Jesus' life and career must be seen as congruent. To claim for Jesus the role of Son of God or Messiah requires adroit interweaving of new stories and old texts. As Stephen L. Harris puts it, "To demonstrate that Jesus' entire career, from conception to resurrection, was predicted centuries earlier by biblical writers from Moses to Malachi, Matthew quotes from, paraphrases, or alludes to the Hebrew Bible at least 60 times" (377). After offering a genealogy of Jesus' ancestors from Abraham forward, Matthew relates the story of Jesus' birth in which a virgin conceives the divine child through the Holy Spirit, linking Jesus' conception to a messianic passage in Isaiah (7:14): "All this took place to fulfil what the Lord had spoken by the Prophet: Behold, a virgin [or young woman] shall conceive and bear a son" (Matthew 2:18–23).[4] Here Matthew repeats the formula he will use several times ("All this took place to fulfil . . . ") to reveal the Old Testament texts prophetic of events in Jesus' life. To accept the concept of "fulfilling prophecy" is in line with the notion of God's Book or plot and corollary propositions of election and predestination. It is also, astonishingly, to embrace willy-nilly the hero's almost puppet-like lack of autonomy.[5]

The prophecies that predict and thus direct the course of Jesus' life affect, of course, not only Jesus, but also all those near him. For example, Matthew finds in Jeremiah's description of Rachel's weeping for the exiled and slaughtered northern tribesmen a presage of Herod's slaughter of the innocents, in which "was fulfilled what was spoken by the prophet Jeremiah: 'A voice was heard in Ramah, wailing and loud lamentation, Rachel weeping for her children . . . '" (Matthew 2:16–18). All those infants, as incidental characters in the plot of Jesus' life, must have led determined lives, however brief, and played their parts, however small, in the grand story of the victory of Life over Death. Jesus' adversaries—Satan and Judas—also play their required parts to advance the plot whose climax in a final apocalyptic battle is anticipated by the enactment of struggle and victory in Jesus' betrayal, crucifixion, and resurrection.

Any system of thought that incorporates notions of plot, design, fate, or providence—call it what one will—*and* prophecy, the mystical linguistic forecasting or revealing of events that will transpire in later stages of the plot, necessarily invalidates or renders problematic concepts of human responsibility and freedom. Oedipus' cry raises the unanswerable question for those who wish to reconcile plot, prophecy, and freedom: "How with any justice could you blame me?" And, if one cannot be blamed, can one be praised?

As observed by New Testament authors, relationships between Old Testament prophecies and the life of Jesus are figurative and imaginative. For example, a verse from Hosea reads, "When Israel was a child, I loved him, and out of Egypt I called my son. / The more I called them, the more they went from me; / they kept sacrificing to the Baals, and burning incense to idols" (Hosea 11:1–2). Matthew reports that Joseph, in response to a dream warning, "rose and took the child and his mother by night, and departed to Egypt, and remained there until the death of Herod. *This was to fulfill* what the Lord had spoken by the prophet, 'Out of Egypt have I called my son'" (Matthew 2:14–15; emphasis supplied). Whereas the Old Testament, looking backward to the Exodus from Egypt and the Israelites' subsequent apostasy, depicts Israel as the figurative son of Yahweh, the verses from Matthew ignore the context and interpret a part of the passage as looking forward to events in the life of Jesus, called the "son of God"—the flight from Herod into Egypt and return. The extraction and reinterpretation of the phrase, "Out of Egypt have I called my son," lends these words in Hosea a kind of mystical italics, requiring them to transcend the strictures of meaning in their context.

If Jesus is destined to die as a guilt offering to God for his followers, if there is no chance that through will or act of his own he can evade the necessity that dogs his steps, can he be a hero? Can he take credit for "saving" his followers? By the same reasoning, can Judas be blamed? Even more terrible than that of Jesus is the lot of Judas, predestined to play the villain in the hero's career, a man said to be the subject of an ancient prophecy by King David: "Even my bosom friend in whom I trusted, who ate of my bread, has lifted his heel against me" (Psalms 41:9), a "prophecy" echoed by Jesus: "*I know whom I have chosen; it is that the scripture may be fulfilled*, 'He who ate my bread has lifted his heel against me'" (John 13:18; emphasis supplied). The phrase, *lifted his heel*, echoing from a document of the remote past, serves as what Michael Riffaterre called a "connective." Connectives, he says, "combine the sign systems of text [the citation in John] and intertext [the Psalms] into new semiotic clusters, thereby freeing the text from its dependency on usage and existing conventions, and subordinating its descriptive and narrative devices to a signifying strategy unique to the text" (58). The resulting new semiotic cluster changes the earlier text by highlighting the repeated phrase, thus merging the identities of two "kings" in the line of Jesse and two acts of betrayal. It has a literariness that distends both of the immediate situations, extends their temporal reach, and emphasizes a mysterious inevitability—a destiny—in each aspect of the moment and scene.

Just as Oedipus was destined before he was born to commit certain crimes, and every attempt to evade that fate led him ever closer to it, so, given the force of "ancient prophecy," Judas has been destined from eternity to betray his bosom friend in the service of an unimaginably powerful divine narrative. Certainly the betrayal was needed to advance the plot, to prepare for Jesus' crucifixion and hence his paradoxical death-as-victory over death. Jesus has even identified the instrument by which Judas—*the one Jesus has chosen*—will be compelled to act: "He who ate my bread." And so the bread becomes a sign as well as the instrument by which Judas is propelled toward his fate: "It is he to whom I shall give this morsel when I have dipped it": "So when he had dipped the morsel, he gave it to Judas.... Then after the morsel, Satan entered into him. Jesus said to him, 'What you are going to do, do quickly'" (John 13:26–27). Like Oedipus, Judas is definitely not a child of chance. Given the weight of prophecy and plot, he moves, as he must, relentlessly toward his fate and performance of the incomprehensible treachery. How with any justice can he be blamed?

YAHWEH AS HERO VS. HIS DIVINE ENEMIES

> And the Lord said to Moses, "When you go back to Egypt, see that you do before Pharaoh all the miracles which I have put in your power; but I will harden his heart so that he will not let the people go."
>
> Exodus 4:21

> The Lord will fight for you, and you have only to be still.
>
> Exodus 14:14

If the Book is God's Book, and if there is a character in it that determines his own acts, it is Yahweh, who as Author depicts himself for the most part in a rather unflattering light. His Book is about a creative, truculent, vindictive, and dramatically murderous deity. Nevertheless, he is his plot's protagonist and hero of his own life. Narrative after narrative demonstrates Yahweh's epic power as he vies with other gods for supremacy and ruthlessly manipulates "other peoples," their kings, and their lesser gods. Yahweh's signature narrative demonstrating his heroic stature is the foundational epic of the Exodus, in which Yahweh vanquishes the Egyptian god-king, Pharaoh. Through Moses and Aaron, with their magic rod, God orchestrates the devastations, cynically disdainful of the plight of the Egyptian populace, and hardens the Pharaoh's heart so that he cannot free the Israelites even when he wishes to do so until all ten plagues have been suffered. As a last demonstration of his supremacy, Yahweh parts the Red Sea, and after the Israelites have fled across on dry land, causes the waters to return and drown the pursuing Egyptian army (14:21–29).[6] A song celebrating Yahweh's heroic victory asks the rhetorical question, "Who is like thee, O Lord, among the gods?" (15:11).

God's heroism is again apparent in the tales of the conquest of Canaan, its peoples, and their gods. The assault begins dramatically with the destruction of Jericho, a victory in which the ark of the covenant on which rests God's mercy seat (and implied presence) appears chiefly responsible for bringing down the city walls. The book of Judges relates a series of tales involving the conquest in which relatively weak Israelite judges with inadequate fighting forces prevail over various Canaanite populations through the active participation of Yahweh (e.g., Gideon, Deborah) or a single God-empowered individual devastates the Canaanites or Philistines (e.g., Jephthah, Samson). In the case of Gideon, Yahweh wishes to leave no doubt that he is the hero of the story, telling Gideon to reduce his fighting force: "The people with you are too many *for me to give the Midianites into their hand,* lest Israel vaunt themselves against me, saying, 'My own hand has delivered me'" (Judges 7:2; emphasis supplied). During the early career of Samuel, last of the judges, the Philistines capture the Ark of the Covenant from God's morally deficient priests (the sons of Eli) at Shiloh. Thereafter, the Ark itself accomplishes what the Israelite army could not—the subjugation of the enemy. A statue of the Philistine god Dagon rather comically falls on his face before the Ark of Yahweh (1 Samuel 5:1–5), acknowledging God's supremacy. God's weapon is once more a plague—this time involving mice and tumors. As panic spreads through the land; the five Philistine lords acknowledge the power of the Israelites' God and determine to return the Ark to Israel, along with a *guilt* offering: "Send away the ark of the God of Israel, and let it return to its own place, that it may not slay us and our people" (1 Samuel 5:11). (The guilt offering is a grotesque collection of golden mice and tumors [1 Samuel 6:4–5]). Yahweh has thus single-handedly defeated the enemy and their god and despoiled the enemy.

THE HERO YAHWEH VS. HIS HUMAN ENEMIES

Woe to him who strives with his Maker . . . !

Isaiah 45:9

I myself will fight against you with outstretched hand and strong arm, in anger, and in fury, and great wrath. And I will smite the inhabitants of this city [Jerusalem], both man and beast.

Jeremiah 21:5–6

[W]hen the Lord God of Heaven and Earth . . . goes to war, there is no limit. He is totally without mercy—he, who is called the Fountain of Mercy. He slays, slays, slays! All the men, all the beasts, all the boys, all the babies; also all the women and all the girls, except those that have not been deflowered.

Twain, *The Bible According to Mark Twain, Letters from the Earth* 257

Moreover, Yahweh, the hero of his own Book, contends not only against and prevails over other gods and their worshipers, he also opposes human beings and makes misery for whomever he wishes. Yahweh is even willing to engage in agonistic contests with his chosen individuals—for example, the murderous attack on Moses discussed in Chapter 8, or the wrestling match with Jacob (Genesis 32:24–31), which Yahweh apparently loses. On a universal scale, the Flood displays not only Yahweh's overwhelming power, but also genocidal impulses against his own creatures. The destruction of Sodom and Gomorrah again shows a divine impatience and resort to genocide regardless of the perhaps innocent women and children of the doomed cities, as does his slaughter of the Egyptian children in the tenth plague. His laws of holy war call for genocide against the Canaanites in furtherance of his promise to give the land of Canaan to Abraham's descendants (Deuteronomy 7). In response to the Israelites' making the golden calf, Yahweh tells Moses, "Let me alone, that my wrath may burn hot against them and I may consume them." Knowing of Yahweh's concern for his position among the gods and his reputation among the peoples of the earth, Moses asks, "O Lord, why ... should the Egyptians say, 'With evil intent did he bring them forth, to slay them in the mountains, and to consume them from the face of the earth?'" (Exodus 32:9–12). Sardonic humor hovers just on the edges of the divine-human dialogue. The man who has insisted that he is "not eloquent" (Exodus 4:10), shows a fair amount of rhetorical facility as well as insight into the divine psyche, for his words have the effect of deflecting Yahweh's murderous impulses. In this instance God is concerned about what the Egyptians will say.

Another dialogue between Yahweh and one of the sons of God, the Satan (a title, not a proper name), in the book of Job, is likewise remarkable. As the sons of God gather in the heavenly court, God singles out one whose job is to go "to and fro on the earth," observe human conduct, and report to God. Yahweh proudly calls to the Satan's attention the man Job, one of the earthlings whom he calls "blameless and upright" (Job 1:8). The Satan claims that Job is righteous only because God has blessed him with children, land, animals, and good health—the rewards for righteous behavior promised elsewhere in the Old Testament. God might have replied, "Of course, that's the way the system works." The Satan suggests that if such blessings were removed, Job would "curse thee to thy face." God accepts the challenge and gives the Satan power over "all that he [Job] has." As a result, the righteous man suffers the loss of his oxen, sheep, camels, servants, and all ten of his children—the God-authored human carnage passing unnoticed in the divine court. In response, Job is obsequious and stoic, declaring, "Naked I came from my mother's womb, and naked shall I return; the Lord gave, and the Lord has taken away; blessed be the name of the Lord" (Job 1:21).

When the Satan returns on another occasion to the heavenly court, God comments that Job "still holds fast his integrity, although *you moved me against him, to destroy him without cause*" (2:3; emphasis supplied). The Satan, however, argues that if Job's good health were destroyed, he would curse God to his face (2:5). God gives the Satan permission to inflict Job with "loathsome sores from the sole of his foot to the crown of his head" (2:7). Even so, Job acknowledges a God like the one described in Second Isaiah, who says of himself, "I am the Lord, and there is no other. I form light and create darkness, I make weal and create woe, I am the Lord, who do all these things" (Isaiah 45:6–7). This God is revealed in Job's question, "Shall we receive good at the hand of God, and shall we not receive evil?" (2:10). From Job's perspective God is an antagonist: "Thy hands fashioned and made me; and now thou dost turn about and destroy me . . ." (10:8–17). At this point in God's narrative, the Satan is not God's enemy. He is wholly under God's control. Whatever he does to human beings, he does with God's sanction. Job's extreme suffering and the deaths of his servants and children are merely collateral damage in the working out of God's wager with the Satan.

It would be impossible to tally up the numbers of the God-slain. The Old Testament God, hero of his own story, has easily and often pronounced the sentence of death, individual or collective, and executed the sentence himself or through some human, natural, or supernatural instrument. In God's Book "other gods" suffer humiliation in the face of Yahweh's greater status in heaven and superior power on earth, and Sheol runneth over with the human casualties of divine indifference (Job's children), prejudice (Egyptians, Canaanites), and wrath (the Flood victims). For the most part, Yahweh suffers no real threat to his hegemony in heaven and earth. Yet, insofar as the stature of a hero is measured by the strength of his opponent, as the story unfolds, it becomes narratively useful for God's story to introduce a villain more powerful than mere human beings or lesser gods. He requires a worthier opponent.

A Necessary Evil

Satan is first, and in some sense always remains, a character in a narrative . . . . [W]e must try to see him as an actor . . . with a role to play in a plot . . . .
Forsyth 4

If no devils, no God.
John Wesley, cited in Forsyth 8

Early in the narrative, God's is the sole "authority." He creates the world, introduces death into it as divine punishment, and struggles to establish his supremacy over "other gods," who gradually evaporate into the insubstantial reaches of failed heavens. He struggles too against his human creatures, destroying in the process untold numbers of men, women, and children. God's story moves in the path of Jewish monotheism, which recognized in Yahweh the sole source of all fortune and misfortune. As Forsyth points out, a strict monotheism, articulated most unambiguously in Second Isaiah and Job, acknowledges that Yahweh is both creator and destroyer, maker alike of good and evil, a being single in his unchallenged and unchallengeable power (107–9). So long as God's Book is theocentric or "autobiographical"—that is, focused on the figure of God as creator and destroyer—his seemingly arbitrary interactions with individuals and peoples are of primary interest, while the absurdity of human existence remains a side issue. However, with the composition of the "philosophical texts" and the emergence of the writing prophets with their litany of human crimes, divine wrath, and punishment, narrative interest begins to shift to the human world and the confused and confusing nature of the human condition: "What has a man from all the toil and strain with which he toils beneath the sun? For all his days are full of pain, and his work is a vexation; even in the night his mind does not rest" (Ecclesiastes 2:22–23).

As the texts reveal, God as author and character gradually appears less explicable. Narrative focus shifts to the human realm as it becomes impossible to reconcile events (especially as they affect his chosen people and select individuals) and any *humanly* understandable concept of divine justice. The shift of perspective from Creator to creatures is dramatic, for example, in the book of Job as the narrative moves from the casual wager between God and the Satan to the resulting human despair of Job: "Let the day perish wherein I was born . . . !" (Job 3:2). Job's anguish is echoed in the cry of Jeremiah, "Cursed be the day on which I was born!" (20:14). Human failure to understand God becomes apparent. Job asks, "Why is light given to a man whose way is hid, / whom God has hedged in?" (3:23). Ecclesiastes, observing that the "righteous and the wise and their deeds are in the hand of God," wonders "whether it is love or hate" (9:1). Look as he might, he fails to find divine justice working in the world: "Moreover I saw under the sun that in the place of justice, even there was wickedness, and in the place of righteousness, even there was wickedness" (Ecclesiastes 3:16). Over time, God's story and his world approach the border of the absurd.

Seemingly to remedy this situation, toward the end of the Old Testament period God's narrative discloses an emerging enemy set free from Yahweh's strict control and acting from his own malevolent, largely inexplicable, motives. It is as if death—God's punishment of humanity—gradually takes on a semiautonomous existence, assumes personal form, grows large, mean-spirited, and spiteful, and gains dominion over the world of human beings. As discussed in Chapter 7, the emerging enemy retains an old appellation—Satan (adversary)—now a proper name, rather than a title; he becomes God's adversary, rather than man's, assuming a new narrative function in God's book. In short, Satan begins to morph from God's minion as prosecutor general into the powerful embodiment of evil depicted in Revelation, a worthy opponent, whose defeat can establish a hero as savior of humanity. As God's narrative has progressed, his relationship with death forms a curious flow: first, God creates death and issues the sentence of death; for a long time, God executes the sentence extravagantly; then, at last, God extricates himself from and renounces his relationship with death: death becomes Death, the enemy, named Satan. Who will defeat Death?

THE BOOK, THE PLOT, THE DEVIL

[T]he world is all the richer for having a devil in it, so long as we keep our foot upon his neck.
William James 52

As mentioned, compilers of the New Testament canon considered their texts a continuation of the Book of the divine author. Paul, especially, argued that it is only in the light of the gospel that the true meaning of the Old Testament texts, especially the law, is revealed (Forsyth 275–76). The good news of their testament was that a savior had come to return to human beings God's original gift of Life—immortality. As part of his three curses culminating in the sentence of death—on the serpent, Eve, and Adam—Yahweh had condemned the serpent to go on its belly, to bruise the heel of the seed of Eve, and to have his head bruised in return (Genesis 3:14–15), a passage, as Forsyth shows, that "would become known as the 'protevangelium,' the first cryptic announcement within the Old Testament of the Christian gospel revealed in the New" (272), a passage, moreover, whose revisionist reinterpretation has perhaps resonated more widely than any other in Christian thought. From the Christian perspective, the serpent is not simply one of God's creatures, but is a shape-shifted form of Satan, the tempter, and the one who will bruise his head is Jesus, seed of Eve.

With the compilation and addition of the New Testament texts, clearly the "old" Book is evolving. The Christian identification of the serpent with Satan and hence with sin, temptation, and death creates an idea cluster from which will emerge the enemy who enjoys great power in New Testament texts. Satan is enemy, tempter, the old serpent, prince of the world, and death. Forsyth reads the confrontation between Jesus and Satan as a "Christian variant of the ancient Near Eastern combat narrative." Satan is a "dark tyrant" who will be "thwarted by the son of God (or man) in the most mysterious episode of the Christian story, the crucifixion, which oddly combines both defeat and victory . . . . The function of Christ, in almost the technical narrative sense of function, is to be the potential liberator of mankind from this tyranny" (7).

Who then is the hero of the Book? The God who "wrote the Book" and created Death? Or the God who would crush the serpent's head, who would die in order to defeat Death? Are they alter egos? Or are they one? Are they one person with divided will? To whom does Jesus say, "not as I will, but as thou wilt" (Matthew 26:39)? If they are one, who speaks to Jesus, saying, "Thou art my beloved son; with thee I am well pleased" (Mark 1:11)? God's acknowledgement of the Son is, it seems, another plot point in the Book, for the following verses introduce the Spirit of God *and* Satan working almost cooperatively: "The Spirit immediately drove him [Jesus] out into the wilderness forty days, tempted by Satan" (Mark 1:12–13). Matthew stresses the relationship between God and Satan even more explicitly, making the Spirit's action purposeful: "Then Jesus was led up by the Spirit [of God] into the wilderness *to be tempted by the devil*" (Matthew 4:1; emphasis supplied).

Given his imaginative appeal in Christianity, Satan has a surprisingly small role to play in the New Testament. The temptation, as described by Matthew, is his rather anticlimactic big scene, an affair of dueling quotations and rhetorical one-upmanship, in which Jesus (the Word) easily defeats Satan. The contest consists of Jesus and Satan exchanging Old Testament quotations. For example, in his final attempt Satan quotes Psalm 91: "For he will give his angels charge of you to guard you in all your ways. / On their hands they will bear you up, lest you dash your foot against a stone" (11–12); Jesus replies with a quotation from Deuteronomy ("You shall not put the Lord your God to a test" [6:16]), which Jesus paraphrases as, "You shall not tempt the Lord your God" (Matthew 4:7). At this Satan gives up (Matthew 4:11), and "depart[s] from him until an opportune time" (Luke 4:13).

Although he seems to have a royal title (prince of demons, prince of the world) (Matthew 9:34; Mark 3:22, Luke 11:15; John 16:11), throughout the gospels Satan withdraws from the action and, if at all, seems to work behind the scenes. Certainly evil has proliferated.[7] There are references to satanic possession—by demons and devils (in the plural)—but no actual confrontation between Jesus and Satan after the temptation. References to him, as in the temptation, depict Satan's parries as *rhetorical*, manifest in his confrontation with and contradiction of the Word. In this role, Satan becomes identified with falsehood, the false words of heretics, soon to be crushed under the feet of true Christians (Romans 16:17–20). In another example, Jesus, explaining the parable of the sower, describes Satan as the one who "snatches away" the "word of the kingdom" from those who do not understand: "He who sows the good seed is the Son of man; the field is the world, and the good seed means the sons of the kingdom; the weeds are the sons of the evil one, and the enemy who sowed them is the devil; the harvest is the close of the age, and the reapers are angels" (Matthew 13:19, 37–39). The battle is a battle of words, and the words are metaphors. The words are the good and bad seed, that grow, again figuratively, into grain and weeds, that are, figuratively, the saved and the damned, based on their having "ears to hear"—good seed (word of the kingdom, sons of the kingdom, those who hear and understand, grain) vs. bad seed (those who hear and do not understand, sons of the evil one, weeds). At the apocalyptic harvest, the culmination of the rhetorical battle, the "weeds" will be "gathered and burned with fire" (Matthew 13:40).

Prophecy that predicts the future is inextricably a part of an idea cluster that includes a supernatural author (the Fates, Yahweh, Allah), whose text with its beginning, middle, and end includes all of human history, as well as all human characters, their acts, and their destinies. As the characters emerge, one by one, they demonstrate if nothing else that they lead their lives as inscribed in the divine texts. Any resistance to one's destiny only proves to be a part of it. Oedipus, Odysseus, Abraham, Jacob, Joseph, Moses, Jesus, and Muhammad all demonstrate the determined way of heroes.[8] But the bad characters, too, lead determined lives—Judas, Satan, all those who do not understand, all the unbelievers. Once the story is written, all the sparrows accounted for, all the fingertips reshaped, all the hairs retrieved, where is there opportunity for deviation from the divine text? What freedom? What power before the majesty of the Author? Such questions raise the issue of the efficacy of prayer, a form of communication with the Unknown in which a human petitioner seeks to influence the progress of the plot of God's authorship. I turn my attention in the next chapter to that subject.

CHAPTER 10

PRAYER, PRAISE, AND THE WAR PLOT

> Evening and morning and at noon
> I utter my complaint and moan
> and he will hear my voice.
>
> Psalm 55:17–18

> And whatever you ask in prayer, you will receive, if you have faith.
>
> Matthew 21:22

PRAYER—TALKING TO GOD

In "Letter to the Earth," Mark Twain's Recording Angel enacts an ironic version of the notion that God answers prayers. He writes to a human petitioner, Abner Scofield, in response to Abner's prayers of a single week: "As regards your prayers . . . , I have the honor to report as follows: 1. For weather to advance hard coal 15 cents a ton. Granted. 2. For influx of laborers to reduce wages 10 percent. Granted." The angel's letter reveals that Abner has asked God for economic rewards for himself and illness, hardship, and death for various troublesome neighbors and employees. The remaining 298 supplications are granted "in a body, except that 3 of the 32 cases requiring immediate death have been modified to incurable disease" (*Letters from the Earth* 103–4).

Abner's prayers are petitions, requests that God grant some desire—health, wealth, success in an undertaking, protection from harm, or defeat of enemies.[1] Other categories include prayers of lamentation, confession, thanksgiving, and, most frequently, ritual praise. Jews are charged to pray three times a day (morning, noon, and nightfall); the first Pillar of Islam requires Muslims to perform ritual prayers (*salat*) five times a day (at dawn, noon, in the afternoon, at sunset, and nightfall). In many Christian denominations, ritual prayers are part of the worship services, varied according to the occasion or events of the Christian calendar. Practice varies.[2] Taking into account both formal, public, liturgically prescribed prayers, and countless occasional, individual prayers, and focusing just on those produced by devotees of the three major Abrahamic religions, one thing is clear: during every second of passing time, billions and billions of petitions, praises, appreciations, and laments ascend from the human world to the infinite Unknown.

In *Letters from the Earth*, considering merely prayers of praise recited before the divine throne, Twain's epistolarian, Satan, describes the "deafening hurricane of sound" issuing from "millions and millions of voices screaming at once" and asks, who would be willing "to endure this strange compliment, this insane compliment" and who "not only endures it but likes it, enjoys it, requires it, *commands* it?" (18). Incomprehensibly, humans believe that it is God who "endure[s] this strange compliment." The object of Twain's satire is the view of God implicit in the human theory of prayer, one that supposes a God who "sits on his throne, attended by his four and twenty elders and some other dignitaries . . . and looks out over his miles and miles of tempestuous worshipers, and smiles, and purrs, and nods his satisfaction. . . ." (ibid.).

The figurative basis for prayer is the same as for prophecy—the impulse to communicate with the Unknown. The ability to do so is assumed, based on the anthropomorphic figuration through which the Unknown talks with humans, speaking Hebrew or Arabic, Greek, Latin, or English, or any other of the thousands of human languages, living or dead, and their dialects. God is language-centered and linguistically astute; he has a "mind" geared to producing and decoding speech, creating by speaking; he is father of the Word; he writes sacred Books. He supposedly cares about what people *say* and responds—"if they believe" (Matthew 21:22).

Unfortunately, as Twain notices, such figuration produces a sublime pomposity privileged to exist in a nightmarish cacophony of words. Like a megalomaniacal human ruler, God observes from his shining throne his narrative of human history unfold, beset by, but feeding upon, a self-scripted, unceasing barrage of petitions, laments, confessions, and reiterations of his greatness and goodness by creatures he created and controls and for whom, through much of his history, he has shown nothing but contempt.[3]

THE PRAYER MANDATE

> Keep up the prayer: prayer restrains outrageous and unacceptable behavior.
>
> Qur'an 29:45

And yet prayer from these same corrupt hearts is mandated: the Jerusalem temple, the House of God, was called a "house of prayer" (Isaiah 56:7; Matthew 21:13), as is the Kaaba (Aslan 106). Christians are admonished, "Rejoice always, *pray constantly, give thanks in all circumstances; for this is the will of God.* . . . " (1 Thessalonians 5:16–18; emphasis supplied). Jesus' parable of the widow and the judge supposedly demonstrates the necessity and efficacy of constant prayer: "[T]hey ought *always to pray* and not lose heart." The narrative presents a cynical figurative representation of the relationship between God and his petitioners. In the parable, God is cast as a judge who "neither feared God nor regarded man." God's elect are represented by a certain widow who "kept coming to him and saying, 'Vindicate me against my adversary.'" Eventually the widow's persistence pays off. After refusing her petitions numerous times, the judge changes his mind, saying to himself, "Though I neither fear God nor regard man, I will vindicate her, or she will wear me out by her continual coming." The parable concludes with an explanation of sorts: "And the Lord said, 'Hear what the unrighteous judge says. And will not God vindicate his elect, who cry to him day and night?'" (Luke 18:1–8).

What is one to make of God's identifying himself with the "unrighteous judge" pestered by the widow's pleas, and hence with the judge's exasperated capitulation? The parable mentions God's elect, but not the reprobate or the necessary failure of their prayers, although they are shadows and echoes in the background. The parable's subtext seems to be that if the "elect" make nuisances of themselves by praying often, continually, and long, they will wear God out (or down), and he will grant their petitions just to silence them. But, like the unrighteous judge, God neither fears God nor regards man.

"For this is the will of God . . . ": Does God delight in prayers? Or does he find them wearying? What does he make of the prayers of the reprobate, or the misbelievers? How many prayers will he endure? Aside from the required ritual prayer, Allah welcomes the praise not merely of humans (five times a day, every day) but of "all who are in the heavens and the earth . . . as do the birds with wings outstretched," for each "knows its [own way] of prayer and glorification" (Qur'an 24:41). Yahweh receives praise even from inanimate creation: "The heavens declare the glory of God; and the firmament sheweth his handywork. / Day unto day uttereth speech, and night unto night sheweth knowledge. / There is no speech nor language, where their voice is not heard" (Psalm 19:1–4).

PRAYER, PLOT, AND PROPHECY

> PRAY, v. To ask that the laws of the universe be annulled in behalf of a single petitioner confessedly unworthy.
>
> Ambrose Bierce, *The Devil's Dictionary*

> It was the divine purpose anyhow; it will gratify you to know that you have not disturbed it.
>
> Twain, *Letters from the Earth*, "Letter to the Earth" 106–7

Not the least of the puzzles associated with prayer is a problem in logic created by the coexistence of the figures of prayer and plot. Insofar as prayer is thought to involve God's acting in response to human requests, it would seem that any positive response must introduce an element of chance and necessarily send the divine narrative off in a new direction. In the process eternal prophecies must fail. Suppose Jesus' prayer at Gethsemane had succeeded. Jesus, anticipating his imminent crucifixion, prays, "Father, all things are possible to thee; remove this cup from me; yet not what I will, but what thou wilt" (Mark 14:36). Matthew, revises the prayer: "My Father, if this cannot pass unless I drink it, thy will be done" (26:42). Jesus' prayer to "remove this cup" could not succeed, given his eternally determined role in the divine plan. Matthew's version shows Jesus' overt recognition that he is in fact playing a part in God's story, and that things cannot happen except as designed. Could any prayer shift the gears of the universe, or as Ambrose Bierce puts it, annul its laws?

King David, often praised by Yahweh as one who followed the Lord, nevertheless commits an act for which his descendents will suffer. He has impregnated Bathsheba, wife of Uriah. To avoid detection, he arranges the death of Uriah in battle and marries Bathsheba. God sends the prophet Nathan to deliver his censure to David:

> Now, therefore the sword shall never depart from your house, because you have despised me, and have taken the wife of Uriah the Hittite to be your wife. . . . Behold, I will raise up evil against you out of your own house; and I will take your wives before your eyes, and give them to your neighbor, and he shall lie with your wives in the sight of the sun.[4]

Nathan explains that Yahweh has "put away [David's] sin," so that David will not die as a result of his behavior; "Nevertheless, because by this deed you have utterly scorned the Lord, the child that is born to you shall die"

(2 Samuel 12:10–14). Subsequently, God causes Bathsheba's newborn baby to become sick. David prays for the child, weeps, and fasts for seven days, until the child dies (as foretold). David immediately "recovers" from his grief, and when his servants remark on his swift change of demeanor, he explains: "While the child was still alive, I fasted and wept; for I said, 'Who knows whether the Lord will be gracious to me, that the child may live?' But now he is dead; why should I fast?" (1 Samuel 12:22–23). David's pragmatism in his dealings with God and God's attack on the child are disconcerting. Nevertheless, had David's prayers succeeded, the prophecy would necessarily have failed, altering God's plot, for the death of this child is a crucial link in the chain of plot; it, along with David's adultery, prepares the way for the birth of Solomon to the "wife of Uriah." Solomon will be David's successor, the wise king, whose bloody ascent to the throne and his later apostasy will follow from God's prophecy to David.

Twain's Recording Angel explains to Abner a distinction between public prayers and "Secret Supplications of the Heart." When prayers of these two types conflict, prayers uttered in public are discounted. Abner's public, "Prayer-Meeting prayer" for "weather mercifully tempered to the needs of the poor and the naked" conflicts with his Secret Supplication for weather to increase the price of coal (and his profits!). Of Abner's hundreds of *public* requests, the Angel reports that only two are granted: "(1) that the clouds may continue to perform their office; (2) and the sun his." The Angel sardonically explains, "It was the divine purpose anyhow; it will gratify you to know that you have not disturbed it" (*Letters from the Earth*, "Letter to the Earth" 106–7). Twain's Angel may suggest that no consideration is given to any petition that disturbs God's purpose, runs counter to the already-written divine plan, or annuls its laws.

Yahweh's purpose and the greater biblical plot involve "giving" Canaan, the Promised Land, to the Israelites. Joshua is his human agent chosen to conquer the land for the Israelites, thus advancing God's narrative. On a decisive day, both the Israelites and their God confront five Amorite kings in a battle in which "the Lord threw down great stones from heaven" upon the enemy and killed more in this way than the entire Israelite army.[5] The stones from heaven are, it seems, in keeping with God's universal laws; supposedly, Yahweh has a divine rock pile "up there," along with the storehouses of rain, snow, and hail. The image in the heavenly mirror briefly displays a primitive, almost prehistoric Yahweh hurling rocks at the Canaanites from on high. This is strange enough, but an even stranger event follows:

> Then spoke Joshua to the Lord . . . ; and he said in the sight of Israel, "Sun, stand thou still at Gibeon, and thou Moon in the valley of Aijalon."

> And the sun stood still and the moon stayed, until the nation took vengeance on their enemies. . . .
>
> Joshua 10:12–14

God apparently approves Joshua's request, for in this unique moment time stops and the great natural laws are for a while annulled as the universal gears grind to a stop. The text remarks on this unprecedented peculiarity: "There has been no day like it before or since. . . . " Did Joshua's prayer request a change in God's plot? Or did it merely cooperate in a God-planned manipulation of the laws of nature in service to that plot? Apparently the whole dramatic affair of the motionless sun was always already written. It must be that Joshua's words were spoken in accordance with the divine will, as Jesus' request to "remove this cup" was not. What is clear is that the tale foregrounds the issue of an irreconcilability in any coexistence of *efficacious* prayer and plot. Twain's Abner prayed that the sun would continue to perform his office, a request that is aligned with divine purpose; Joshua prays that the sun pause in his duties. More than likely, the Recording Angel would have reported that the prayer was granted because "[i]t was the divine purpose anyhow."

As discussed in Chapter 9, the institution of prophecy defines a world in which the future is fixed and not only are human lives determined in all aspects, but so also is God's participation in the unfolding narrative (e.g., Yahweh's heavenly stones; Allah's wind and invisible host). Prophecy can predict events because they are part of the divine text. Though the related events may be millennia apart, page 3 and page 1009 are co-present between the covers of God's Book (a fact that, however figurative, makes possible the Christian reading of God's curse on the Eden serpent as prophetic of Jesus' life, death, and resurrection). Thus, when two kinds of speaking—prayer and prophecy—impinge on the divine plot and its unfolding, prophecy arrives to confirm the narrative's inevitability; prayer, conversely, to attempt to alter it on behalf of a petitioner. A logical way to resolve the difficulty is to assert that human petitions and prayers in all their particulars, along with the divine response or lack of it, were written into the text from the beginning.

THE GOD OF BATTLES AND WAR PRAYER

> The Lord . . . will roar mightily against his fold, and shout, like those who tread grapes, against all the inhabitants of the earth. The clamor will resound to the ends of the earth, for the Lord has an indictment against the nations; he is entering into judgment with all flesh, and the wicked he will put to the sword, says the Lord.
>
> Jeremiah 25:30–31

War provides a particularly rich context in which to examine the figure of prayer. Early in *The Iliad*, the Greek general, Agamemnon, offers a fat ox in sacrifice and prays to Zeus for victory over the Trojan king: "[L]et not the sun go down upon this day / . . . before I tumble / Priam's blackened rooftree down. . . . !" The Fates have other plans for the upcoming battle, however. Of Zeus' response to Agamemnon, Homer remarks, "But Zeus would not accomplish these desires. / He took the ox, but added woe on woe" (2:49). When war gods are thought to frame and oversee human history, their plot will naturally privilege conflict, glorify heroes, and celebrate slaughter and victory. It is inevitable within such a figurative domain that those divine authors of history be written into the action. We have seen that Yahweh enthusiastically participates in the battles required to advance the narrative. It is he, for example, who kills the Egyptian firstborn sons and drowns the Egyptian army. In the example from Joshua, God hurls stones from heaven upon the hapless, helpless, *fated* Amorites.[6] God's and the Israelites' victory over the Amorites had long been "written." A half a millennium earlier God had prophesied to Abraham that he would give Canaan to his descendants once the iniquity of the Amorites was complete (Genesis 15:16). Their *necessary* iniquity, determined in the plot and foreshadowed by prophecy, becomes complete in the time of Joshua, when God participates in the battle to defeat them, seize their homeland, and hand it over as promised to Abraham's descendants.

Could any prayer have been efficacious to change the designed outcome and avert the slaughter? Could the Amorites have converted, repented, prayed, and saved their land? No, for given God's prophecy, the victory is necessary to the plot. God's text focuses always on the unfolding of his plan and his role in the conquest. The story understandably gives no attention to the pain, anguish, terror, grief, and despair suffered by the Egyptian parents of their God-slaughtered firstborn sons or that of the Amorite warriors and their surviving families. The narrative is all about God and his heroes; other human beings, like extras on a movie set, are for the most part inconsequential, and to dwell on their anguish would distract from God's triumph. God's story of the world has a beginning, middle, and end, when his sustained account of conflict will culminate in the ultimate battle of battles and a victory good for all eternity. The laws of God's world are linguistic—written, created by the Word. To the extent that human petitions, if granted, would change the detailed unfolding of God's plot in any of its particulars, they are reduced to mere sound. Nothing can be altered in the beginning or middle without changing the glorious end.

An Ironic Aside

It is instructive to compare God's persona and actions during the conquest of Canaan with an anomalous tale of his dealing with Nineveh, capital of the despised Assyrian Empire. The account appears in the book of Jonah. Although included among the books called the latter prophets, Jonah, unlike the others, contains a single oracle, a prophecy directed not to the Israelites, but to the Ninevites. The coherent, sustained narrative, showing signs of careful crafting, constitutes a charming and comical satire on the assumptions of other prophetic books, as well as much of the rest of biblical history and its legacy in the Qur'an. The objects of its satire include repeated xenophobic themes associated with Yahweh as war god: that Yahweh is a national god partial to the Israelites; that he is typically wrathful, destructive, genocidal, and relentlessly hostile toward non-Israelites (and their animals); that prayers fail to influence God's grand design; that God-inspired speaking by true prophets is inevitably "true"; and that an appropriate mindset for his prophets is one of alienated anger and bloodlust.

The story contains the often-repeated motif of the reluctant prophet (for example, Moses, Gideon, Jeremiah, Muhammad [Aslan 37]), the one who when God assigns him a task protests that he is incapable of fulfilling it. God sends Jonah on a particularly dangerous mission: "Arise, go to Nineveh, that great city, and cry against it; for their wickedness has come up before me" (Jonah 1:2).[7] Unlike Moses, Jonah does not verbally protest; he simply boards a ship heading to Tarshish (Spain), thereby attempting to escape the realm of the "national" God's supremacy. Using a storm, a great fish, and a ship full of non-Israelite converts (all goodhearted fellows), God dunks Jonah in the sea, recruits a fish to swallow him, finally returns him to land, and patiently reiterates his command: "Arise, go to Nineveh, that great city, and proclaim to it the message that I tell you." What is that message? "Yet forty days, and Nineveh shall be overthrown" (Jonah 3:2, 4). And so Jonah travels through the city repeating God's message. Jonah has a lot at stake, for the unusually specific prophecy of destruction at the end of forty days is one on which Jonah's prophetic reputation must hang.

Nevertheless, a strange thing happens, unique in all biblical prophecy. "The people of Nineveh believed God"! Usually even God's people pay little attention to the prophets who rant in the streets reiterating God's anger and relaying his dire warnings. But the "foreign" Ninevites not only believe, they repent, fast, don sackcloth, and pray to God. The Ninevite king proclaims,

> Let neither man nor beast, herd nor flock, taste anything; let them not feed, or drink water, but let man and beast be covered with sackcloth, and

let them cry mightily to God, let every one turn from his evil way and from the violence which is in his hands.

Moreover the king's decree and motive sound like David's as he fasted and wept: "Who knows, God may yet repent and turn from his fierce anger, so that we perish not?" (Jonah 3:5–9). The situation is ludicrous, of course—the strange effectiveness of God's/Jonah's pronouncement and the fasting, sackcloth-wearing, praying population are odd enough, but rendered absurd when one imagines the animals—the herds and flocks—similarly "repenting," fasting, "crying mightily" to God, and wearing sackcloth![8] In any case, unlike David's, the fasting and prayers of Ninevites prove sufficient. God changes his mind: "When God saw what they did, how they turned from their evil way, God repented of the evil which he had said he would do to them; and he did not do it" (Jonah 3:10).

God's about-face has humiliating consequences for Jonah, for he is thereby proven to be a false prophet. God's change of heart "displeased Jonah exceedingly, and he was angry":

> And he prayed to the Lord and said, "I pray thee, Lord, is not this what I said when I was yet in my country? [There is no record of this.] That is why I made haste to flee to Tarshish; for I knew that thou art a gracious God and merciful, slow to anger, and abounding in steadfast love, and repentest of evil."
>
> Jonah 4:1 2

Jonah's characterization of God ironically paraphrases God's own self-description (Exodus 34:6; Numbers 14:17–19), which, to say the least, neglects his history of interaction with humans—chosen and enemy peoples alike—as well as his usual demeanor. The prophet is "angry enough to die." Nevertheless, still desiring to be vindicated, Jonah hopes that the power of God's word, the prophecy, will yet destroy Nineveh: "Then Jonah went out of the city and sat to the east . . . till he should see what would become of the city" (Jonah 4:5).

Jonah's big problem is that he is a nationalist prophet who serves an anomalously universalist Yahweh—a God for all peoples. Jonah believes, reasonably, that he receives instructions from the God who destroyed the human population in the Flood; who rained fire and brimstone on the cities of Sodom and Gomorrah; who slaughtered the Egyptian firstborn sons, the Pharaoh, and his army; who ordered the destruction of the Midianites and the sexual enslavement of the virgin females; the God who killed more of the Amorites than the entire Israelite army. But, in this case to Jonah's dismay, Yahweh "repents" of his intended "evil." Jonah perhaps does well to be angry.

God raises a plant to shield Jonah from the burning sun as he watches Nineveh from a hillside. Then God destroys the plant, and Jonah is again "angry enough to die." At last God offers the comically sulking Jonah an unprecedented lesson in mercy and tolerance:

> You pity the plant for which you did not labor, nor did you make it grow.... And should not I pity Nineveh, that great city, in which there are more than a hundred and twenty thousand persons who do not know their right hand from their left, and also much cattle?
>
> Jonah 4:9–11

Perhaps they are the Ninevite children who do not know their right from their left hands, or perhaps they are just ordinary people—ignorant, afraid, and vulnerable. In any case, God abandons for this moment the destructive fury that so frequently defines his approach to living things and replaces it with pity, a compassion that extends even to the hungry, praying, and sackcloth-wearing flocks and herds: "and also much cattle."

With responsibility for both war and peace projected onto the mirror of heaven, God bears a heavy burden. He is both war Lord and Prince of Peace. As the saying goes, we pray for peace, but prepare for war. But we not only prepare for war, whether spiritual or actual, we make it our prevailing metaphor for life—of the individual and the species—and many relish the prospect of vanquishing "enemies" of whatever ilk. Many anticipate with the ardor of John of Patmos the "coming of the kingdom,"[9] with its scarcely imaginable slaughter, bloodshed, and eternal suffering of those whom they oppose, while they, the righteous ones, evade death and enjoy an eternity of peace in the Holy City or Gardens of Paradise. Many accept as true the declarations of ancient prophecy and consider the predicted events inevitable. At the same time, they imagine that prayers from what the sacred Book describes as sinful, contemptible, and ignorant human beings can sway the Unknown, annul the universal laws, and disturb the divine purpose.

CHAPTER 11

HOLY MADNESS

> The prophet is a fool, the man of spirit is mad. . . .
> Hosea 9:7

> For the foolishness of God is wiser than men. . . .
> 1 Corinthians 1:25

> As things are, the greatest of good things come into being for us through madness, when, that is, it is given with a divine giving.
> Plato, *Phaedrus* 244a

> My argument is that grasping [the] concept [of the overlap of psychosis and spirituality] fully . . . lies at the heart of making sense of the universality of the sacred and religion in human culture.
> Clarke 110

REASON IN MADNESS

In Chapter 9 I discussed predictive prophecy and its problematic relationship to history and human freedom within a Book and a plot ascribed to a divine Author, the end of whose story is contained in its beginning. Now I want to turn my attention to prophecy as a cover term for a cluster of phenomena that in ancient thought constituted the "prophetic experience" and manifested a state of mind variously referred to as holy madness, divine folly, the foolishness of God, and crazy wisdom. These "mad"[1] phenomena include prophecies, dreams, visions, oracles, divination, and ecstasy—all grounded in the figure of a talking deity. Debate, ancient and modern, swirls around the epistemological implications of the prophetic experience. As Laura Nasrallah shows, at the center of debate are questions of "how the divine communicates with humans" and "how to understand [such communications] properly"—their intelligibility:

> Arguments about the phenomenon . . . to which I shall refer using the term "prophetic experience(s)" . . . are launched in contexts of struggle and debate. These struggles are especially concerned with epistemology, with what can and cannot be known, and with the authority gained and religious identity constructed from claims to perceive the communication and intervention of the divine. . . .
>
> Nasrallah 1–2

Common occurrences within such debates were accusations by one group about another that its prophets were "false." Either they were frauds, or they were "in fact just crazy, not divinely inspired," engaged in "an ecstasy of folly" (Nasrallah 2–3). That is, credibility was an issue, both within and between communities. For instance, the prophet Micah accuses other prophets within his community of a failure of vision, those who God says "lead my people astray," by crying "Peace." Micah, however, claims for himself true vision and hence knowledge: "But as for me, I am filled with power, / with the Spirit of the Lord" (Micah 3:5–8).

Like beauty, the truth or falsity of prophecy lies in the eye of the beholder. Ezekiel announces that the "word of the Lord came to me," proclaiming the falsity of Israel's other prophets who "prophesy out of their own minds," yet declare, "Hear the word of the Lord." Both sides of the debate assert that theirs is the true reception of the "word of the Lord." Ezekiel says that Yahweh calls their vision "delusive," they having "uttered a lying divination" (Ezekiel 13:1–7). No doubt Ezekiel's opponents made similar claims about his pronouncements. Ezekiel's God-voice explains that the delusive vision is one of peace: "[T]hey have misled my people, saying 'Peace,' when there is no peace" (Ezekiel 13:10; cf. Jeremiah 23:16–20). Yahweh promises to "spend [his] wrath" on such prophets. Those who "prophesy out of their own minds" are perhaps afflicted with garden-variety forms of madness, rather than having been stricken by an influx of the "Holy Spirit." The average citizen must have had difficulty determining who was the true and who the false prophet. Yahweh tells Jeremiah, "Behold I am against those who prophesy lying dreams . . . and who tell them and lead my people astray" (23:32).

Credibility or lack thereof lay too at the center of a second struggle, which emerged in a debate about the relative values of reason and madness and their roles in the production of knowledge. To the reasonable god Apollo and his worshipers the wild behavior of Dionysus and his ecstatics appears absurd, unproductive of knowledge, while at the same time the rationality of the Apollonian appears epistemologically limited (blind and deaf) to the one who undergoes a "prophetic experience." Religious craziness, when valued and given "authority," is explained as the result of an infusion of a divine knowledge into the individual, as in Micah's case. The inspired one gains a kind of wisdom unavailable not only to "false" prophets, but also to the uninspired, the reasonable, and the empirically minded—those who live within the limits of the senses and sensible. In general, and as far back as the sacred texts reach, divine communication has been taken for granted. The problems arise in determining who among the "prophets" has actually received divine communication, and then in determining the epistemological freight such experiences carry.

THE ANGRY, ALIENATED PROPHET

> I did not sit in the company of merrymakers, nor did I rejoice.
> I sat alone, because thy hand was upon me,
> for thou hadst filled me with indignation.
>
> Jeremiah 15:17

Prophecy is often joyless work. Prophecy, dreams, visions, divination, and oracles—all are based on the notion that God, the gods, or spirits talk to certain humans, and conviction that such communication gives the prophet, visionary, or dreamer special knowledge. His[2] difference is manifest in behaviors that, as judged by the non-visionary, are strange, threatening, anti-social, deleterious to domestic tranquility, and even self-destructive. Such effects of divine communication (the majority of which is angry and accusatory) establish an antithetic relationship between the recipient of messages and his society, especially society's power structure. The prophecies of Amos, chronologically first among the Old Testament's "writing" prophets, are in some ways paradigmatic of prophetic texts that follow. All are characterized by extreme anger, opposition to society, visionary or hallucinatory episodes, and bizarre, symbolic behavior. Amos's denunciations exceed the bounds of ordinary anger, manifesting an inspired fury that serves as a conduit for Yahweh's superhuman wrath. Concerning Amos's "ecstatic fury of the negative," Herbert Marks comments,

> Where does the energy for the prophet's wrath come from? How and why does he persist against all odds in rejecting accommodation? To speak of the social context of prophecy, of schools and support groups, only evades the central question of a poetic power which in its hallucinatory intensity recalls the megalomania, the magic words and obsessional ideas, of the paranoiac.
> "The Twelve Prophets" 223

Marks speculates that, "like paranoid delusions, prophetic zeal may be a function of repression, or, more precisely, of the failures of repression." When repression fails, the liberated will may impose on the world its "own structures of psychological and social affliction" (223). Amos's alienation from Israel, its king Jereboam, and its priest Amaziah is wide and bitter.[3] When Amaziah instructs the raging Amos to leave Israel and go prophesy to the land of Judah, Amos invokes the authority of divine animosity: "Therefore thus says the Lord: 'Your wife shall be a harlot in the city, and your sons and daughters shall fall by the sword . . . ; you yourself shall die in an unclean land'" (Amos 7:16–17). This retaliatory language, whether Yahweh's or Amos's, certainly exceeds the bounds of civil exchange ("Your wife shall be a harlot in the city"). Such curses are unlikely to produce any desired change either in Amaziah's attitude or Israel's behavior. The language not only resists accommodation, it is rhetorically inept. From the perspective of the king and the priest, Amos's behavior is outrageous; from Amos's (Yahweh's?) perspective, the king, his priest, and his people are ignorant and guilty of capital crimes.

Anger again characterizes Jeremiah's career. Like Amos, he suffers isolation and a failure of repression. He is alienated from his society by his constant shouting of the divine message, "Violence and destruction!" As a result, he has become "a laughingstock all the day" and "everyone mocks" him; all his friends call him "Terror . . . on every side!" (20:7–8). At one point Jeremiah imagines that the people plot against him (18:20). As angry as Amos, he asks Yahweh to send famine, war, childlessness, and plague: "Deal with them in the time of *thine* anger" (18:21–23; emphasis supplied). His isolation, so complete as to be nearly unendurable, results directly from what he perceives is divine communication: "For *the word of the Lord* has become for me a reproach and derision all day long." And yet as with Amos, repression fails; he is compelled to repeat the divine message: "If I say, 'I will not mention him, or speak any more in his name,' there is in my heart as it were a burning fire shut up in my bones, and I am weary with holding it in, and I cannot" (Jeremiah 20:7–10; emphasis supplied). When the "burning fire" breaks forth, it emerges as language—"the word of the Lord." Purportedly positioned somewhere between a wrathful Yahweh and the society that is the object of wrath, the mad prophet has about as much choice as a lightning rod about whether to conduct the heaven-sent electricity. He must speak, with or against his will.

Earlier figures among the "former" prophets exhibited similar anger and alienation. Elijah stands alone as Yahweh's spokesman against King Ahab and his Israelite society of Baal worshipers; the king calls him a "troubler of Israel" (1 Kings 18:17). When Elijah's God prevails in the "contest" between Yahweh and Baal, Elijah's anger is manifest in his single-handed slaughter of the 450 prophets of Baal (1 Kings 18:40). Elisha, Elijah's spiritual heir and successor, likewise manifests a divine anger, as he curses the small boys who have called him "bald-head" (2 Kings 2:23–24). It is as if Elisha's anger had been embodied in bears. Like Amos's reply to the priest, Elisha's response to childish insults is so insanely disproportionate as to border on the comic.[4]

Sometimes the prophet's alienation is attributable to Yahweh's requirement that he engage in symbolic behavior—behavior that appears mad but is thought to constitute a "sign" of divine intention. Yahweh instructs Isaiah, for example, to walk "naked and barefoot" as "a sign and portent" (Isaiah 20:2–4). In another instance, God commands Ezekiel to lie on his left side for 390 days and on his right side for forty days, assuring the prophet's compliance by promising to "put cords" on Ezekiel "so that [he] cannot turn from one side to the other" (Ezekiel 4:4–8).[5] This bizarre behavior, too, is "a sign," supposedly, of impending punishment of Israel and Judah. In neither case is the relationship between the extravagant symbolic behavior and the divine sign/message apparent, nor can multiple interpretations be ruled out.

The seemingly closer analogy in the case of Hosea's symbolic behavior (discussed in Chapter 4) is *only apparent* and its significance equally obscure. When Yahweh abruptly and inexplicably commands Hosea, "Go, take to yourself a wife of harlotry and have children of harlotry, for the land commits great harlotry by forsaking the Lord" (Hosea 1:2), he in effect demands that the prophet become a living, human metaphor *for a metaphoric relationship* between Yahweh and Israel, his figurative bride. Hosea's wife, Gomer, and his yet unborn children likewise are made figures in a figurative world.[6] The anger of Yahweh and Hosea, the betrayed "husbands," merges in the "domestic abuse" of Israel/Gomer, the bride: "Now I will uncover her lewdness in the sight of her lovers, / and no one shall rescue her out of my hand" (Hosea 2:10). It is unclear what divine message Hosea's fellow citizens might glean from all this.

Ezekiel borrows Hosea's figuration of the harlot-bride and names her Jerusalem. The divine/prophetic anger and anticipated abuse are intensified, as Yahweh promises to gather her lovers against her, "and they shall stone you and cut you in pieces" as a means of satisfying his fury (Ezekiel 16:35–42). In all cases of the prophets' use of the marriage metaphor,[7] an exchange of particles occurs—between a human husband's anger in response to the wife's sexual betrayal and God's anger that the people betray their covenant by worshiping other gods; the violation of a marriage contract and violation of the Mosaic covenant; the shared "sexual" nature of the violation (pursuing other lovers) and worshiping other gods (including participating in sexual rituals); the unequal relationship between husband and wife and that between Yahweh and Israel/Jerusalem; and the stoning of an adulterous wife and Yahweh's destruction of the people/land. Not least, of the interactive effects of the metaphor is the way in which it permits a glimpse of an erotic dimension of holy passion—human and divine.[8] As a prominent metaphor throughout biblical writings, the marriage metaphor provides the prophet an odd sort of "knowledge" (spiritual by way of the carnal) of the Unknown, *his* divine passion and fury, both of which resonate with and from the prophets, their passions, and their divinely inspired madness and alienation.

MADNESS AND ALIENATION IN THE QUR'AN

Muhammad continues the prophetic tradition of alienation and antithesis. Through his prophetic claims he opposes himself to his society and its earlier prophets by rejecting both the accepted polytheism of pre-Islamic Arabia and its center of ritual observance, the Kaaba. In so doing, he launches an assault on the very livelihood of the ruling clan of Mecca, the Quraysh, whose wealth and power are derived from their control of religious practices. Aslan explains that Muhammad places himself in the tradition of the Book, but unlike previous Arab prophets claims to speak not "from his own authority," nor to relay divine messages as mediated by the Jinn, but instead uniquely claimed to be the "Messenger of God," identifying himself with the biblical prophets before him, and, in particular, with Abraham (Qur'an 6:83–86; 21:51–93). "Muhammad was the *new* Abraham": "And it was precisely this self-image that so greatly disturbed the Quraysh. For by proclaiming himself 'Messenger of God,' Muhammad was blatantly transgressing the traditional Arab process through which power was granted" (Aslan 44).

Like Jeremiah, Muhammad endured the torment of dream visions that "were so disturbing that they made him seek solitude." Yet he found no relief in solitude, for when alone he was said to experience "aural and visual hallucinations" in which, for example, the stones and trees would speak to him, saying, "Peace unto thee, O Apostle of Allah." Yet, also like Jeremiah and, as Aslan suggests, like "all prophets before him," Muhammad "wanted nothing to do with God's calling. So despondent was he about the experience that his first thought was to kill himself" (Aslan 37). Muhammad identified as charlatans and madmen those who claimed divine communication, and he had no wish to join their ranks. Indeed, the Qur'an records that Muhammad's opponents suggested as much about Muhammad: "Are we to forsake our gods for a mad poet?" (ibid. 38; Qur'an 37:36). Allah himself offers Muhammad reassurance that he is not insane: "Your Lord's grace does not make you [prophet] a madman: you will have a never ending reward . . . and soon you will see, as will they, which of you is afflicted with madness" (Qur'an 68:1–6). From his society's perspective, Muhammad, like the prophets before him, was simply mad: his message ran counter to accepted truth and proved disruptive of established practice. From Allah/Muhammad's point of view, it is the others who are afflicted.

THE EXAMPLE OF DIONYSUS AND PENTHEUS

Those whom the gods would destroy they first make mad.
Anonymous ancient Greek proverb

Society at large, then, sees the prophet (ecstatic, visionary, dreamer, diviner) as mad. In the view of the prophet, society is blind and deaf, unable to perceive the "truth" of the divine vision—"They have . . . eyes, but do not see. They have ears, but do not hear" (Psalm 115:5–6; cf. Isaiah 6:10; Mark 4:11–12). Records of the meeting of the mad with the blind and deaf reveal a tragic center in this opposition. From the narrative perspective, it often amounts to an unequal contest between the supernatural and the natural, between a deity, through his spokesman, and a "reasonable" man or men. Such is the situation displayed in Euripides' *The Bacchae*.

Written in a period when mystery religions were spreading throughout Greece, the play is an admittedly ironic, yet deeply disturbing, treatment of a common occurrence: the confrontation between mystery and common sense, divine madness and human reason. Although ambiguously, these two conditions are personified in the god/prophet Dionysus and the young king of Thebes, Pentheus. Dionysus, in the form of a man, has returned to Thebes, his "birthplace," to vindicate his mother Semele against charges that she fabricated the story of having been impregnated by Zeus. It is said that, pregnant with Dionysus, she was struck dead by the unbearable magnificence of an undisguised Zeus. As one account goes, Zeus took the unborn child and sewed him into his own thigh, from which the child was later "born again."

While Pentheus has been away from Thebes, Dionysus has arrived with a company of ecstatic followers, the Bacchae or Maenads, infused the city's women with divine madness, and led them away from their homes to dance on the holy mountain and participate in his mysterious rituals. On returning and discovering the situation, Pentheus vows to capture the effeminate stranger and the wayward women and restore order to the city. The reasonable Pentheus is a devotee of Apollo, on whose temple walls appear, among others, the aphorisms, "Keep women under rule," "Nothing too much," and "Know thyself."

From this initial situation the action proceeds, revealing the power of the god, with his divine madness and mysterious knowledge, to confront the "blindness" and ignorance of Pentheus. Pentheus' grandfather and the blind prophet Tiresias try to warn him: "Be not so sure / That force and order rule all-powerful / Over humanity." The old prophet is talking about epistemology and access to another sort of knowledge: "There is too much / We do not know" (Euripides 177). Pentheus, an empiricist, trusts only that knowledge he can gain through his physical senses. When he questions Dionysus, he asks, "This god of yours; you say you saw him clearly. / What was he like?" Dionysus responds cryptically, "What he wished to be; / I have no command over the god's face and shape." A bit later, Dionysus emphasizes Pentheus' "blindness," his lack of knowledge, telling Pentheus that "disbelief stops you from seeing the sign" and, when Pentheus orders the god bound, "You do not know what you are doing. What life / You are living. You do not know who you are" (Euripides 183–85). The mysterious epistemological claim: "You do not know."

As the play progresses, Dionysus gradually drives Pentheus "out of his mind into ecstatic madness" (199). So addled is Pentheus that he agrees to dress in women's clothing and be led through his city to the mountainside to observe the Bacchic rituals. The Chorus describes the god's pursuit of the king as strength like "a faithful hound" that trails and points "[a]t the arrogant two-footed prey, / Who, isolated in his senseless pride, / Does not submit to the god's advice / In the whisper of the leaves" (200). To hear the god's advice in the "whisper of leaves" would require a "crazy" kind of hearing—one unavailable to the commonsensical Pentheus.[9] At last, Pentheus, dressed as a Bacchant, primping and posing, reveals a fearfully altered vision, seeing double: "a second sun behind the sun," "a second city behind the city," and Dionysus as a bull with horns (201). Pentheus, the empiricist, has been infused with holy madness. He experiences a visionary seeing, giving him access to a terrible knowledge previously unavailable. On the mountainside he will be torn to pieces and eaten by the ecstatic celebrants of Dionysus, thus reenacting the agony and "death" of Dionysus at the hand of the Titans.

Pentheus' resistance to the unreasonable god and his ecstatic rituals has been the death of him.[10] As the Chorus comments, echoing the advice of Cadmus and Tiresias, the appropriate approach to holy madness is "balance":

> Justice is balance.
> In his unbalanced state

> An impious anger rages
> Against the almighty wind.
> His mind is stark vacant
> And his will, unhinged,
> Flaps unavailingly
> Against the almighty wind.
> Death is the only corrective.
>
> 205

It is an unequal and tragic battle as the "unhinged" will "flaps unavailingly" against the Spirit, against divinely inspired insanity, against "the *almighty* wind." Death *is* the only corrective.

THE TRAGEDY OF SAUL

> And on the morrow an evil spirit from God rushed upon Saul, and he raved within his house.
>
> 1 Samuel 18:10

> And when Saul inquired of the Lord, the Lord did not answer him, either by dreams, or by Urim, or by prophets.
>
> 1 Samuel 28:6

Joel Rosenberg is correct when he comments, "There is no biblical character quite like Saul" (128), for Saul more closely resembles Greek tragic heroes than any other biblical character. Israel's first king, Saul was a handsome man, standing head and shoulders above the crowd. Yet, he modestly describes himself as a Benjaminite, "from the least of the tribes of Israel" and a member of the "humblest of all the families" (1 Samuel 21). However, as he and a servant are seeking some lost animals, this quite ordinary man meets an extraordinary fate in the person of the prophet Samuel. As it develops, Saul's life and career are as determined as those of Oedipus, and no less tragic than those of Pentheus. Without preamble, Samuel announces, "[T]he Lord [has] anointed you to be prince over his people" to "save them from the hand of their enemies" (1 Samuel 10:1). Saul almost immediately enters a visionary landscape where he encounters three "signs" of his divine appointment: news that the animals have been found, three men who give him two loaves of bread, and a band of prophets "coming down from the high place with harp, tambourine, flute, and lyre before them, prophesying" (1 Samuel 10:2–5).[11]

Unlike Pentheus, Saul does not move gradually into holy frenzy, but from the first teeters on its edge, from which his fall is precipitated by his meeting with Samuel: "When he turned his back to leave Samuel, God gave [Saul] another heart" (1 Samuel 10:9). What sort of "heart" has God given him? Part of the answer lies in his susceptibility to prophetic ecstasy: "When they came to Gibeah, behold a band of prophets met him, and the spirit of God came mightily upon him, and he prophesied among them." This is strange behavior for Saul, for those who know him ask, "What has come over the son of Kish? Is Saul also among the prophets?" (1 Samuel 10:10–11). The band of prophets Saul joins is like the troop of ecstatic Bacchae that accompany Dionysus. They too make boisterous, rhythmic music, dance, and repeat spontaneously and half-consciously "messages," however incoherent, received through an altered consciousness—a version of the New Testament's "talking in tongues." The image of the tall countryman dancing frenziedly in the company of ecstatics and murmuring divine messages that must sound like gibberish might almost be comic, were it not so ominous. Saul's basic instability makes him susceptible to control and suggestion, hence his rapid transformation to whirling, ecstatic, "prophesying" holy madness.

That mania soon takes a dark turn toward paranoia, "irrational" fears, and fits of rage. The narrative explains this "unholy" madness as the result of God's repeatedly sending an evil spirit to torment him. David, a poet skillful with the lyre, is brought into the king's household to soothe him in his periods of madness (1 Samuel 16:14–23). Nevertheless, Saul soon becomes fearful that David is seeking to replace him. Saul's fear will prove well founded, for Samuel has told him, "The Lord has torn the kingdom of Israel from you this day, and has given it to a neighbor of yours, who is better than you" (1 Samuel 16:28). Yet Saul continues in his office, waiting for the axe to fall. In fact, Samuel/Yahweh has already anointed David to succeed Saul as king. A transformation occurs at the anointing: "[T]he Spirit of the Lord came mightily upon David from that day forward." At the same time, "the Spirit of the Lord departed from Saul, and an evil spirit from the Lord tormented him," accounting for the degeneration of Saul's holy madness into paranoia (1 Samuel 16:12–15). As in the example of Dionysus and Pentheus, Yahweh drives Saul mad and leads him relentlessly toward his destruction.

At one point David flees from Saul and takes refuge with Samuel and a band of ecstatics at Ramah.[12] When Saul attempts to capture David, a divine madness overtakes successive groups of Saul's messengers, causing them to "prophesy," and finally it overwhelms the fragile, unstable Saul himself. When he finds Samuel and David and the band of prophets, "the Spirit of God came upon him also, and as he went he prophesied. . . . And he too stripped off his clothes, and he too prophesied before Samuel, and lay naked all that day and all that night" (1 Samuel 19:23–24). In this disconcerting scene, a crowd of naked men (including judge, king, and future king), raves, whirls, and gibbers under the effects of holy madness.

Saul's situation continues to deteriorate. Samuel dies. David's fame and following increase. At last, abandoned by God, facing overwhelming odds in an upcoming battle against the Philistines (whose fighting force includes David), contending with the "evil spirit from the Lord," Saul seeks some sort of counsel, perhaps some comfort, through the only means available. He consults a witch or medium, requesting that she "call up" the ghost of his nemesis, Samuel. She does so, whereupon Samuel, still showing his old animosity, offers neither counsel nor comfort. Instead, he berates Saul, reminds him that God has torn the kingdom from him, and predicts Saul's and his sons' deaths the following day. Samuel's prophecy proves accurate. Saul, perhaps the first suicide, suggestive to the end, insures its veracity by falling on his own sword (1 Samuel 28; 31:4–6). Death *is* the only corrective.

Saul's story explores the theme of divinely induced madness—both benign and delusional. At first, Yahweh gives Saul "another heart," which opens the door for his prophetic mania or ecstasy; later, he sends the "evil spirit," which torments Saul and renders him delusional, paranoid and, ultimately, self-destructive. In either case, and from the moment of his meeting with Samuel/Yahweh, Saul is God-maddened and doomed.

FORMS OF PROPHETIC EXPERIENCE

> To one is given through the Spirit . . . prophecy, to another the ability to distinguish between spirits, to another various kinds of tongues, to another the interpretation of tongues. All these are inspired by one and the same Spirit. . . .
>
> 1 Corinthians 12:8–11

> I feared what word would split high noon with light
> And lock my life, and try to drive me mad. . . .
>
> Thomas Merton, "St. Paul"

The "prophetic experience" takes several forms—direct address by God or the gods (which may or may not be figurative), divinely induced dreams (which are usually figurative, requiring "interpretation"), visions (often in symbolic forms), oracles (often ironic, obscure, or ambiguous), inspired/compelled speaking (ecstatic "prophesying" or "speaking in tongues"), and signs (often conveyed through symbolic action). Several of these forms of holy madness are indistinguishable from common, garden-variety insanity, hence the frequent accusations against "false" prophets. Hence, also, St. Paul's hesitation about encouraging the speaking in tongues (as if it were a matter of choice) and his reservation about epistemological gains therefrom. He expresses a preference for the engagement of the "mind" in *public* religious discourse:

> I thank God that I speak in tongues more than you all; nevertheless, in church I would rather speak five words with my mind, in order to instruct others, than ten thousand words in a tongue. . . . If, therefore, the whole church assembles and all speak in tongues, and outsiders or unbelievers enter, will they not say that you are mad?
>
> 1 Corinthians 14:18–25

By traditional dating, approximately a thousand years intervene between Saul's "prophesying" at Ramah and St. Paul's address to the Corinthians (when, he understands, the practice of speaking in tongues would appear "mad"). In St. Paul's time, bands of ecstatics seldom roamed the land, as they had in the times of Elijah or Samuel. Yet Elijah, as first among his prophetic guild, does find his first-century CE counterpart in the visionary St. Paul; and the prophetic guild, its counterpart in an assembly like the Corinthians, who placed great value on "speaking in tongues" or "prophesying" in the older sense. But things have changed. It is interesting to notice a strain of rationalism in St. Paul's discourse. Five words spoken *with the mind* "to instruct others" are to be desired over ten thousand spoken in the incomprehensible, God-sent language of tongues. At the same time, however, St. Paul values the experience of holy madness; it is just that he recognizes that such behavior appears mad to outsiders.

PROPHECY, OBSCURITY, AND MEANING

> Pharaoh told them his dream, but there was none who could interpret it to Pharaoh.
>
> Genesis 41:8

> If there is a prophet among you, I the Lord make myself known to him in a vision, I will speak with him in a dream.
>
> Numbers 12:6

One theory holds that during a prophetic experience the recipient becomes privy to "knowledge" of that which exists outside the bounds of the material realm as known through the physical senses. Thus Joseph "knows" the meaning of Pharaoh's dreams of fat and lean cows (Genesis 41) and Daniel reads the "meaning" of the handwriting on Belshazar's wall (Daniel 5). Ultimately, many participants in the debate reached a rather Platonic consensus that holy madness is valuable because it permits *an immortal soul* to transcend the limits imposed by the body's physicality. Knowledge, when constrained by the senses and what they can know of the sensible world, is limited, misleading, and largely useless. It is knowledge merely of a realm of appearance. A "spiritual reality" exists beyond the reach of reason as an authentic dimension of *insensible* knowledge. One gains access to that dimension through the mysteries of prophetic experience—its distortions of physical sensation, especially sight and hearing, its symbolic language, and eerie occurrences.

As philosophical theories evolved, the old texts became grist for a Platonic mill of inquiry and interpretation. Apparently for the spiritually astute any sacred text could conceal a spiritual meaning beneath that of the "letter." As an example of such philosophical understanding, Nasrallah examines a text by Philo, first-century Jewish philosopher and contemporary of St. Paul. Philo merges a form of neo-Platonism with the language of Greek mystery religions to explicate the "spiritual meaning" of a biblical passage: "Now the Lord said to Abram, 'Go from your country and your kindred and your father's house to the land that I will show you'" (Genesis 12:1). Philo addresses *his soul or understanding*, urging it to be like Abram:

> Therefore, soul, if some yearning to inherit the good and divine things should enter you, leave not only "the land"—that is, the body—and "kindred"—that is, sense perception—and "your father's house"—that is, *logos*, but also flee from yourself and stand outside of yourself; as those who are possessed and corybants [celebrants of Greek mysteries], be inspired with frenzy and be possessed by some prophetic inspiration.
> Philo, *Who Is Heir of Divine Things?* Quoted in Nasrallah 38

Nasrallah draws attention to the fact that *knowledge* of the realm of "good and divine" things is obtained through inspired frenzy and by abandoning not only the body and sense perception, but reason itself (38). Thus, the everyday functions of seeing, hearing, speaking, and understanding are surrendered in favor of "spiritual" (i.e., figurative) seeing, hearing, speaking, and understanding, as one abandons the realm of sense and reason for metaphor and ecstasy.

PROPHECY FOR THIS WORLD

Some assumptions about the prophetic experience have been implicit throughout prophecy's long history in the pre-biblical, biblical, and Greco-Roman experience, especially the notion that God can communicate special knowledge to an individual. However, as mentioned, a major transformation occurs as gradually a Platonic disdain for the world and the flesh privileges knowledge of a realm of "good and divine things." Before the spread of the idea of immortality, emphasis fell not on knowledge of the spiritual, but on the ways divine communication could enhance the satisfactions of the world, life in the world, and pleasures of the flesh. In its time, God's address to Abram would have constituted an example of holy madness, divine communication, and instruction, but would have been heard and acted upon not figuratively, but literally. Thus, in response to Yahweh's communication, Abram simply leaves his land (Haran), his clan, and the house of his father, Terah, and travels to Canaan, land of promise.

Ancient prophecy tended to speak of this world, its limitations and enjoyments, and to argue against the possibility of knowing "good and divine things." This, for example, is the lesson Gilgamesh learned in his failed quest for immortality. Siduri, mystical alewife and Babylonian prophet, asserts that immortality is unavailable to human beings, but explains that nevertheless humankind has compensations appropriate to its mortal condition:

> Thou, Gilgamesh, let full be thy belly,
> Make thou merry by day and by night.
> . . . . .
> Let thy garments be sparkling fresh,
> Thy head be washed; bathe thou in water.
> Pay heed to the little one that holds on to thy hand,
> Let thy spouse delight in thy bosom!
> For this is the task of [mankind]!
> *Epic of Gilgamesh*, Pritchard 64

Over a millennium later, the rational, philosophical writer of Ecclesiastes reiterates the alewife's advice:

> Go, eat your bread with enjoyment, and drink your wine with a merry heart; for God has already approved what you do. Let your garments be always white; let not oil be lacking on your head. Enjoy life with the wife whom you love, all the days of your vain life which he has given you under the sun, because that is your portion in life and in your toil at which you toil under the son. Whatever your hand finds to do, do it with your might; for there is no work or thought or knowledge or wisdom in Sheol to which you are going.
> Ecclesiastes 9:7–10

Death is the common lot; no one inherits "good and divine things." If there is a place where wisdom may be found, it is in and of the world, not of some transliminal place or time and not in Sheol certainly, where there is "no work or thought or knowledge or wisdom." In his long discourse on wisdom, Job asserts that knowledge "is hid from the eyes of all living" (Job 28:20–22).

Homer leads Odysseus to a similar conclusion when in Hades Odysseus learns not of "good and divine things," but of mortality's grim realities. Saul learns that the once powerful Samuel molders in Sheol in a perpetually unconscious state in which his old animosity slumbers. Since Sheol is the common destination, proverbial wisdom describes *earthly,* rather than "good and divine," rewards and punishments for wise and foolish behavior: "[T]he righteous will flourish like a green leaf. / He who troubles his household will inherit wind, and the fool will be servant to the wise. / The fruit of the righteous is a tree of life, but lawlessness takes away lives. / If the righteous is requited on earth, how much more the wicked and the sinner!" (Proverbs 11:28–31). Job's "prophetic experience" consists of God's monologue from the whirlwind. God offers Job no knowledge of "good and divine things," but rather confirms his ignorance and insignificance. The role of prophecy and the sorts of "knowledge" it provides change remarkably with acceptance of the concept of an immortal soul.

PROPHETIC IRONY

Nay, but by men of strange lips and with an alien tongue
The Lord will speak to this people....

Isaiah 28:11

Legend has it that Oedipus, having been told by a drunken companion that he was not his father's son, consulted the oracle at Delphi and posed the question, "Who are my parents?" Apollo inspired his mad oracle's answer, which she conveyed in half-conscious gibberish to the attendant priests, who "translated" her ironic reply: "Avoid your homeland." Oedipus, of course, believed that home was Corinth, whereas his native land was actually Thebes, the very city toward which he fled in order to avoid his homeland. One can almost hear the grim laughter originating on Mt. Olympus.[13]

Prophecy predates history. Through the millennia it seemed to provide a means of communication between gods and mortals. As the example of the Delphic oracle suggests, however, the gods' communications could be enigmatic, symbolic, obscure, or ironic. Yahweh's very first message to his newly created man is a case in point: "You may freely eat of every tree of the garden; but of the tree of the knowledge of good and evil you shall not eat, for in the day that you eat of it you shall die" (Genesis

2:16–17). As discussed in Chapter 6, this is a sophisticated message to a naïve listener. The implications of the message are staggering; what is said is dwarfed by what remains unsaid. The message itself (like the name and placement of the tree) is curiously tempting, but also misleading and ambiguous. And, if, as seems necessary, the Author God required the first couple to eat the fruit as a major plot point (without "disobedience," no story), the entire situation is ironic in the extreme.

The parables of Jesus, as divine communication, are similarly ironic. Jesus tells his disciples that the parables are intended to be misunderstood. Whereas they are addressed to the multitudes who normally depend upon "common sense," they carry a message only for those with spiritual sight and hearing: he tells the disciples, "To you has been given the secret of the kingdom of God, but for those outside everything is in parables; so that they may indeed see but not perceive, and may indeed hear but not understand" (Mark 4:11–12). The parables possess a degree of sadistic irony equaled only by the Delphic oracle's reply to Oedipus.

DREAMS AND VISIONS

... I will pour out my spirit on all flesh;
your sons and your daughters shall prophesy,
your old men shall dream dreams,
and your young men shall see visions.
Joel 2:28–29; cf. Acts 2:17

If the gods send us these unintelligible and inexplicable dream-messages they are acting as Carthaginians and Spaniards would if they were to address our senate in their own vernacular without the aid of an interpreter.
Cicero, quoted in Nasrallah 1

In biblical narratives from Genesis to Revelation, dreams and visions are common modes of divine communication. An early example of a dream vision is Jacob's dream at Bethel. While visionary (the stairway or ladder reaching to heaven) and numinous (the presence of ascending and descending angels and God himself standing above it), the dream's message is fairly direct: "I am the Lord, the God of Abraham your father and the God of Isaac; the land on which you lie I will give to you and your descendants...." (Genesis 28:12–13). Often, however, the divine communications are so cloaked in metaphor and symbol that only God can interpret them, or "inspire" a human interpreter to explain their meanings.

The most interesting uses of metaphor and symbol in vision and dream reveal a poetic dimension of the divine being, who, while delighting in ambiguity, presents an abstract situation in vivid concrete terms.

Sometimes God, the assumed metaphor maker, himself serves as interpreter, as in Ezekiel's bizarre vision of a valley "full of bones" (Ezekiel 37:1). The scattered bones, on being addressed by the prophet, begin to rattle: "and the bones came together, bone to its bone. And as I looked, there were sinews on them, and flesh had come upon them, and skin had covered them" (37:7–8). This stunning view of a valley full of manikins, or zombie like semi-animate figures, changes as Ezekiel prophesies "to the breath" or spirit, "Thus says the Lord God: Come from the four winds, O breath, and breathe upon these slain, that they may live." Then, "the breath came into them, and they lived, and stood upon their feet" (37:9–10). God interprets the metaphor. The bones are the "whole house of Israel" who have lost hope in exile. He promises to raise them from exile, their figurative graves, and return them to the Promised Land (37:11–14).[14]

Prophetic concern shifts away from the world and survival only with the advent of dualisms (Zoroastrian, Platonic), when mortal body separates from immortal soul, when nature, no longer "very good" as at the creation, is seen as corrupt, *material*, and delusive, when physical perception no longer provides knowledge, and when life is not valued for its pleasures—eating, drinking, making merry, raising families, working—but is rather devalued as a condition to be endured until one can escape, in St. Paul's term, from "this body of death." "Do not love the world or the things in the world," John admonishes, "For all that is in the world, the lust of the flesh and the lust of the eyes and the pride of life, is not of the Father but is of the world. And the world passes away, and the lust of it. . . . " (1 John 2:15–17). With this change, the messages of the dreams and visions focus no longer on the world, but on "good and divine things," Old Testament texts are read "spiritually," and apocalypse becomes the prominent mode of prophetic experience.

REVELATION—VEILING OR UNVEILING?

> It cannot be denied that the apocalyptists had visions, but it is quite another question how far these experiences have been deposited in the Literature.
>
> Vielhauer 584

Some view John of Patmos as the epitome of holy madness, for his visions rise to unprecedented levels of unreason and illogic. He introduces his prophetic experience to readers in both auditory and visual details, obscure symbols, and intertextual allusions. He announces at the beginning that he heard a loud voice and in a sort of synesthetic expectation turned to "*see* the voice." What he sees is a vision of Jesus, the voice having taken on life, shape, and color. He saw, he says,

> one like the son of man, clothed with a long robe and with a golden girdle round his breast; his head and his hair were white as white wool, white as snow; his eyes were like a flame of fire, his feet were like burnished bronze, refined in a furnace, and his voice was like the sound of many waters; in his right hand he held seven stars, from his mouth issued a sharp two-edged sword, and his face was like the sun shining in full strength.
>
> Revelation 1:12–16

The vision, in ways horrific, even repellent, is reminiscent of Ezekiel's vision of Yahweh and his chariot throne. Elements like the flame, the burnished bronze, and the sound of many waters might have been transported directly from the earlier vision. The responses of the prophets too are similar and typical: Ezekiel says, "[W]hen I saw it [the vision of God], I fell upon my face" (1:28); and John says, "When I saw him, I fell at his feet as though dead" (1:17). Literary borrowings, echoes, and allusions are characteristic of the apocalyptic genre. Scholars have noticed the presence of many precursor texts in Revelation. Of particular interest in this theophany is the influence of John, the gospel writer, who calls Jesus the *Word* (the Logos, Reason) of God. John of Patmos embraces the metaphor, representing the *heard* word, the *voice*, in the visual image of Jesus, whose tongue (language, words) is a "sharp, two-edged sword." For John of Patmos, the gospel writer's Word does indeed "become flesh" or at least the appearance of flesh.

The numerous literary influences in Revelation prompt questions: Has John been stricken by holy madness? Or is he a creative writer working in a popular genre and following literary precedent? Is his Revelation merely wordcraft? Vielhauer, discussing the literariness of apocalyptic texts, suggests that "the work of distinguishing neatly between actual experience and literary activity in the Apocalypses will scarcely be successful." He then quotes Thomas Mann on *Doctor Faustus* as noticing that perhaps rapture may occur not independently but "in something like a process of borrowing" (Vielhauer 2:584). Perhaps borrowed rapture is like the infectious frenzy of group "prophesying" seen in the case of Saul at Ramah. Perhaps, that is, a power of *textual* suggestion and contagion operates in the literary genre of apocalypse.[15]

John of Patmos presents Chapters 1 to 3 as a vision in which he acts as recording secretary for God/Christ. His astonishing claim is that "the Alpha and Omega" (Jesus), as did Yahweh to Moses, *dictated* John's text in the form of letters to the seven churches, each addressed to "the angel" of the church. In his letters the epistolary Jesus commends, admonishes, and exhorts the various congregations. His language is often radically figurative and mysterious. He admonishes the congregation of Smyrna, for example, to reject heretical teachings and false prophets, warning, "I will come to you soon and war against them with the sword of my mouth." If they repent, he says, he will give them "some of the hidden manna" and "a white stone with a new name written on the stone which no one knows except him who receives it" (2:16–17). What might be "hidden manna"? Why a stone? Why a *white* stone? Why write a secret name on a stone? One of the false prophets Jesus mentions is a prophetess (called Jezebel), who has approved eating food sacrificed to idols, a practice also condoned by St. Paul (1 Corinthians 10:25–27). It is unsurprising that John's Jesus shares John's disposition in matters of religious practice. John's Jesus goes so far as to identify a real woman, the "false" prophetess, with the figurative harlots of the Old Testament. Jesus says, "Behold, I will throw her on a sickbed, and those who commit adultery with her I will throw into great tribulation . . . ; and I will strike her children dead" (Revelation 2:22–23).[16] Such violence and anger suggest something archaic about Revelation. As John depicts him, Jesus of the gospels might never have existed, for here his persona appears as the true ideological heir of the Old Testament's wrathful Yahweh, whose attitudes and figurative realities have passed intact to the son. Likewise, in his stark black-and-white world, in his embrace of violence, vengeance, and anger, in his identifying difference of opinion with heresy, figured as sexual crimes, the prophet is himself the true heir of the angry Old Testament prophets.

As John moves into the second phase of his vision, he makes the apocalyptic journey into heaven so common in earlier Jewish apocalypses. Jesus invites John to "come up hither," whereupon John sees in heaven "an open door" (a challenging image!) and hears the voice of Jesus announce, "I will show you what must take place after this" (4:1). The only detailed description of heaven in the Bible, John's draws on figurative capital of the ages to depict the Unknown. He presents the storm god, king, court, throne room and throne, crowns, attendants, heavenly armies, warrior angels, weapons, books, scrolls, fathers and sons, harlots and brides, slaughtered lambs, horses, horsemen, composite beasts, plagues, battles, trumpets, and old enemies. The result is a baroque scene lorded over by an unforgiving tyrant who orchestrates the suffering of the vast majority of earth's populace and the slow progress of the earth's destruction. At its culmination,

> [t]he seventh angel poured his bowl into the air, and a loud voice came out of the temple, from the throne, saying, "It is done!" And there were flashes of lightning, voices, peals of thunder, and a great earthquake. . . . The great city was split into three parts, and the cities of the nations fell, and God

remembered great Babylon, to make her drain the cup of the fury of his wrath. And every island fled away, and no mountains were to be found; and great hailstones, heavy as a hundred weight, dropped on men from heaven, till men cursed God for the plague of the hail, so fearful was the plague.

Revelation 16:17–21[17]

Even more disquieting than the vindictive wrath evident in the passage is the consequent heavenly joy at the destruction and eternal suffering of "enemies." The "great multitude in heaven" rejoice over the devastation of Babylon (the old world): "Hallelujah!" they shout. "The smoke from her goes up for ever and ever" (Revelation 19:1–3). One looks in vain for sympathy or regret in heaven, for a hint of "Christian" charity, for *any* humane response at all.

Once the enemies are disposed of in a place of eternal torment, God's obsequious and robotic subjects look forward to a future that would drive anyone still in his or her senses stark, staring mad. The text manifests the sort of thinking associated with what I referred to in the introduction as doom eagerness. It dismisses the world, its lives, and its business as inconsequential. Love, laughter and tears, life, work, and death—these too are dismissed in favor of "salvation" of the righteous whose destiny is to participate in a mindless eternal chanting of praises, against a ground bass of agonized cries of "enemies."

Holy Madness and "Knowledge"

> By tapping into the deep mine of myth in order to give meaning to history, apocalyptic literature introduced ambiguity and polyvalence that increase fascination while compounding obscurity....
>
> McGinn 527

The common claim about holy madness is that it offers knowledge of a dimension of reality unavailable to those who abide in the sane and sensible world of ordinary experience. As Nasrallah shows, in ancient Greco-Roman times prophetic experience was taken seriously and constituted a "hot topic" of intellectual discourse "in conversation with the religions of antiquity" (30). Nasrallah identifies the sorts of questions such ancient authors addressed: "What is the human soul, and how is it susceptible to dreams and ecstasy? What capacities for knowledge does a human have? How does the divine communicate to the human? What exactly happens to a person in death, or sleep, or madness?" (9).

If one using physical senses gains knowledge of the physical world, and if one assumes that there exist metaphysical realms, what means are available to gain knowledge of those realms? The quick answer is that *one takes leave of his or her senses*; or, in the idiom of the time, one undergoes prophetic experiences during which one enjoys a mind-altering influx of spirit and knowledge—holy madness. That ancient authors raised and attempted to answer such questions is not surprising. The situation is more curious when a modern psychologist, Isabel Clarke, revisits such questions "in conversation with" religion, and, like the ancients, argues that madness—holy or not—is the high road to valuable "knowledge" and spiritual experience undreamt of in the philosophy of the logical, the commonsensical, and the sane. She asks, "Where does God, and that yearning for the irrational and infinite, fit into the tidy world view of the scientist?" In a debate a between science and religion, she declares, "I value both [science and religion] as different but essential aspects of the human experience and *of human knowing*. . . . " (Clarke 5–6; emphasis supplied). She proceeds, as she puts it, to approach religious "knowledge" through "association with madness," and begins by comparing experiences of modern insanity with the spiritual encounters of St. Teresa and St. John, as examples of those who walk "that fine line between the mystical vocation and madness" (59).

But, what is knowledge? What can human beings know? What sorts of tests can be brought to the answers? A child may "know" that if he puts a tooth under his pillow a fairy will come in the night and exchange it for a nickel. Like most "knowledge" of the Unknown, his is language created. No doubt he "knows" of the fairy and the process of exchange through a story told by his parents, authorities in whose assurances he has confidence. Having heard the story, he may even encounter the tooth fairy in a dream, prophetic or not. Is the child's knowledge real knowledge? Is his dream a vision? Has he willingly suspended disbelief? Are the parents false prophets? This sort of deception may be harmless. The tale of the generous night visitor may satisfy the child's "yearning for the irrational" by offering hints of a "supernatural" realm where fairies abide. Certainly he has "assurance of things hoped for" and "evidence" of things not seen—the lost tooth and the found nickel. The exchange of coin for tooth gives the child "knowledge" that will no doubt be surrendered with the last of his deciduous teeth. Perhaps the experience will lead to skepticism, but probably not. Likely other authoritative voices will speak of other wonders, "knowledge" of which has been gained by those who have been "out of their senses," undergone prophetic experiences, and passed along to the child as "truth"—sacred text and personal testimony.

I have referred to any realm of the metaphysical, and all its aspects, as the Unknown, whereas the underlying proposition of prophecy is that the *Unknown may be known*—through those maddened by an almighty wind or a holy spirit who then report their dreams, visions, and hallucinations for the edification of others. Of course, the credulous hearer of prophecy may find it impossible to distinguish the "true" from the "false" prophet, the one stricken with holy madness from the fraudulent or insane.[18] John of Patmos or St. Paul, both or neither—which prophet offers "knowledge" of the divine attitude toward sacrificial food consumption? One's eternal blessedness may have depended on one's choice.

LANGUAGE AND THE INSANE CREATIONS OF HOLY MADNESS

> O Jerusalem, Jerusalem, killing the prophets and stoning those who are sent to you! . . . you will not see me again, until you say, "Blessed is he who comes in the name of the Lord."
>
> Matthew 23:37–39

The underlying proposition of prophecy requires scrutiny. The prophet portends to relay "knowledge" of the Unknown and unknowable that lies beyond the boundaries of human empirical understanding. The "knowledge" comes in the form of language, either the prophet's own or his rendering of that spoken by some divine figure. Whichever the case, the words are taken from the world of the senses to convey information about a realm one supposedly accesses when one is out of one's senses. The process involves the embedding of metaphor, symbol, and other figures within figures, layer upon layer. For example, John of Patmos "sees" a figure from the insensible realm and "hears" him dictate letters, forms of earthly communication. In those missives, the figure uses language of the physical world of sense. The figure (called figuratively "the Alpha and Omega"), figuratively "visible" to John as the Word with a sword-tongue, promises a figurative reward to those who repent: "a white stone with a new name written on the stone. . . ."

What "knowledge" can the Christians at Smyrna (or anyone else) glean from John's prophetic experience? Perhaps they "learn" that some sort of spiritual food (manna) from the time of the Exodus lies hidden in their world, or that white stones are better than gray stones, or that secret names written on stones are important. In his letter the figure cautions against the "false" prophetess who, like St. Paul, advocates a practice condemned by John. Those whom the prophet and prophetess address must decide in each case whether the madness is indeed holy and the message "true." Is he a true prophet, and is she a fraud or a garden-variety lunatic? Or is the situation reversed? Examining the textual evidence suggests that many in a prophet's audience from ancient to modern times have judged him a fraud or lunatic. And often they have been correct.

THE LIMINAL AND THE TRANSLIMINAL

My people are destroyed for lack of knowledge....

Hosea 4:7

I applied my mind to know wisdom and to know madness and folly. I perceived that this also is but a striving after wind.

Ecclesiastes 1:17

My term *the Unknown* stands at odds with claims that the prophetic experience, as undergone and transmitted to others (often in sacred texts), provides "knowledge." There are limits to the knowable, but none, it seems, to the human imagination and its story-telling abilities. It is these that transcend, that go beyond, and, with the figurative devices of language, create persons, acts, scenes, and plots. The narratives of prophets and their prophetic experiences are things made of words—words drawn from the realm of sense to serve the story-telling requirements of one who has been "out of his senses," stricken with holy madness, wandering in realms without limits.

As suggested in the discussion of Revelation, the fruits of one imagination may be ingested and transformed by another, and one sort of rapture borrowed by another. Soon there is a labyrinth of textual realities and a population of those willing to "know" what the texts relate. How many accounts of alien abduction make an alien abductor? How many nickels left under how many pillows conjure up a tooth fairy? God only knows.

An accumulation of accounts of mysterious night visitors—supernatural, alien, or fairy—cannot, I think, yield knowledge, although it can produce for some belief. The question is often posed, "Do *you* believe in UFO's and alien visitors?" And among the younger set, "Do *you* believe in the tooth fairy?" I reiterate my claim that we simply *cannot know* what if anything lies beyond that line (the boundary, the limit, the threshold), in language-created space (transcendental, metaphysical, supernatural realms) where aliens, fairies, and gods abide. They have always been and remain unknowable. Nietzsche said, "If you gaze long into an abyss, the abyss will gaze back into you." It is equally the case that if you gaze long into the mirror of heaven, the mirror will gaze back at you with strangely familiar eyes, face, and expression.

CHAPTER 12

REFLECTIONS

[God] is not jealous, trivial, ignorant, revengeful . . . ; He has personal dignity—dignity answerable to his grandeur, his greatness, his might, his sublimity; He cares nothing for men's flatteries, compliments, praises, prayers; it is impossible that he should value them, impossible that He should listen to them, these mouthings of microbes. . . . His sun does not stand still on Gibeon to accommodate a worm out on a raid against other worms. . . .
     Mark Twain, "Mark Twain's God," *The Three R's* 155

How clean the sun when seen in its idea,
Washed in the remotest cleanliness of a heaven
That has expelled us and our images. . . .
     Wallace Stevens, *Notes Toward a Supreme Fiction* I

WHEN MARK TWAIN LOOKED INTO THE MIRROR OF HEAVEN and the book of nature, he saw what for him was the "real God," the "One who created this majestic universe and rules it." He would not have human characteristics like jealousy, "a trait so small that even men despise it in each other"; "He would regard self-praise as unbecoming the dignity of His position"; "He would not have the spirit of vengeance in His heart" ("Mark Twain's God," *The Three R's* 153–54). Twain recognized that our sacred texts throughout history, especially the Bible (his immediate concern), have created as objects of worship preposterous personae—a grandmother slaughtering and dismembering Marduk, a tyrannical, womanizing, child-abusing Zeus, or an angry, jealous, biased, sex-preoccupied, self-promoting, vengeful Yahweh. Twain found the biblical God repellent and responded with sardonic laughter directed toward those who created and perpetuate his story. Even so, Twain was unwilling to relinquish the metaphor of a masculine, divine author, king, and originator. *He* is the "one who created this majestic universe and rules it."

Wallace Stevens goes further than Twain and imagines the "cleanliness of a heaven / That has expelled us and our images." He advises, "Never suppose an inventing mind as source" of the idea of the sun, "nor for that mind compose / A voluminous master folded in his fire." Let Phoebus (Apollo), the sun god, "slumber and die in autumn umber." Phoebus is dead, he says, "But Phoebus was / A name for something that never could be named" (*Notes Toward a Supreme Fiction* I). The impossibility of naming that ineffable "something" has not, of course, prevented its naming. Xenophanes was making a similar point when he referred to the "something" as *Thing*; it has been my point also in adopting *the Unknown* to designate the something that cannot be named.

In the preceding chapters, I have examined some of the ways that we and our images are reflected in the mirror of heaven. It is not a pretty picture, nor clean or coherent. We have littered heaven with our names, labels, figurations, and plots, all inevitably reflecting human prejudices, preoccupations, superstitions, desires, fears, and hatreds. We have, in short, populated the heavens with monsters. Richard Dawkins' description of the Old Testament's Yahweh might apply to a greater or lesser degree to a host of other deities, including Marduk, Zeus, Kronus, Uranus, Jupiter, Odin, and Allah. Dawkins says that the Old Testament God is "arguably the most unpleasant character in all fiction." He is,

> jealous and proud of it; a petty, unjust, unforgiving control-freak; a vindictive, bloodthirsty ethnic cleanser; a misogynistic, homophobic, racist, infanticidal, genocidal, filicidal, pestilential, megalomaniacal, sadomasochistic, capriciously sadistic bully.
>
> 31[1]

It is of course impossible that the mirror itself can expel the images we have held up to its reflective surface: so well established are our linguistic peopling and structuring of the heavens, so full are they of our images and stories that, in all probability and even with good intentions, neither can we. To do so would involve asking new questions, changing the language, the metaphors, and the narratives (indeed editing the divinely authored, inerrant Book). It would involve nothing less than re-creation. And, of course, the recreated Unknown would, like the old one, suffer similar *human* limitations. As Xenophanes noticed so long ago, "a Thing whose true description must owe nothing to the characters of those who describe it is beyond our reach: whatever we find it plausible to say It is will be what we find plausible" (Stephen R. L. Clark 12).

RELIGION, PHILOSOPHY, AND MORALITY

Are all these tales of the gods true . . . ?

Plato, "Euthyphro"

Without God, there is no virtue, because there's no prompting of the conscience.

Ronald Reagan[2]

With or without religion, good people can behave well and bad people can do evil; but for good people to do evil—that takes religion.

Stephen Weinberg, quoted by Stenger 215

Philosophy and theology have been largely unsuccessful in expunging us and our images from the mirror of heaven. A disjunction exists between philosophical/theological interpretations and explanations of the Unknown, and the persons, acts, and images inerrantly "revealed" (supposedly *by* or through the inspiration of the deities) in the texts. In general, philosophers and theologians have created a parallel textual tradition, which they superimpose on the sacred texts. The philosopher/theologian writes narratives about the narratives. Greek philosophy, responding to the Homeric texts, began a process of "making sense" of the nature, motives, characters, and values of the gods and their relationships to human beings. Hesiod, essentially a philosopher/theologian, was among the first to attempt to absolve Zeus of his pre-Homeric and Homeric indiscretions. Hesiod's Zeus personifies justice and righteousness. He oversees the actions of humans, meting out rewards and punishments as appropriate. "Otherwise," Hesiod asserts, "I would not myself be righteous among men / nor have my son be so. . . . " (*Works and Days* 270–72). Hesiod's position is common. As he and like thinkers see it, humans naturally behave badly; the only reason to behave well is the promise of divine rewards for good behavior and threat of punishments for unjust or bad behavior.

Philosophy's difficulty with the traditional texts that tell of God or gods and their exploits is "sometimes called 'the Euthyphro dilemma'": "If we try to define the holy as what is loved by the gods (and goddesses), we will be faced with the question 'Is the holy holy because it is loved by the gods, or do they love it because it is holy?'" (Hare 4). Is war, for example, holy because the gods love it, or do the gods love it because it is holy? As suggested in the epigraph, Socrates, a pious believer, rejects accounts of the gods and their arbitrary, violent, immoral behavior; he rejects also the claim that a thing will be holy if the gods love it. He understands that the gods are just and, therefore, advances the notion that the gods will love a thing only *because* it is holy. The Bible offers a different response to the question. One might ask, for example, are the "chosen people" holy because God loves them, or does God love them because they are holy? The answer is apparently that they are holy because God loves them, despite their stubborn and stiff-necked behavior, their faithlessness and "harlotry."

Through its long tradition, the philosophical tactic has been to evade troublesome aspects of the texts and assume a priori that God or the gods are embodiments of the Good, the Just, and the True, and that humans should aspire to be like them. It is thus not within the ancient tales or sacred texts themselves, but in the philosophical tradition that the stronger link between religion and morality is forged and maintained. In its origins, biblical morality was associated with and defined as obedience to divine laws, many of which strike modern readers as silly ("you [priests] shall not go up by steps to my altar, that your nakedness be not exposed on it" [Exodus 20:26] or "[the priests] shall not make tonsures upon their head, nor shave off the edges of their beards" [Leviticus 21:5]), and others as patently immoral ("you must utterly destroy them [the Canaanites]; you shall . . . show no mercy to them" [Deuteronomy 7:2]).

The contrast between the Greek and biblical traditions has been described as one in which the "Greeks favor *the good*, in their account of the relation of morality and religion, and the Judeo-Christian account favors *the right* or obligation." The ensuing philosophical development consists of a "cross-fertilization of these two traditions or lines of thought" (Hare 9). In other words, even though the two traditions are irreconcilable, philosophy attempts through carefully selected texts to make them cohere. For example, a strong current of Greek Platonism runs through the theology of St. Augustine. It is then through his authority that Platonism maintains its force in subsequent philosophical/theological discussions. In the *City of God*, seeking to reconcile Platonic and biblical texts, Augustine claimed that Plato "thought that to be a philosopher is to be a lover of God"; he joins this idea with the admonition in 1 John to "love one another; for love is of God, and he who loves is born of God and knows God. He who does not love does not know God; for God is love" (1 John 4:7–8; Hare 9–10). Augustinian authority subsequently established the metaphor, "God is Love," even in the face of numerous biblical texts announcing, on the contrary, that if God is a personification of a human emotion, it is not Love, but Wrath. Through the centuries philosophy has continued to associate religion and morality by assigning to God such metaphors as Love, Right, Good, and Truth. In this tradition, God's will is the righteous source of all moral law.

The religious, then, encounter two kinds of authority that speak at cross-purposes as regards religion and morality. There are the sacred texts themselves, and then there is the superimposed tradition of philosophy and theology. To the extent that they know the sacred texts, average religious believers consider the narratives and their figurations compelling (e.g., the story of Adam, Eve, and the serpent, or the story of Noah and the Flood). They accept the premise of the texts' origin in the divine Author. Yet such readers are unlikely actually to have read the whole Book on which they place such value.[3] As Stenger states the matter, "While the Judeo-Christian-Islamic God described in scriptures is hardly benevolent, the faithful of these religions are far more likely to ignore unpleasant scriptural passages than abandon belief in a benevolent God" (222). An alternative tactic is to acknowledge God's outrageous behavior in the various tales, but to defend it as the inevitable or necessary divine response to human disobedience and irremediable "sinful nature." According to this argument, human behavior has given God no choice but to be angry, vengeful, and murderous—to send the plague of AIDS in response to human sexual or homosexual behavior, for example, or to devastate a "sinful city," Sodom or New Orleans, with fire, brimstone, hurricane and flood. And yet John and Augustine said that God is Love. The Qur'an reiterates that Allah is "merciful and compassionate." Both are silent concerning the logical gap between such claims and God's militant history or his promised apocalyptic judgment of eternal suffering.

One of the difficulties involved in cleansing the mirror of us and our images is the widespread, but patently false notion that inasmuch as morality originates in the heavens, moral behavior in humans depends upon religiosity—an idea of ancient origin, as the claim of Hesiod demonstrates, or this from the Bible:

> The fool says in his heart, "There is no God."
> They are corrupt, they do abominable deeds,
> there is none that does good.
>
> Psalms 14:1

Moral behavior in this view does not come naturally to sinful or "fallen" human beings—heirs of the "evil seed." All are sinners; no one deserves salvation. Salvation falls from on high; codes of conduct are imposed from on high. Good behavior is prompted by divine rewards—hence believers' pitiless scorn for "disbelievers" who, they assert, cannot help but behave badly. The conclusion follows inevitably: to be moral one must be religious.

I have argued that the messages emblazoned on the mirror of heaven, like the fly-over messages of advertisers, are of human rather than divine origin, as a single brief passage from the laws in Exodus illustrates:

> You shall not permit a sorceress [witch] to live. . . .
> Whoever sacrifices to any god, save to the Lord only, shall be utterly destroyed.
> You shall not wrong a stranger or oppress him.
> 22:18–21

Religion and morality? It is easy to see the difficulty. "You shall not wrong a stranger or oppress him" sounds, for lack of a better word, "moral." However, if that stranger happens to practice witchcraft or to worship the Unknown under a name other than Yahweh, he or she is to be killed or "utterly destroyed"—a pious atrocity that sounds not moral at all, but brutal and intolerant. A moment's thought reveals that throughout history, immoral acts have been and continue to be performed in the name of religion.[4] Are religion and morality really a compatible pair?

Answering in the affirmative, Isabel Clarke asserts blithely that, "morality and religion have always gone hand in hand" (32). Nevertheless, if one assumes, as I do, *a human origin* of moral behavior (a basic core of human morality nearly universal to all peoples and times) and does not reduce "morality" to local custom and habit (as recorded in sacred texts and practiced by the religious), clearly this traveling "hand in hand" has not "always" been the case, nor is it today. Clarke can be right only if we concede that "morality" is a flexible system of behavior that changes with changing locales, times, motives, and gods.[5] Rape, plunder, and infanticide, acts most humans consider abominable violations of any minimal standard of behavior, were perfectly acceptable—"moral"—to the ancient Greeks; it was the right of gods to rape human women, and the customary right of human victors to rape and enslave women, plunder cities, and slaughter children. Similarly in ancient times, Yahweh's laws of "holy war" directed the Israelites to kill every living thing in a conquered city, or to kill the men, women, and boys, but to save for themselves the virgin girls. The "moral" status of rape and genocide (however *divinely* established) must always have been judged immoral by human sensibility. To take another example, slavery, a repulsive practice, and an idea antithetical to democracy and other political and social systems that value human rights, has traditionally been considered "moral"—condoned by the gods and practiced by the pious.[6] But while slavery has been considered moral, even divinely mandated, other rather innocuous practices (e.g., performance of religious rituals by non-Israelites) were considered "immoral"—heinous acts involving "harlotry"—acts that Yahweh condemned passionately and punished ruthlessly. To claim that religion and morality have always constituted an inseparable pair, that religious behavior must be moral behavior, or that behavior by the non-religious must be immoral manifests a profound ignorance or misinterpretation of the facts.

The changeless, inerrant Book will continue to offer the image of the wrathful warrior God alongside the New Testament's masochistic victim God as models for twenty-first century humans; it will continue to present a world divided—friend and foe, chosen and excluded, saved and damned; it will still speak of rewards for divinely sanctioned behavior and the harshest of punishments for disbelief. It will still contain such pearls of wisdom as, "Spare the rod, and spoil the child," and the command to kill a disrespectful son. Is child abuse moral? Is filicide? Were such behaviors ever moral in any reasonable sense? The mirror of heaven can only reflect the "morality" of those who project their images onto its surface. When morality is "frozen" in textual form representing a particular culture and time, when, moreover, the "inerrant" text carries divine Authority, the way is clear for an archaic, brutal "morality" to remain, as it were, "on the books."[7] And so religious spokespersons today can cite the ancient laws and justify the killing of "infidels," the beating of children, the persecution of homosexuals, and the stoning of women. In this sense only, religion and morality have "always gone hand in hand."

Doom Eagerness

Apocalypse [Revelation] is not a book of catastrophes, but rather a book of hope.

Alessio Geretti[8]

Why does any of this matter? Why not leave the heavenly figures to their ongoing performance of the tragi-comedy composed for them? Why—even if it were possible—cleanse the heavens of us and our images? Even with monsters in the heavens and their servants on earth, the world would probably tumble on, however violent and riddled with hate and anxiety. Probably. But one reason to be concerned is the fact that many of us, whose images litter the heavens and whose "plot" plods relentlessly toward its inscribed ending, continue to act to bring that ending about. Joseph Campbell has described the danger implicit in the master plot now in progress:

> In the old Near East, where in Sargon's time the idea appears to have been implemented of politically exploitive wars of territorial conquest,

contending armies of the only three monotheistic monads of the planet . . . in this delicate moment of imminent global unification . . . are threatening the whole process of global unification with the adventure of their scripturally prophesied Armageddon.

The Inner Reaches of Outer Space 22

Having created the means for destroying earth's inhabitants and their civilizations, we face the fact that the plot progresses, supposedly written by the divine Author, but hastened by believers whose heavenly monsters approve its End Times devastation. A popular sentiment among the faithful seems to be that the sooner *we* blow up the earth, the sooner *they* (the faithful) will be singing hymns in heaven or enjoying the Gardens of Paradise, while the evil others roast in the eternal fires of hell.

While End Times speculation has been in vogue since the early years of the Common Era, in 1970 Hal Lindsey began what would be a trend in best-selling Doomsday literature with his book, *The Late, Great Planet Earth*, in which he "explained" the "relationship" between biblical prophecy and current events. While his End Times prophecies[9] were happily mistaken (as had been all earlier predictions, including those of Jesus), still people were eager to read the "signs" of immanent disaster, and by 1990 some twenty-eight million copies of the book had sold.[10] Even more popular are the currently best-selling novels in the *Left Behind* series by Tim LaHaye and Jerry B. Jenkins. My copy of the first of these bears the legend, "Over 65,000,000 Sold in Series."

For the past century and a half, many of the faithful have vested their hope of heaven in an interpretation of End Times that includes a phenomenon known as the Rapture. Briefly put, Rapture is the notion that Jesus will whisk away those intended for salvation and take them to heaven, leaving the rest of humanity to End Times "tribulation."[11] Apparently an eternity of suffering in hell is insufficient. There must be a period of fear, anguish, and universal devastation for unbelievers. Just how this whisking away of the faithful is to be accomplished is usually (and wisely) left unspecified, but the intrepid LaHaye and Jenkins offer details. *Left Behind* opens in a commercial aircraft just after the Rapture has occurred. (Neither the pilot nor the copilot is among the saved, and so the plane does not crash.) A panicky flight attendant informs the Pilot, "People are missing. . . . A whole bunch of people, just gone!" The pilot believes that they must be hiding or playing a joke. The flight attendant points out that the missing passengers have left stark naked: "Their shoes, their socks, their clothes, everything was left behind" (16). In the case of Harold, one of lucky raptured passengers, his "clothes were in a neat pile on his seat, his glasses and hearing aid on top. The pant legs still hung over the edge and led to his shoes and socks" (22). I suppose readers are fortunate that Harold had no glass eye, pacemaker, false teeth, wig, steel plates and screws, or prosthetic limbs. The pile might not have appeared so neat. And when did Harold disrobe? Why? Or did someone or something else simply strip him naked willy-nilly? And what about Jesus, the savior? What was his role in the stripping and whisking? The novel is silent on these matters. It seems there are places even the apocalyptic imagination cannot go.

As is no doubt obvious, I find the idea of the Rapture ludicrous, even without all that naked streaking through the skies. One would think that only in bizarre circumstances could people take the possibility of such an occurrence seriously or find its perpetrator worthy of worship. I try to imagine droves of naked, disoriented, half-blind people ascending like rockets, joyously leaving behind their lives, loves, families, and work, along with their hearing aids and dentures. I do not think that the authors of *Left Behind* intended their post-Rapture scene to be amusing or satiric—another cause for concern.

BIBLICAL LAUGHTER

He that sitteth in the heavens shall laugh; the Lord shall have them in derision.

Psalm 2:4

If humans are primarily distinguished from other creatures by their ability to speak, write and use symbols and figures, perhaps a second defining feature is their sense of humor and their laughter. Yet oddly there is no humor, no joyous laughter echoing from the heavens, and no image in that mirror of God as a merry old soul. The Romans did imagine Jupiter as a kind of heavenly Old King Cole. In fact the word *jovial* derives from a form of his name, Jove: "Characterized by hearty mirth, humour, or good fellowship; merry, jolly; convivial" (*OED*). One looks in vain for friendly laughter or humor in most mythologies or in God's Book and its Author. Of the thirty-eight occurrences of *laugh* in the King James Bible, twenty-two describe scornful or derisive laughter. In Proverbs, for instance, Wisdom (a primordial emanation of God) tells the fools who reject her counsel, "I also will laugh at your calamity; I will mock when panic strikes you . . . when distress and anguish come upon you" (1:26–27). One hears a sort of divine version of the playground "na, na, na, na!" chanted appropriately with rising and falling intonation. What sort of divine "Wisdom" could take delight or satisfaction in extreme human suffering, however self-inflicted?

Or consider the case of Sarah—the ninety-year-old woman who overhears Yahweh tell her husband that she will have a child in the spring. Sarah is sensibly incredulous, thinking perhaps that this is a divine jest: "So Sarah laughed to herself." One might expect a wise, benevolent deity to laugh with her, but Yahweh is offended, hearing in her laughter a question as to his power: "Why did Sarah laugh . . . ? Is anything too hard for the Lord?" Sarah, frightened by God's reaction, denies laughing, but God accuses, "No, but you did laugh" (Genesis 18:10–15).

Most commonly biblical laughter is demeaning: Job decries the fact that he is "mocked of his neighbor," one who "calleth upon God, and he answereth him: the just upright man is laughed to scorn" (Job 12:4). God's laughter, too, is triumphant and scornful: "But thou, O Lord, dost laugh at them; / thou dost hold all the nations in derision" (Psalm 59:8).

CELESTIAL CHARACTERS IN SEARCH OF AN AUTHOR

In the name of religion we perpetuate the "moral values" of a brutal, misogynistic, and naïve society because its laws are "carved in stone" by the divine hand—or so the story goes. As those figures and images in the mirror of heaven continue to exert their influence, we goose-step to the rhythms of a war god's music, possibly toward an apocalyptic end of everything.

While I doubt that it is possible, it would be interesting to wipe the mirror clean of us and our images; to start anew. Even so, the mirror would probably not stay clean, nor would we find that we had no need of a peopled sky. The old motives for creating the images would not evaporate from the human scene. We have lived too long with the "truth" that we are despicable sinners unworthy of divine approval; with the truth, too, that some of us, by the "grace of God," will live happily ever after—if we just believe, follow the rules, or such of them as we are familiar with. The question is, would the old images return, the old contentious, self-righteous, suspicious, ethnocentric, proud, jealous, wrathful, murderous, humorless characters of other times and places, or might we find there other sorts of celestial figures in search of modern authors?

NOTES

PREFACE

1. Sumerians no doubt inherited a version of their tale from earlier, preliterate societies.

INTRODUCTION

1. Unless otherwise noted, quotations from the Bible and Apocrypha are from *The Oxford Annotated Bible with the Apocrypha*, Revised Standard Version.
2. I have included quotation marks for these first mentions of *reality* to indicate my skepticism—not about the real, but about human access to it. Henceforth I omit the visible quotation marks and merely suggest here their ghostly hovering.
3. Farhad Khosrokhavar speaks of the mindset that produces an eagerness for doom as "mortiferous religiosity," a "phase . . . often reached in radical forms of religiosity"; further, "practically no religion is immune to it" (59).
4. *Logocentrism*, a term from Deconstruction, refers to a Platonic tradition in Western theology and philosophy in which mental/verbal constructs (for example, the duality of body and soul or holy and unholy) are afforded the status of "truth." "Greek questions" are those that interrogate the presumption of truth in such constructs.
5. See Frederic Jameson's *The Prison-House of Language*. Lacan suggests a similar sense when he argues that an individual's entry into language makes each one a "slave of language," a participant in a discourse "in the universal movement in which his place is already inscribed at birth" (*Écrits* 148).
6. Historiographer Hayden White also speaks of ways in which narrative "creates reality" (*The Content of the Form* 1–25 and *Tropics of Discourse* 121–34).
7. When such accounts arise from the sciences or social sciences, they are called grand *theories*—for example, Darwinian evolution, Einsteinian unified field theory, or intelligent design. A Postmodern tendency is to call such accounts "grand narratives,"—that is, stories, not theories. See Prickett (Chapter 1, 14–53) and Rée for astute discussions.
8. Quotations from the Qur'an are from M. A. S. Abdel Haleem's translation, Oxford University Press, 2004.
9. Scientific models are figures—forms of analogy, for example, the "Bohr model" of atomic structure.
10. The classical designation of metaphor as "an implied comparison between two things of unlike nature that yet have something in common" (Corbett 479) will not serve well in thinking about the figuratively metaphysical, for it implies, first, "two [existent] things," whereas in the situation at hand, the metaphor may be said actually to create

one of the "things." Second, the definition implies a preexistent similarity between the two "things," whereas the metaphor actually creates a similarity between the known ("man of war") and a "thing" of which no one has or can have knowledge.

11. I. A. Richards, "The Philosophy of Rhetoric," Max Black, "Metaphor," and Mark Johnson, "Metaphor in the Philosophical Tradition," discuss the interactive theory of metaphor.
12. In Book 10 of *The Republic*, Plato posits a divine maker who produces a perfect idea (e.g., of a bed); the human maker merely "imitates" that ideal bed in the material bed; the artist, in images, or the poet, in words, still further removed, imitates the material representation of the perfect bed in the mind of the Creator.
13. Elsewhere I have called *nothing* the ultimate linguistic form of the metaphysical—naming a concept that stands in opposition to all "thingness" (*Wordsworth's Biblical Ghosts* 26). *Creatio ex nihilo* implies the infinite potential of this No-thing.
14. From John Vignaux Smyth, *Maxims* (Athenopolis Press, forthcoming 2012).
15. Burke's analysis of the "principle of the negative" makes it central to language use in general (the word is not the thing), to forms of irony, and to figurative language of whatever sort. "The negative is a peculiarly linguistic marvel" (18–19). This marvel is manifested in theology as the Negative Way (apophasis).
16. Burke notices that in the fourth paragraph of his *Confessions*, St. Augustine addresses God in ten superlatives, "highest, best, most powerful," etcetera, and then resorts to "epithets typical of negative theology," "incomprehensible," "immutable" (52).
17. Corbett says that, historically, the rhetorical term *catachresis* implied a "wrenching of words" and might be applied to the use of "mixed metaphors" (480). Since Freud, the term has taken on a special significance in analyses of religious language.
18. I take "praxis of the 'para'" to suggest the rhetorical practice at the boundary or limit of language by which words are nudged into an infinitesimally narrow borderland between meaning and absurdity.
19. Critics often claim that it is impossible to analyze metaphor without resort to metaphor; in a similar way, they resort to parapraxical writing to explain parapraxis.
20. I use the term "Old Testament" throughout, while recognizing that it is a Christian revision and reorganization of the Hebrew Bible. See Bloom, "Before Moses Was, I Am" 291.
21. The imposition of grammatical gender on an understanding of the Unknown is carried to extremes in the earliest written accounts of the gods. Sumerian narrators use two dialects—the main dialect and a second called *Emesal*, used exclusively for "rendering the direct speech of a *female*, not male, deity" (Kramer, *Sumerian Mythology* 31).
22. Texts concerning this first creation are found in Proverbs 8:22–31 and John 1:1–18. Patai discusses the evolution of Wisdom from Hokhma to Shekhina (*The Hebrew Goddess* 96–111).
23. Owen Barfield explains that in Indo-European languages the same words were used for sky and "Supreme Being, the Father of all the other gods—Sanskrit 'Dyaus pitar', Greek 'Zeus pater', Illyrian 'Deipaturos', Latin 'Juppiter'." In English the word *heaven* is "still used for a similar double purpose, and . . . it was once not a double purpose at all" (84–85).

CHAPTER 1

1. This is time measured by clocks and calendars. The calendar may say that this is the year 2011 or 5771, designations which have no relationship to cosmological time/process.

2. "Time shelter" is a term Wood uses in his analysis of Paul Ricoeur's *Time and Narrative*, an attempt "to test a hypothesis—that the resources of narrative remedy a fatal deficiency in any purely phenomenological approach to time" (1). The phrase "imposition of a plot on time" is Kermode's, describing world history as a "substitute for myth" (*The Sense of an Ending* 43).
3. Quotations are taken from the introduction to Kramer's *History Begins at Sumer* (xxi), and the first sentences of the Books of Job and Ruth.
4. Time as both creator and destroyer is found in Zurvanism, a form of Zoroastrianism, where the primordial divine being is Time who fathers twin sons—two eternal principles of the universe, Creator and Destroyer. Chronos in Orphism is a similar primordial being.
5. Kermode comments, "Broadly speaking, apocalyptic thought belongs to rectilinear rather than cyclical views of the world, though this is not a sharp distinction . . . " (*The Sense of an Ending* 5).
6. Sigmund Freud, and his successors (e.g., Jacques Lacan) make much of the notion of "penis envy." They do not notice that the world's myths are essentially silent on the subject, while speaking often and clearly about something one might call "womb envy."
7. Traditionally the waters of the deep (*Tehōm*) were envisioned as a serpentine beast and opponent of God, a descendent of Tiamat, and referred to in the Bible variously as Rahab and Leviathan (cf. Psalm 89:9–10; Psalm 77:16–20; Job 7:12). I shall return to this opposition in Chapter 3.
8. Burke analyzes the terms Being and Non-Being in regard to the Heideggerian idea of Nothing: "When you have arrived at a term as highly generalized as 'Being,' there is one notable dialectical 'advance' still available. You can add the negative, and thereby arrive at 'Non-Being' . . . which can be treated as the contextual ground of your highly generalized term, 'Being.' For such an absolute opposite is all that's left. Whether or not it actually refers to anything, it is a 'reasonable' operation linguistically" (21).
9. Philo, first-century Jewish philosopher and theologian, interpreted God's work as explicitly procreative, the things to which he gives birth fathered upon an internal mother: "The Architect who made this universe was at the same time the father of what was thus born, whilst its mother was the Knowledge possessed by its Maker. With his Knowledge God had union . . . and begat created things" (quoted in Patai, *The Hebrew Goddess* 77).
10. Hesiod's negative reinterpretation of her name "giver of all gifts" (long an epithet for the ancient earth goddess) provides an example of what Campbell calls "mythological defamation," a device in "constant use . . . by Western theologians" (*Occidental Mythology* 80).
11. That Hesiod's vision was socially legitimate and constructive of realities that endure is evident in works by the Greek tragedians and philosophers. Toward the end of Aeschylus' *Oresteia*, the argument that sways judgment in Orestes' favor (he was right to kill his mother to avenge his father) is that the woman is merely a field (like the Earth, matter) in which the male seed is planted; her blood does not run in his veins (*Eumenides*). In Euripides' *Medea*, Jason rages at fate and laments that men cannot produce heirs without women, "for there would have been no race of women then" (41). Like Hesiod, Euripides speaks of women as a distinct breed or species. Aristotle went so far as to assert that a girl child is not only "a mutilated male" (lacking a penis), but that she lacks "the principle of soul," thus identifying penis with soul (*De Generatione Animalium*, II, 3 (737a, 26–31).

12. The so-called J writer's account in Chapter 2 is some three to four hundred years older than the Priestly writer's in Chapter 1.
13. Harold Bloom has commented on the incongruity of this situation in which God—great, universal maker of heaven and earth—gives mouth-to-mouth resuscitation to a little, lifeless, clay form (*Ruin the Sacred Truths* 6–11).

CHAPTER 2

1. William Dever identifies difficulties in treating the Bible as "a single story with a structured plot and believable characters" (1–2)—the many "books" by many authors, its thousand-year period of composition, to name just two. Nevertheless, processes of redaction, editing, and canon formation, combined with intertextual allusions by later authors to earlier texts and the fiction of presenting a narrative of events from "beginning" to "end"—all such factors, while complicating meaning and creating critical puzzles—have lent to untold readers a sense of consistency and congruence.
2. Indo-European notions of fate or necessity (personified as three powerful female divinities) are similar. The Greek Morai, the Latin Parcae, and the Norse Norns were said to determine the course of events for individuals, the people as a whole, and even gods.
3. Old Testament texts are nearly silent on the matter of an otherworldly abode in eternity. In later texts the authors look forward to the end of an age, the restoration of the temple, and the return of God to the people (e.g., Ezekiel 43:1–4). The Lord promises to dwell in the renewed *earthly* city of Jerusalem in the midst of his people "for ever" (Ezekiel 43:7); the river of life will flow from the throne of God (Ezekiel 47:1–12). It is the *chosen people* who will endure forever, not individuals.
4. As Kaufmann Kohler has it, "The belief that the soul continues its existence after the dissolution of the body is a matter of philosophical or theological speculation rather than of simple faith, and is accordingly nowhere expressly taught in Holy Scripture" (1).
5. I do not wish to imply that the testaments, taken together, or either testament by itself, presents, in William Dever's definition of theology, "a unified body of propositions about the nature of God [and] his revelation of himself" (19). That is simply not the case. Nevertheless, broad propositions concerning such subjects sharply differentiate the two testaments.
6. I concur with Vielhauer's assertion that the "essential feature of Apocalyptic is its dualism which, in various expressions, dominates its thought-world" (588).
7. A parallel might be drawn between this ancient literary fashion and Greek tragedy, Elizabethan sonnets, or the recent proliferation of "near-death" and "alien-abduction" narratives. Vielhauer points to the traditional character of apocalyptic imagery, and remarks that apocalyptic is "book-wisdom," a "literature" and, "in fact a collected literature." Goldsmith distinguishes between prophetic and apocalyptic, making the case that prophecy is essentially an oral form; apocalypse is a written genre (Chapter 1).
8. As Vielhauer explains, the apocalyptist generally borrows his authority from the great figures of the past by writing under an assumed name, for example, Enoch and Solomon. A "fictitious antiquity" may also attach to the text (Vielhauer 583).
9. The book of Enoch (1 Enoch) shares many features with the roughly contemporaneous book of Daniel (Barnstone 485).
10. The phrase occurs in Ezekiel's description of Yahweh's chariot-throne (1:24), and again in Revelation in reference to the voice of God (1:15; 14:2).

11. This notion of transformation of the "human" at the end of This Age is echoed more explicitly in St. Paul's claim that "flesh and blood" does not inherit the kingdom of God: "We shall not all sleep, but we shall all be changed, in a moment in the twinkling of an eye" (1 Corinthians 15:50–52). The nature of the transformation is from the physical "man of dust" to the "spiritual body" (1 Corinthians 15:44, 47), from the human to something other than human.
12. Babylon has rich figurative associations, therefore, not merely with the city of the Israelites' captivity, but with the old, corrupt world of This Age (Goldsmith 63).
13. There is a long tradition of similar tales of a divine being's treading or wading in human blood in a furious move to destroy humanity (Kramer, *Mythologies of the Ancient World* 197–99).

CHAPTER 3

1. Qur'an 17 is devoted to "The Night Journey"; see especially 1 and 60, and also 53:13–18. See Molloy 441.
2. Ezekiel's living creatures appear to be an elaboration of the image of the cherubim (Patai, *The Hebrew Goddess* 70), the figures that adorn the mercy seat (or throne), per God's instructions (Exodus 25:17–20; cf. Isaiah 6:1–2).
3. For a discussion of cherubim as God's mounts, see Patai, *The Hebrew Goddess* 72–75.
4. See, for example, Exodus 19:9.
5. The "rider-on-the-clouds" is a title given to Mesopotamian storm gods (Forsyth 48).
6. Patai observes that "Clouds—winds—Cherubim—horses and chariots, all these appear as interchangeable concepts in the imagery of the Bible in speaking of the vehicle or mount on which Yahweh appears" (*The Hebrew Goddess* 73).
7. The Destructive, the Pitiless, the Trampler, and the Flier—"sharp of tooth, bearing poison" (Heidel 38–39). The creatures that draw Marduk's chariot may well be precursors of the biblical "living creatures" of the Merkabah.
8. Canaanites depicted the god Baal in the form of a bull. Zeus takes the form of a bull when he carries off Europa; Pasiphae conceives the Minotaur (man-bull) by mating with the bull form of Poseidon. Couchant bulls held the temple laver at Jerusalem; golden calves adorned Yahweh's sanctuaries at Dan and Bethel. In the notorious incident in Exodus, Yahweh is depicted as a golden calf.
9. The persistence and antiquity of this figure—the mother-bride of the dead and resurrected god—are apparent in the fact that her earliest known representations now date to about 5500 BCE (Campbell, *Occidental Mythology* 43). And see the whole of Chapter 2, "The Consort of the Bull" 42–93.
10. Such behavior does not seem especially wicked; God understands, however, that it is intended to provoke him.
11. Barfield comments, "[O]ne of the most remarkable characteristics in which Aryans [Indo-Europeans] differed from the races they supplanted was their patriarchal system" (94). The same claim may be made for the Semitic invaders into Sumer and their difference from the "races they supplanted."
12. The "heroic" ages in Greece, India, and northern Europe are characterized by (1) "a period of national migrations," and (2) contact between people operating on a "relatively primitive and tribal level" and "a civilized power in the process of disintegration." A parallel pattern occurred in Sumer (Kramer, *History Begins at Sumer* 235–36).

13. People still tell the story of the God who urges his followers to engage in "holy wars." In 2005, President Bush claimed that God instructed him to invade Iraq as part of a divine plan, and in 2008, vice-presidential candidate Sarah Palin, told a group at the Wasilla Assembly of God Church that the war in Iraq is a "task . . . from God"; "there is a plan and that plan is God's will."
14. Similarly, in the Qur'an, Allah remarks that people in Noah's time called his servant mad, and that as a result he "opened the gates of the sky with torrential water . . . " (54:9–11).
15. Aslan has pointed out that the "idea of killing nonbelievers who refused to convert to Islam" became "the foundation of the classical doctrine of Jihad ['just' or 'holy' war]" (85).
16. Just as Moses received the law or "commandments" on Mt. Sinai, so Muhammad receives instruction—laws—for appropriate behavior. "Thou shalt not kill" of the Decalogue is echoed in Sura 17: "And slay not the soul that God has forbidden you, except for just cause" (35).

CHAPTER 4

1. Cf. the Egyptian god Ra's self-insemination (Chapter 1).
2. The belief that the prosperity of a kingdom depended upon the virility of the king is ancient and ubiquitous. One finds statements of the idea in Indo-European, Semitic, and pre-Semitic mythologies. Perhaps its most elaborate development occurs in the Christianized Arthurian legends of the Fisher King (see Weston, *From Ritual to Romance*).
3. Given the "economic, political, strategic, [and] sentimental" value placed on "fruitfulness and multiplication," the commandment was also an often-repeated blessing to God's chosen (Patai, *Sex and the Family* 71–74).
4. Patai observes that "the sin of idolatry was . . . almost indistinguishable in Biblical mentality and phraseology from the sin of adultery. Both resulted in the same punishment: barrenness among the humans and the disruption of the normal course of nature. . . ." (*Sex and the Family* 85).
5. Baal was frequently depicted as a bull, the ultimate image of male virility, and Yahweh as a bull or bull calf (Exodus 32; 1 Kings 25–29; cf. Hosea 8:5). Although the second commandment, requiring imageless worship, rejects such representations for Yahweh, it is clear that he was nevertheless so conceived and represented (Patai, *The Hebrew Goddess* 45).
6. "The sons/children of God are found as well in Phoenician and Ammonite inscriptions, referring to the pantheon of subordinate deities, indicating that the term was widespread in the West Semitic religions (Metzger and Coogan 713).
7. It is difficult to reconcile this message with the fact that it is addressed to the "*sons* of God."
8. Ancient law would have denied Israel/Gomer the opportunity to return to her first husband; the Qur'an has a similar, more complex, prohibition (Patai, *Sex and the Family* 114, 116; Deuteronomy 24:1–4; Qur'an 2:229–31). But see Jeremiah 3:1.
9. Even at Yahweh's Shiloh sanctuary, sacred prostitutes were in evidence. The priest Eli castigates his sons (also priests of Yahweh), who have been lying "with the women who served at the entrance to the tent of meeting" (1 Samuel 2:22).
10. Despite the importance of the sexual aspect of life in biblical thought, "practically no sexual terminology proper is found in the Bible." Rather, "reference to sexual activities and sexual organs is always couched in euphemistic terms." One of the more

resonating of such euphemisms is the verb "to know" for sexual intercourse (Patai, *Sex and the Family* 157–58).
11. A measure of the metaphor's influence may be seen in the fact that Ezekiel uses the words *whoredom* and *harlot* thirty-three times to refer to Jerusalem.
12. According to tradition, Abraham was an Amorite, and Bathsheba, mother of Solomon, was a Hittite, hence Jerusalem's Hittite-Amorite lineage.
13. See Patai, *Sex and the Family*, for a discussion of a man's gesture of spreading his cloak or skirt over a woman (92–98).
14. Details of the bloody business of capturing, killing, and skinning animals are happily omitted, as are those of tanning, cutting and stitching.
15. The passage proceeds to list fourteen sorts of "near of kin" with whom sexual relations are forbidden. A curious omission from the list is a man's daughter. The passage implies that Canaanites and Egyptians (the evil others) are wildly and indiscriminately sexual, suffering no restrictions as to choice of partner. Speaking generally of the sexual regulations of Middle Eastern cultures, Patai remarks, "Perhaps no other field of human life is so heavily surcharged with such rules, both positive and negative, as the sexual one" (*Sex and the Family* 158).
16. A similar tale of seduction and incest concerns Lot and his daughters (Genesis 19).
17. Details of these stories repeat motifs, including that of virgin birth, whose nature Rank interprets as reflecting characteristic psychic processes (9). See also Raglan, "The Hero of Tradition," and Campbell, *The Hero with a Thousand Faces*.
18. As the cases of Semele and Mary illustrate, however, the pregnant virgin might well come under suspicion.
19. According to this doctrine, Mary "was preserved exempt from all stain of original sin at the first moment of her animation, and sanctifying grace was given to her before sin could have taken effect in her soul." As a result, "every stain and fault, all depraved emotions, passions, and debilities, essentially pertaining to original sin, were excluded" (Holweck 1).
20. Watchers/Nephilim, "Watchers in Jewish Midrash," http://www.deliriumsrealm.com/delirium/articleview.asp?Post=186, accessed August 23, 2010.
21. The concept of immortality through one's descendants is behind the levirate, a law by which the brother of a man who dies childless is obligated to marry his widow, "and the first son whom she bears shall succeed to the name of his brother who is dead, that his name may not be blotted out of Israel" (Deuteronomy 25:5–6).
22. A sort of New Testament Tamar, the woman appears to be a "beneficiary" of the levirate.
23. This idea was also the basis for God's berating of the "Watchers" who fathered children with the "daughters of men" (Genesis 6:1–4). Because they [humans] perish I gave them wives so they might impregnate them, have children. . . . " (2 Enoch, Barnstone 187).
24. Compare this parable with that in Luke 22, placed in the setting of heavenly feast hall, where entry to the hall is predicated on one's hating father, mother, wife, children, brothers, sisters, and self (Luke 14:25–27). Luke has Jesus repeat a similar idea when he tells the disciples about the necessity of severing all familial relationships in the cause of achieving eternal life (18:29–33).
25. How different the world might have been if instead of the Whore of Babylon, the metaphor for sin had been the War Monger or Child Abuser of Babylon.
26. The jinn, masculine sexual beings with free will, will be judged with mankind at the end of days (Qur'an 55).

NOTES

27. The so-called Satanic Verses imply that Allah fathered three of the lesser goddesses of neighboring tribes and, further, that Muhammed recognized their divinity. The day after he had read the offensive verses, Mohammed repudiated them and explained that Satan had "put the blasphemous words in his mouth." The passage was recited again, to read, "Have ye considered Allat and Al 'Huzza and Manat the other third? Shall there be male offspring for Him and female for you? That, then, were an unfair division! They are but names which ye have named . . . ." (Palmer xxvii). Aslan describes the roles of these lesser deities in pre-Islamic Arabia (6–7). The Qur'an makes a clear distinction between "fathering" and "creating."
28. The Islamic Houris do not achieve citizenship in the Gardens. They are "mere appurtenances meant to serve the pleasure of the men who feared God in their lives . . . simply part of that idealized physical environment" (Patai, *The Hebrew Goddess*, 203). Patai would make more room for the feminine in the Christian heaven, but clearly it is a scene dominated by the masculine. The "females" are little more than sexual stereotypes—feminine *figures* rather than women: the pregnant "woman clothed with the sun," the Whore of Babylon, and the virginal bride of the Lamb. The 144,000 "redeemed from the earth" are specifically those "who have not defiled themselves with women" (Revelation 14:3–4; emphasis supplied).

CHAPTER 5

1. Freud remarked, "The task before each new human being is to master the Oedipus complex; one who cannot do this falls into a neurosis" (Freud 585).
2. The epigraph from *The Táin* exemplifies the "Laius Attitude" and the father's murderous intentions. The son in the quotation is Connla, illegitimate son of the semidivine Irish hero, Cuchulainn, fathered merely to be killed. Cuchulainn remarks, "[T]he blood of Connla's / body will flush my skin with power" (43–44). One might also identify the "Polybus heroism," characteristic of Oedipus' foster father, a man who lovingly receives the infant Oedipus as a gift. Freud likewise gives scant notice to the relationships of other Greek fathers and sons, for example, the hero worship of Orestes for Agamemnon, or of Telemachos for Odysseus.
3. The Aztecs refrained from totally annihilating neighboring peoples so as to have a continuing supply of prisoners to appease the insatiable goddess Tlateutli's craving for human hearts (Campbell, *The Sacrifice* 37). "Scapegoat" phenomena in general, including sacrifice, Girard asserts, are "the very basis of cultural unification, the source of all rituals and religion" (*Violence and the Sacred* 302). In the story of the Exodus, Yahweh exacted from the Egyptians an enormous sacrifice of first-born children and animals, thus claiming an ironic sacrifice to the Israelites' God (Exodus 11:4–7). The biblical rules of holy war (Deuteronomy 7:1–6) place enemy peoples "under ban," requiring the slaughter of man, woman, child, and beast, consecrating the enemy to the Israelites' God (Stephen L. Harris 152).
4. Exposure was a way of eliminating unwanted children without suffering the miasma associated with homicide.
5. From this injury Oedipus, "swell foot," received his name, with suggestively Freudian implications.
6. The Latin phrase means, "You give so that I must give." As explained in an earlier chapter, the Babylonian creation narrative states that the sole purpose for which humans were created was to serve the gods—till their fields, reap their harvests, and offer their food sacrifices; Adam's purpose was to tend Yahweh's garden.

7. David and his men were on one occasion given the "shewbread," which had been placed before Yahweh and then removed: "So the priest gave him hallowed bread: for there was no bread there but the shewbread, that was taken from before the Lord, to put hot bread in the day when it was taken away" (1 Samuel 21:5–7).

8. Bloom notices the weirdness of this picnic on the ground, during which the Incomprehensible washed his feet and consumed "roast calf, curd, milk and bread" (*Ruin the Sacred Truths* 6).

9. In the *Homeric Hymn to Hermes*, Hermes participates in a ritual sacrifice with Hephaistos. Like Yahweh and the Babylonian gods, he is drawn by the savor of the burning sacrifice: "Then glorious Hermes longed for the sacrificial meat, for the sweet savour wearied him, god though he was" From http://ancienthistory.about.com/library/bl/bl_text_homerhymn_hermes.htm, accessed August 24, 2010.

10. See, for example, Jill Robbins' analysis of the tale and her brief survey of approaches ("Sacrifice"). She remarks that the "proportion of commentary that this text has received is staggering in relation to its nineteen verses" (291).

11. See Auerbach's perceptive analysis of the unsaid in the narrative. He observes, for example, that only "the decisive points of the narrative ... are emphasized, what lies between is nonexistent ...." He enumerates these lacunae: "[T]ime and place are undefined ...; thoughts and feeling remain unexpressed, are only suggested by the silence and the fragmentary speeches; the whole, permeated with the most unrelieved suspense and directed toward a single goal .... remains mysterious and 'fraught with background'" ("The Sacrifice of Isaac" 14–15).

12. Kierkegaard is among those who consider God omniscient: "God sees in secret and knows the distress and counts the tears and forgets nothing" (*Fear and Trembling* 88).

13. The Yahwist, not the Elohist, tells the tale of Sodom's destruction. Abraham seems two different characters as depicted by the two narrators.

14. The question of duty to authority was raised, too, at the Nuremberg trials.

15. The Norse high god Odin sacrificed himself on the world tree Yggdrasil in order to learn the wisdom of the runes: "I hung on that windswept tree, hung there for nine long nights; ... I was an offering to Odin, myself to myself" (Crossley-Holland 15).

16. Long before Jesus, Greek philosopher Xenophanes (570–478 BCE) observed that the principle of divine immortality presents a conundrum for those who worship gods who die and are resurrected: "If you think he's a god, you shouldn't mourn him; if you think he died, you shouldn't worship him" (cited in Brennan 1).

17. Modern scholarship has uncovered what appears a sacred pathology in practices of various religions and what William R. LaFleur discusses as a power struggle at the very "*center* of religious traditions, not merely in some later corruption or deformation." In the case of the "sacrifice" (of Jesus), he calls attention to recent exegetical studies that "analyze the anatomical details of the crucifixion, dismemberment, and resurrection of Jesus to suggest the extent of the New Testament's dependence upon themes of submission, torture, penetration, and erection—often with only lightly disguised sexual referents" (46).

18. For instance, as its books are arranged, the New Testament begins with Matthew's genealogy of Jesus, tracing his descent from Abraham through David to Joseph in forty-two generations, although, of course, Joseph's relationship to Jesus is said to be that of stepfather. In a sense, the invocation of Old Testament narratives and events serves to "legitimize" Jesus' place in a divinely ordained history of the world. (In a similar way, Muhammad takes his place in world history through the selective appropriation of biblical history.)

19. I take the ambiguous title of this section from Jan Kott's book, *The Eating of the Gods*.
20. A centuries-old debate among Christian sects concerns whether the ritual consists of the *literal* transformation (transubstantiation) of the "substance" (not the appearance) of the sacramental bread and wine into the flesh and blood of Christ. As so often in his *Devil's Dictionary*, Ambrose Bierce's definition of *Eucharist* is curiously on point: "A sacred feast of the religious sect of Theophagi [god-eaters]. A dispute once unhappily arose among the members of this sect as to what it was that they ate. In this controversy some five hundred thousand have already been slain, and the question is still unsettled."

CHAPTER 6

1. The major difficulty in defining *death* arises with the introduction of "immortality": if all souls are eternal, what does it mean to die? For the most part, the difficulty does not arise in ancient Sumerian, Babylonian, Greek, and Hebrew texts,
2. Given the identification of Yahweh and Allah, a side issue in the language use of the God concerns the radically different speaking/writing styles and forms of self-presentation and self-contradiction in the Old Testament, the New Testament, and the Qur'an. (See "Stylistic Features," Qur'an xix–xxi.)
3. Jerry Falwell spoke for a multitude of twenty-first century advocates of this view: "The Bible is the inerrant . . . word of the living God. It is absolutely infallible, without error in all matters pertaining to faith and practice, as well as in areas such as geography, science, history, etcetera" (Mark Morford, "The Sad, Quotable Jerry Falwell," *San Francisco Chronicle*, May 18, 2007.)
4. Of this sort of linguistic invention, Umberto Eco remarks, "It is evident that we use linguistic expressions or other semiotic means to name 'things' first met by our ancestors; but it is also evident that we frequently use linguistic expressions to describe and to *call into life 'things' that will exist only after and because of the utterance of our expressions*" (*Semiotics* 76; emphasis supplied).
5. From the Code of Lipit-Ishtar (http://staffwww/fullcoll.edu/amande/sumerian.pdf, accessed September 2, 2010). Kramer dates the Lipit-Ishtar code, a Sumerian document, to approximately one hundred fifty years before Hammurabi. A Semitic code, the Bilalama code, precedes the Lipit-Ishtar code, and a Sumerian document, the Ur-Nammu code, is even earlier, dating to c. 2050 BCE, some three hundred years before Hammurabi (*History Begins at Sumer* 51–55).
6. The Code of Lipit-Ishtar (http://staffwww/fullcoll.edu/amande/sumerian.pdf).
7. Richard Hooker, ed., and L. W. King, tr., "The Code of Hammurabi," http://www.wsu.edu/~dee/MESO/CODE.HTM, accessed August 24, 2010.
8. Palmer notes that "[t]he relations of a murdered man are always allowed to choose the fine instead of the blood revenge" (Qur'an, n. 1, 6, 25). However, in modern Tehran (2008–2009), Ameneh Bahrami, blinded by acid, rejected monetary remuneration and demanded that the criminal defendant himself be blinded; the court has complied by issuing a verdict to that effect (the blinding of one eye), the punishment having been ruled legal under Islamic law.
9. Code of Ur-Nammu, http://en.wikipedia.org/wiki/Code_of_Ur-Nammu, accessed August 24, 2010.
10. The law endures in Muslim law. In 2009 a Saudi court sentenced a Lebanese man, Ali Hussain Sibat, to death for "sorcery." He had made predictions and offered advice on a Lebanese television network.

NOTES

11. The fact that the first four commandments are explicitly religious in nature raises the issue of separation of church and state. The principle of inherited guilt in the second commandment raises other issues.
12. Justifying God's response, the Midrash explain that the monoglots of Babel were proud, arrogant, and intent on wresting power from God; the biblical narrative says merely that they wanted to "connect"—with God, but also with each other ("lest we be scattered abroad").
13. As John puts it, "nothing unclean shall enter it, nor any one who practices abomination or falsehood, but only those who are written in the Lamb's book of life" (Revelation 21:27).

CHAPTER 7

1. In one version of Zoroastrian origins, Ahura Mazda produces twin brothers, one good and one evil, who exist as eternal foes. In Gathas (Y.30.3–4), Zarathustra (Zoroaster) describes his vision of the twins: "And when these two Spirits met, they established at the origin life and non-life . . . ."
2. The logocentric dualism questioned by deconstructionists.
3. A. Powell Davies attributes to Paul a world-changing role in his shaping of Christianity: "Nor is it likely that events would have turned out as they did if at this time [first century CE] there had not appeared on the scene the Greek-speaking Jew who would reshape the faith of the early believers into a gospel for the Gentiles—Paul, the first Christian" (118). Robert Wright argues that Paul used the "information technology" of his day (in the form of epistles) to forge the far-flung Christian community: "Paul wasn't satisfied to just have a congregation in Corinth; he wanted to set up franchises—congregations of Jesus followers—in cities across the Roman Empire" (41).
4. Problematic in two senses: (1) The apparent power of Satan, and (2) The prominence given to a universal battle between God/Jesus and Satan anticipated at End Times.
5. Aslan calls attention to a similarity of ideas current at the emergence of both Christianity and Islam. Having outlined the pre-Islamic Arabian religious experience, the author summarizes the era as one "in which Zoroastrianism, Christianity, and Judaism intermingled in one of the last remaining regions in the Near East still dominated by paganism" (13).
6. Cyrus, the Great, founded the period of Persian hegemony (the Archaemenid period). Isaiah calls Cyrus "anointed," a term earlier used for Israelite kings and later applied to Jesus—"Messiah." The anointed one, Cyrus, was led by Yahweh "to subdue nations before him," among them Babylon, and end the exile (Isaiah 45:1). At the same time, however, Babylon hailed Cyrus as the *anointed one of Marduk*, chosen to defeat the heretical Babylonian king Nabonidus (Stoyanov 49).
7. Nowhere is this Persian influence more evident than within the Qumran community, whose texts (The Dead Sea Scrolls, 200 BCE–70 CE) reveal a Jewish sect, similar to or identical with the Essenes. Self-isolated in the desert, its members anticipated End Times and prepared to participate in an eschatological battle against Yahweh's enemies, the sons of darkness.
8. Pythagoras and the Orphics coupled the belief in an immortal soul with a doctrine of reincarnation, in which the soul progresses through a series of "bodies"—human and animal—until it is freed from the material realm (35).
9. It is not clear the extent to which agricultural deities had continued to be worshiped in Greece. Hesiod's *Theogony* suggests the ongoing worship of Hekate, ancient Earth

Mother, who retains her "ancient rights" and enjoys power in heaven, earth, and sea (410–52).
10. Davies notices that the "close similarity between the mystery cults and Christianity was acutely embarrassing to the early church." As a result, the church fathers argued that Satan "had forseen what the Christian ritual would be and had caricatured it in advance" (124).
11. Stoyanov provides a concise account of the spread of Zoroastrianism through the originally Babylonian prophetic figures of the Magi and evolution of Zoroastrianism from its original account of the twin sons of Ahura Mazda as good and evil to a strict dualism which embodies the principles of good and evil (or creator and destroyer) in Ahura Mazda (Ohrmazd) and his coeternal opponent, Ahriman.
12. This idealist interpretation of the material realm is given concrete exposition in Plato's "Allegory of the Cave," Book 7, *The Republic*. There Plato explains that what we take to be reality is like "shadows thrown by fire-light" on the wall of a cave (228).
13. Platonic devaluation of the world, the body, and life, creates a divisive dualistic system in which one member of each pair is "privileged," and members of each pair are placed at strife. Friedrich Neitzsche and others, most influentially Jacques Derrida, attacked this tendency of Platonism and of the broader philosophical tradition of Western metaphysics, finding it a source of violence and injustice. Derrida's response was to deconstruct the hierarchies.
14. Stoyanov cites this verse from the "Call to Cyrus," a Zoroastrian, as "a probable reaction to the Zoroastrian type of ethical dualism of good and evil" (56–57).
15. In Catholicism, demonic possession, the most dramatic of Satan's behaviors, is said to occur at the direction of God, who uses Satan's evil for some "good purpose" (Baglio 58–59). Indeed, various schools of Christian theology hold (quite logically) that Satan and his deeds are subject at all times to God (as divine Author), and that he does not pose a genuine threat—an intellectual stance lost in New Testament narratives and overlooked in the popular understanding.
16. The identification of Satan with the talking serpent in Eden, the seduction of Eve, Adam's disobedience, and evil retroactively draws the battle lines and enables Jesus' heroism as the one who defeats Death.
17. Paternal favoritism and brother strife are repeating themes in the Bible—Cain and Abel, Ishmael and Isaac, Esau and Jacob, Joseph and his brothers, Absalom and Amnon. The theme appears in Egyptian religion as the opposition of Osiris and Seth.
18. Lactantius' claim has implications for understanding not only the beings called "Sons of God," but of the phrase, "only begotten Son."
19. The problem of evil in a system of belief that embraces cosmic monism results in some creative retelling. See Forsyth's discussion of Augustine on this topic, at the conclusion of which Forsyth remarks, "Thus doctrine, as the interpretation of narrative, becomes in turn a new narrative" (15)
20. Whereas Michael confronts Satan in a battle (Revelation), Jesus through his death and resurrection achieves a passive victory, merely revealing his opponent's impotence.
21. Such reassurance in both the mystery religions and early Christianity would come in part through the worshiper's sense that he or she had received special knowledge (*gnosis*) or revelation of "secret" information intended for the few (Matthew 11:27).
22. In the brief gospel of Mark, for example, there are some twenty accounts of possession and exorcism. "One of the chief tasks of Jesus, as Mark, Matthew, and Luke tell it, was the struggle against unclean spirits or evil demons" (Forsyth 285).

23. The recently discovered Gospel of Judas (third century CE) interprets Judas' role in the crucifixion drama as foreordained, and portrays Judas as Jesus' friend, who obeys Jesus' instructions in the "betrayal" (http://www.nationalgeographic.com/lostgospel/).
24. The oldest recorded tale of death's unbearable nature relates Gilgamesh's fear and revulsion as his friend Enkidu lies in a benighted sleep and his "heart does not beat." When after seven days "the worm" attacks the corpse, the grieving Gilgamesh sets out on a failed quest for "life." (Pritchard 61).
25. The blessed immortal is envisioned as male.

CHAPTER 8

1. I exclude from "empirical evidence" first- or third-person narratives of "visionary" journeys into the Otherworld, the Underworld, or Heaven, including those divine or semi-divine figures from earliest times, various Greek demigods, the warrior Er, Enoch, John of Patmos, Dante, Muhammad, and so on, a subject to which I return in Chapter 11.
2. Such arguments have not gone uncriticized. Sam Harris, for example, refers to Kierkegaard's and Pascal's arguments as "epistemological ponzi schemes" (63).
3. A crass recent reiteration of the economics of belief emphasizes its quid pro quo aspect: "God sent his only son to get the crap beaten out of him, die for our sins and rise from the dead. If you believe that, you're in. Your sins are washed away from you . . . because of the cross" (Ann Coulter, Human Events.com, 1/6/10, "If You Can Find a Better Deal, Take It!").
4. Circumcision as a mark of identity among the chosen is a form of body alteration that takes its place with other religious practices of "malleation," including fasting, flagellation, tattooing, and eunuchization. Both Jews and Muslims "put a rite of malleation, circumcision, at the center of their religious identities" (LaFleur 39).
5. Circumcision as the enigmatic sign of membership in the community of chosen in effect excludes women from the covenant. "The people" are the males, as is evident, for example, on Mt. Sinai when Moses addresses "the people" with the instruction, "Be ready by the third day; do not go near a woman" (Exodus 20:15).
6. Signs as words, marks, images, or wounds deceive those who approach them, seeming to offer meanings, to make sense of something, but as Roland Barthes thought, "Language in its sense-making function is a veil of Maya," a system "with little responsibility toward the real" (Blonsky xv).
7. Most cultures that practice the ritual circumcise males either at puberty, or at marriage, associating the rite with sexual maturity or sexual intercourse. Islam understands that Abraham circumcised himself at the age of 100 with an axe! And then Sarah conceived.
8. Given the notion of inward circumcision, Christianity seems to find the unseen wound on the first page a heart-wound, one that involves a mental or spiritual laceration.
9. A side issue, given the promise of happiness for the blessed, is the grim possibility of a sort of heavenly *Schadenfreude:* malicious joy experienced by the blessed on hearing (perhaps "spiritually") the anguished cries of the damned issuing from the fiery pit.
10. So persistent is the theme of belief in the New Testament that the word *believe* or one of its forms occurs 260 times; in the Qur'an, over 600 times. The exact numbers for "the few" who will be redeemed remains uncertain: Revelation records the number of redeemed as 144,000 (12,000 from each of the twelve tribes of Israel) plus a "great multitude" from among the non-Israelites (Revelation 7:4, 9); in one of the Hadith, Mohammad is quoted as saying, "Verily! 70,000 or 700,000 . . . of

my followers will enter Paradise altogether; so that the first and the last amongst them will enter at the same time" (Sahih Bukhari, Vol. 4, Bk. 54, No. 470). As of 2007, estimates placed the number of Christians in the world at 2.1 billion, and of Muslims, 1.5 billion, numbers which reduce the scriptural figures to *very* few.
11. Coleridge explained that his inclusion of supernatural elements in poems like *The Rime of the Ancient Mariner* required the reader's "willing suspension of disbelief . . . which constitutes poetic faith" (*The Major Works* 314). It is interesting that Coleridge's definition of poetic faith is nearly identical with Kierkegaard's leap into faith.
12. To become exempt from the "Last Day" and its judgment and to "proceed directly to paradise," Muslims must believe, but beyond that they must become martyrs (Steven L. Harris 35; cf. Qur'an 4:74–76).
13. The term "heart" has connotations of both mind or thought and feeling, hence the phrase, "understand with their hearts."
14. Other texts reinforce the notion that the Qur'an participates in this tradition of privileged "knowledge." Allah tells Muhammad of the "spider's house," explaining that "those who take protectors other than God" build for themselves spiders' houses. "The spider's is the frailest of all houses—if only they could understand." The text continues with a comment of similar import to Jesus' reference to those who have "ears to hear," "Such are the comparisons We draw for people, though only the wise can grasp them" (Qur'an 29:41–43).
15. The operative word in the statement is *faith*, not *righteous*. Notice the change when one says, "He through doubt is righteous shall die."
16. The term *stubborn* is used numerous times for the Israelites, God's chosen people. At times, God recognizes that he has selected badly. He tells Moses, for example, "I have seen this people, and behold, it is a stubborn people; let me alone, that I may destroy them and blot out their name from under heaven" (Deuteronomy 9:13–14).
17. Ellerbe points out that in the early centuries of the Common Era, a controversy arose between Pelagius, an Irish monk, who championed the notion of human free will, and St. Augustine, who argued that salvation is entirely a matter of God's choosing: "Augustine believed that our freedom of will to choose good over evil was lost with the sin of Adam. Adam's sin, that in Augustine's words is in the 'nature of the semen from which we were propagated,' brought suffering and death into the world, took away our free will, and left us with an inherently evil nature" (31).
18. Since the early centuries of the Common Era, Christian theologians have debated whether the fall itself was preordained. There is the *infralapsarian* view, explained as "A term applied in the 17th c. to Calvinists holding the view that God's election of some to everlasting life was consequent to his prescience of the Fall of man, or that it contemplated man as already fallen, and was thus a remedial measure: opposed to supralapsarian." The Supralapsarian view makes Predestination anterior or logically superior to the fall, and views the creation, fall, and saving of some as parts of God's eternal purpose. *Infralapsarian* is generally used as synonymous with *sublapsarian*, the earlier and, in English writers, the more usual term. But some distinguish the two, associating *sublapsarian* with the view that the Fall was foreseen, and *Infralapsarian* with the view that it was permitted, by God (*OED*).
19. As I have discussed elsewhere, the Yahwist's images are older than the story he tells. The cluster that includes the tree(s) of life and death, the oracular serpent, and the "mother of all living" evokes the neighboring religions that worship the great goddess. The story is in one respect about the clash of religions, and the superior power of Yahweh over "other gods" ("Paradise and Paradox").
20. The later-developed biblical concept of immortality complicates any commonsensical reading of "death" in the origin story.

21. Forsyth argues that the account of the Fall in Genesis 3 and the abbreviated Watcher myth in Genesis 6 formed a basis for ascribing blame to women for the initial corruption of God's perfect world. The dangerous sexuality of women revealed in the narratives seemed to confirm the legitimacy of a cultural bias against the feminine and the view that women were the source of sin, guilt, and estrangement from God (212–18).

CHAPTER 9

1. Laura Nasrallah groups prophecy with divination, dreams, visions, and ecstasy, referring to the collocation as "prophetic experience(s)" (2). These, in turn, can be seen as instances of the state known as "holy madness." I shall explore this dimension of prophecy in Chapter 11.
2. The gods themselves are not exempt from the workings of Fate. Uranus and Kronus, for example, attempt to avert prophecies of their sons displacing them, but their evasive actions lead to the prophecies' fulfillment.
3. An ancient middle-eastern tradition allowed a man to indicate his desire to leave his property to a son-in-law by giving him his household gods.
4. In the Septuagint, the Hebrew word *'almah*, "young woman," is translated by the Greek word *parthenos*, "virgin." What started as a translator's decision produced implications that may well have contributed to or provided a sacred textual "authority" for Matthew's account of the virgin birth.
5. Allah reiterates the doctrine of predestination, explaining, "No misfortune can happen, either in the earth or in yourselves, that was not set down in writing before we brought it into being . . ." (57:22). In his Introduction to the Qur'an, E. H. Palmer notices that Allah's divine authorship of the story of humankind is impossible to reconcile with the concept of human freedom and the "difficulty . . . of avoiding the ascription of evil as well as good to God": "Islam inculcates the doctrine of predestination, every act of every living being having been written down from all eternity in . . . 'the preserved tablet'" (lxxv).
6. Thomas Paine, particularly scornful of this tale of God's heroism, remarks that the Red Sea victory consists of God's setting a trap "in the dead of night" for Pharaoh, his host, and his horses to "drown them as a rat-catcher would do so many rats. Great honor indeed!" (*The Age of Reason* 144).
7. Paine remarks that when the New Testament texts were written, the "affair of people being possessed by devils, and of casting them out, was the fable of the day." It is not evident in the Old Testament: "It starts upon us all at once in the book of Matthew" (*The Age of Reason* 153).
8. The themes that repeat in accounts of heroes carry with them attendant "truths" that may go unrecognized. Aslan, describing the signs and prophecies of future heroism (of Muhammad, Jesus, and David), remarks, "It is not important whether the stories describing the childhood of Muhammad, Jesus, or David are true. What is important is what these stories say about our prophets, our messiahs, our kings: *that theirs is a holy and eternal vocation, established by God from the moment of creation*" (21; emphasis supplied).

CHAPTER 10

1. Prayers of petition (intercessory prayer) were the subject of a 2006 Harvard experiment (Study of the Therapeutic Effects of Intercessory Prayer [STEP] in cardiac bypass patients) published in the American Heart Journal (Vol. 151:4, 934–42).

The study's conclusion: "Intercessory prayer itself had no effect on complication-free recovery from CABG, but certainty of receiving intercessory prayer was associated with a higher incidence of complications."

2. Major denominations have specifically designated times and prayers, for example, the Catholic Liturgy of the Hours or the Anglican Book of Common Prayer. Some denominations, for example, Baptists, eschew formal liturgical practice in favor of individual communication with God.
3. As Yahweh observes both before and after the Flood, "[T]he imagination of man's heart is evil from his youth" (Genesis 6:5; 8:21), and as he tells Jeremiah, "The heart is deceitful above all things, and desperately corrupt" (Jeremiah 17:9). Jesus concurs, announcing that, "from within, out of the heart of man, come evil thoughts, fornication, theft, murder, adultery, coveting, wickedness, deceit, licentiousness, envy, slander, pride, foolishness" (Mark 7:21–11).
4. This prophecy refers to Absalom's revolt against David (2 Samuel 16: 20–23)—another instance in which an individual's crimes are divinely determined.
5. In a similarly decisive battle in the evolution of Islam, Mohammad prays for a sign before entering the Battle of Bader against "the largest and most powerful tribe in Arabia." Regarding Mohammad and the Muslim army's siege of the Confederates, Allah acknowledges his role in the defeat and admonishes the believers, "remember God's goodness to you when mighty armies massed against you: We sent a violent wind and invisible forces against them" (Qur'an 33:9).
6. God's act is similar to that of Apollo who, in *The Iliad*, shoots arrows of plague down onto the Greek forces (1:13).
7. Isaac Asimov comments that the task would have been as perilous as that of a Jew sent to Berlin during Hitler's ascendancy to "cry against it" (1:646).
8. It is only in context of the rules of "holy war" that the animals of enemy populations would be in jeopardy ("you shall save alive nothing that breathes" [Deuteronomy 20:16]).
9. Christians have repeated the request that the "kingdom come" untold times in "The Lord's Prayer" (Matthew 6:9–11).

CHAPTER 11

1. Another term for such experiences is *transliminal*—those occurring at or beyond the threshold of physical perception or reason. *Enthusiasm*, used with both positive and negative connotations in Christian Europe and America, is similar. See Taves, *passim*.
2. For simplicity's sake, I use masculine pronouns for the prophet, while acknowledging that female prophets have been recognized in most traditions.
3. A repeated motif in accounts of the relationships between kings and prophets is the relative powers of the king and the gods' spokesman, for example, King Pentheus and Dionysus, Oedipus and Tiresias, Samuel and Saul.
4. The story of the small boys occupies a precarious position—somewhere between outrageously funny and appallingly disgusting. Certainly a reader might "identify" with the angry prophet, but the outcome for the rude boys emerges from anger-driven fantasy. Whatever its lesson, the tale is one that offers no opportunity for accommodation or reform.
5. The image prompted by this divine promise is of one of sadistic torture: a helpless prophet in the hands of a powerful anthropomorphic figure wielding a supply of the biblical equivalent of duct tape.

6. From the moment of their conception, the children's lives are narrowed to the confines of the metaphoric situation and their figurative names: "God Sows," "Not Pitied," and "Not My People" (Hosea 1:4–9).
7. For other examples, see Ezekiel 23, Isaiah 54:1–10 and Jeremiah 3:1–14.
8. The inclusion of the very erotic Song of Solomon in the biblical canon is no doubt made possible by the prophets' repeatedly characterizing the divine-human relationship as sexual.
9. I am struck by this image of hearing the god's advice in the "whisper of the leaves" and am reminded of Muhammad's experience of hearing the stones and trees convey divine messages.
10. Inasmuch as Dionysus' death and rebirth offered his initiates a model for their own existence, the play makes it possible to ask whether Pentheus in undergoing a similar agony earned immortality. Euripides dark play offers little evidence for optimism.
11. As with other "signs," the relationship between sign and significance is arbitrary and ambiguous.
12. Some early prophets banded together into schools, guilds, or brotherhoods. Their prophesying, accompanied by music and manic dancing, consisted of each individually gibbering or shouting divine messages only he could hear. Elijah was a leader of such a band; so, apparently, was Samuel. Independent prophets such as Amos, likewise hallucinatory, also roamed the land.
13. The Sybil was the ironic Roman counterpart of the Delphic oracle. She recorded her prophecies *in Greek* on palm leaves, which she then allowed to be scattered by the wind. Those who received the prophecies could read only fragments of god-talk, and those in a foreign tongue,
14. As is the case with metaphors, however, God's interpretation does not foreclose others. A Christian "spiritual" reading of the vision finds it allegorical of the resurrection of Jesus and his followers.
15. One is tempted to compare this phenomenon of textual contagion with the numerous reported incidents of "alien abduction" in the modern world. That is, one's dream experience may take the form of texts, circulated widely, reported routinely, and then "experienced" by others in the wider society.
16. John's Jesus would perhaps have been equally harsh as regards St. Paul's position; presumably he would have called St. Paul a false prophet, thrown him, too, on a sickbed, and punished his followers with "tribulation." Allah seems to side with John as to the consumption of food dedicated to other gods (Qur'an 2:173).
17. The stones from heaven suggest the battle against the Amorites at Gibeon (Joshua 10). Reminiscent also of the ten plagues of Egypt, the disasters of John's apocalypse have the effect of making Yahweh's often praised destruction of Egypt and the bringing out of the chosen people an elaborate antetype for and "prophecy" of universal destruction and the rescue of the blessed.
18. I am thinking of modern apocalyptic prophets—the Reverend Jim Jones, David Koresh, and Marshall Applewhite and Bonnie Nettles. Each prophet's followers received the prophet's "knowledge" of "good and divine things," made it their own, and fled like lemmings into the Unknown.

Chapter 12

1. Dawkins cites Thomas Jefferson to similar effect: "The Christian God is a being of terrific character—cruel, vindictive, capricious and unjust" (31).

2. Remarks at an Ecumenical Prayer Breakfast in Dallas, Texas, 23 August 1984.
3. The situation is similar in Islam, for the Qur'an incorporates by allusion the Bible, Old and New Testaments, but few Muslims have actually read the Bible. When they do begin to read it, my Muslim students are routinely shocked and amazed at what they discover there.
4. Helen Ellerbe chronicles the "dark side" of Christian history with its enforcement of "moral religious behavior," the wars, tortures, slaughters, and miscellaneous patterns of abuse in the service of "domination and control of spirituality and human freedom" (185 and *passim*). She cites the chronicle of Raymond of Aguilers, who described a massacre by crusaders of Muslims and Jews: "In the temple of Solomon, the horses waded in the blood up to their knees. . . . *It was a just and marvelous judgement of God*, that this place should be filled with the blood of unbelievers" (65; emphasis supplied). The ongoing strife, suffering, and acrimony at large in Middle Eastern countries emerge directly from religion or are made possible through manipulation of the religiously naïve. The disaster of the Twin Towers was probably considered a religious act, a moral act, by its perpetrators, if not by its engineers. And see James A. Haught, *Holy Horrors*.
5. "The term 'moral' comes from the Latin *mos*, which means custom or habit, and it is a translation of the Greek *ethos*, which means roughly the same thing . . ." (Hare 1–2).
6. In the years leading to the Civil War in America an array of religious leaders joined to defend slavery, citing biblical authority. Heyman writes, "Baptists and Methodists rose readily to defend slavery in the 1830s" (248). This argument by Baptist minister Thornton Stringfellow illustrates how easily this could be accomplished: "He who believes the Bible to be of divine authority, believes those laws were given by the Holy Ghost to Moses. . . . [God] *has given them [the laws concerning slavery] his sanction, therefore, they must be in harmony with his moral character.*" The abolitionist stance is therefore *immoral*, holding "God himself in abhorrence" (cited in Noll 389).
7. A modern instance of the staying power of morally outgrown laws is the case of Oregon's eugenics laws that called for sterilization of the "socially unfit." The laws remained "on the books" from 1920 until 1983, a date long after the "science" on which the laws had been based had been rejected.
8. Geretti was curator of an exhibition in the Sistine Hall of the Vatican Museums containing one hundred masterpieces illustrating the Book of Revelation (Malcolm Moore, "Let's celebrate the Apocalypse, says Vatican," October 19, 2007).
9. Lindsey predicted, for example, that the world would end during the decade of the 1980s .
10. The sequel, *The 1980s: Countdown to Armageddon*, was on *The New York Times* bestseller list for over twenty weeks.
11. A variation of the Rapture prompted the suicide of thirty-nine members of the Heaven's Gate cult, who expected to be "taken up" not by Jesus but by a spacecraft trailing the Hale-Bopp comet.

WORKS CITED

Angier, Natalie, "Mirrors Don't Lie. Mislead? Oh, Yes." *New York Times*, July 22, 2008, Science Section On Line 1–2.
Aristotle. *The Works of Aristotle*. J. A. Smith and W. D. Ross, trans. Oxford: Oxford University Press, 1912.
Asimov, Isaac. *Asimov's Guide to the Bible*. 2 vols. Garden City, NY: Doubleday, 1968.
Aslan, Reza. *No god but God: The Origin, Evolution, and Future of Islam*. New York: Random House, 2006.
Auerbach, Erich. "The Sacrifice of Isaac." *Genesis: Modern Critical Interpretations*. Harold Bloom, ed. New York, New Haven, and Philadelphia: Chelsea House, 1986.
Baglio, Matt. *The Rite: The Making of a Modern Exorcist*. New York and London: Doubleday, 2009.
Barfield, Owen. *History in English Words*. London: Faber and Faber, 1953.
Barnstone, Willis, ed. and intro. *The Other Bible*. San Francisco: Harper & Row, 1984.
Bernstein, J. M. "Grand Narratives." *On Paul Ricoeur: Narrative and Interpretation*. David Wood, ed. and intro., pp. 102–23. London and New York: Routledge, 1991.
Bierce, Ambrose. *The Unabridged Devil's Dictionary*. Lexington, KY: Feather Trail Press, 2010.
Black, Max. "Metaphor," in *Philosophical Perspectives on Metaphor*. Mark Johnson, ed., pp. 63–82. Minneapolis: University of Minnesota Press, 1981.
Bloom, Harold. "Before Moses Was, I Am." *Modern Critical Views: The Bible*. Harold Bloom, ed., pp. 291–304. New York, New Haven, Philadelphia: Chelsea House, 1987.
———. *The American Religion: The Emergence of the Post-Christian Nation*. New York and London: Simon and Schuster, 1992.
———. *Ruin the Sacred Truths: Poetry and Belief from the Bible to the Present*. Cambridge, MA, and London: Harvard University Press, 1989.
Boethius. *The Consolation of Philosophy*. H. R. James, trans. New York: E. P. Dutton; London: George Routledge & Sons, 1874.
Borges, Jorge Luis. *Ficciones*. Anthony Kerrigan, ed. New York: Grove, 1962.
Brennan, Tad. "Immortality in Ancient Philosophy." In *Routledge Encyclopedia of Philosophy*. E. Craig, ed. London: Routledge, 2002. Retrieved May 10, 2010, from http://www.rep.rotledge.com/article/A133SECT1.
Bultmann, Rudolf. *Primitive Christianity in its Contemporary Setting*. R. H. Fuller, trans. Cleveland and New York: Meridian Books, 1969.
Burke, Kenneth. *The Rhetoric of Religion: Studies in Logology*. Berkeley: University of California Press, 1970.
Campbell, Joseph. *The Hero with a Thousand Faces*. 2nd ed. Bollingen Series 17. Princeton: Princeton University Press, 1968.
———. *The Inner Reaches of Outer Space*. New York: A. van der March, 1986.

———. *The Masks of God: Occidental Mythology*. New York: Viking, 1964.
———. *The Masks of God: Oriental Mythology*. New York: Viking, 1962.
———. *The Way of the Seeded Earth*, pt. 1, *The Sacrifice*. Vol. 2, *Historical Atlas of World Mythology*. New York: Harper & Row, 1988.
Cassirer, Ernst. *Language and Myth*. Suzanne K. Langer, trans. New York: Dover, 1946.
Certeau, Michel de. "What We Do When We Believe." *On Signs*. Marshall Blonsky, ed., pp. 192–202. Baltimore, Maryland: The Johns Hopkins University Press, 1985.
Clark, R. T. Rundle. *Myth and Symbol in Ancient Egypt*. London: Thames and Hudson, 1978.
Clark, Stephen R. L. "Ancient Philosophy." *The Oxford History of Western Philosophy*. Anthony Kenny, ed. Oxford and New York: Oxford University Press, 1994.
Clarke, Isabel. *Madness, Mystery and the Survival of God*. Winchester, UK, and Washington, D.C.: O Books, 2008.
Coleridge, Samuel Taylor. *Biographia Literaria. The Major Works*. H. J. Jackson, ed. and intro. Oxford and New York: Oxford University Press, 1985.
Corbett, Edward P. J. *Classical Rhetoric for the Modern Student*. 2nd ed. New York: Oxford University Press, 1971.
Crane, Frank, and William N. Guthrie, intro. and ed. *The Lost Books of the Bible and The Forgotten Books of Eden*. New York, Scarborough, Ontario, and London: New American Library, 1974 (1926, 1927).
Crossley-Holland, Kevin. *The Norse Myths*. New York: Pantheon Books, 1980.
Davies, A. Powell. *The First Christian: A Study of St. Paul and Christian Origins*. New York: Farrar, Straus and Cudahy, 1957.
Dawkins, Richard. *The God Delusion*. Boston and New York: Houghton Mifflin, 2006.
Dever, William G. *What Did the Biblical Writers Know & When Did They Know It? What Archaeology Can Tell Us about the Reality of Ancient Israel*. Grand Rapids, MI, and Cambridge, UK: William B. Eerdmans, 2002.
Doria, Charles, and Harris Lenowitz, ed. and trans. *Origins: Creation Texts from the Ancient Mediterranean*. Garden City, NY: Anchor Books, 1976.
Eco, Umberto. *Semiotics and the Philosophy of Language*. Bloomington: Indiana University Press, 1984.
Eliot, Alexander. *The Universal Myths: Heroes, Gods, Tricksters and Others, with Contributions by Joseph Campbell and Mircea Eliade*. New York: Meridian Books, 1990.
Eliot, T. S. "Burnt Norton." *The Complete Poems and Plays, 1909–1950*. New York: Harcourt, Brace & World, 1962.
Ellerbe, Helen. *The Dark Side of Christian History*. Windermere, FL: Morningstar & Lark, 1995.
Euripides. *Medea, Hippolytus, Alcestis, The Bacchae*. Robert W. Corrigan, ed. and trans. New York: Dell Publishing, 1965.
Forsyth, Neil. *The Old Enemy*. Princeton, NJ: Princeton University Press, 1989.
Freud, Sigmund. *The Basic Writings*. A. A. Brill, trans. and ed. New York: The Modern Library, 1995.
Gerhart, Mary, and Allan Melvin Russell. *Metaphoric Process: The Creation of Scientific and Religious Understanding*. Fort Worth, TX: Texas-Christian University Press, 1984.
Girard, René. *Violence and the Sacred*. Patrick Gregory, trans. Baltimore and London: The Johns Hopkins University Press, 1977.
Goldsmith, Steven. *Unbuilding Jerusalem: Apocalypse and Romantic Representation*. Ithaca and London: Cornell University Press, 1993.
Gombrich, E. H. *A Little History of the World*. Caroline Mustill, trans. New Haven and London: Yale University Press, 1985.

González, Justo L. *Essential Theological Terms*. Louisville, KY: Westminster John Knox, 2005.

Gordon, Cyrus H. "Canaanite Mythology." *Mythologies of the Ancient World*. Samuel Noah Kramer, ed. New York: Doubleday, 1961.

Haleem, M. A. S., trans. and ed. *The Qur'an*. Oxford: Oxford University Press, 2005.

Hare, John. "Religion and Morality." In *Stanford Encyclopedia of Philosophy*. Edward N. Zalta, ed. September 27, 2006 (http://plato.stanford.edu/entries/religion-morality/).

Harries, Karsten. "Metaphor and Transcendence." *On Metaphor*, pp. 71–88. Sheldon Sacks, ed. Chicago and London: The University of Chicago Press (1978).

Harris, Sam. *The End of Faith: Religion, Terror, and the Future of Reason*. New York and London: W. W. Norton, 2004.

Harris, Stephen L. *Understanding the Bible*. 7th ed. New York: McGraw Hill, 2007.

Haught, James A. *Holy Horrors: An Illustrated History of Religious Murder and Madness*. Amherst, NY: Prometheus Books, 2002.

Heidel, Alexander. *The Babylonian Genesis: The Story of Creation*. 2nd ed. Chicago and London: The University of Chicago Press, 1951.

Hennecke, Edgar. *New Testament Apocrypha*. Wilhelm Schneemelcher, E. R. McL. Wilson, trans. 2 vols. Philadelphia: Westminster Press, 1964.

Herodotus. *The Histories*. Rev. ed. and trans. Aubrey de Selincourt. John Marincola, intro. London and New York: Penguin Books, 2003.

Hesiod. *The Works and Days, Theogony, The Shield of Heracles*. Richmond Lattimore, trans. and intro. Ann Arbor: The University of Michigan Press, 1959.

Heyman, Christine Leigh. *Southern Cross: The Beginnings of the Bible Belt*. New York: Alfred A. Knopf, 1997.

Homer. *The Iliad*. Robert Fitzgerald, trans. Garden City, NY: Anchor Books, 1975 (cited by book and page number).

———. *The Odyssey*. Robert Fitzgerald, trans. Garden City, NY: Anchor Books, 1963 (cited by book and page number).

Holweck, Frederick. "Immaculate Conception." *The Catholic Encyclopedia*. Vol. 7. New York: Robert Appleton Company, 1910. Accessed 7 May 2010 from http://www.newadvent.org/cathen/07674d.htm.

Jabes, Edmond. *The Book of Questions*. Rosmarie Waldrop, trans. Middletown, CT: Wesleyan University Press, 1976.

James, William. *The Varieties of Religious Experience. Writings 1902–1910*. New York: Library of America, 1986.

Jaynes, Julian. *The Origin of Consciousness in the Breakdown of the Bicameral Mind*. Boston: Houghton Mifflin, 1976, 1982.

Johnson, Mark, ed. and intro. "Introduction: Metaphor in the Philosophical Tradition." *Philosophical Perspectives on Metaphor*, pp. 3–47. Minneapolis: University of Minnesota Press, 1981.

Kafka, Franz. "Franz Kafka." BrainyQuote.com. Retrieved September 2, 2010, from http://www.brainyquote.com/quotes/authors/f/franz_kafka_2.html.

Kermode, Frank. *The Sense of an Ending: Studies in the Theory of Fiction*. New York: Oxford University Press, 1967.

Khosrokhavar, Farhad. *Suicide Bombers: Allah's New Martyrs*. David Macey, trans. London and Ann Arbor, MI: Pluto Press, 2005.

Kierkegaard, Sören. *Fear and Trembling*. Radford, VA: Wilder, 2008.

Kinsella, Thomas, trans. *The Táin: From the Irish epic Táin Bó Cuailnge*. Oxford and New York: Oxford University Press, 1969.

Knox, Bernard. "Introduction." *Sophocles. The Theban Plays: Antigone, Oedipus the King, Oedipus at Colonus.* Robert Fagles, trans. New York: Penguin Books, 1984.

Kohler, Kaufmann. "Immortality of the Soul." In jewishencyclopedia.com, 1.

Kott, Jan. *The Eating of the Gods: An Interpretation of Greek Tragedy.* Boleslaw Taborski and Edward J. Czerwinski, trans. New York: Vintage, 1974.

Kramer, Samuel Noah. *History Begins at Sumer.* Philadelphia: The University of Pennsylvania Press, 1981.

———. *Mythologies of the Ancient World.* New York: Doubleday, 1961.

———. *Sumerian Mythology,* ed. Rev. ed. New York, Evanston, and London: Harper & Row, 1961.

Kuhn, Thomas S. *The Structure of Scientific Revolutions.* 3rd ed. Chicago and London: The University of Chicago Press, 1996.

Lacan, Jacques. *Écrits: A Selection.* Alan Sheridan, trans. New York and London: W. W. Norton, 1977.

LaFleur, William R. "Body." *Critical Terms for Religious Studies.* Mark C. Taylor, ed., pp. 36–54. Chicago and London: University of Chicago Press, 1998.

LaHaye, Tim, and Jerry B. Jenkins. *Left Behind: A Novel of the Earth's Last Days.* Colorado Springs, CO: Tyndale House Publishers, 1995.

Lattimore, Richmond, trans. and ed. *Hesiod, The Works and Days, Theogony, and The Shield of Heracles.* Ann Arbor: The University of Michigan Press, 1959.

Leeming, David. *The Oxford Companion to World Mythology.* Oxford and New York: Oxford University Press, 2005.

Lévi-Strauss, Claude. *The Savage Mind.* George Weidenfeld and Nicolson, trans. Chicago: University of Chicago Press, 1966.

———. "The Structural Study of Myth." *Myth, A Symposium.* Thomas A. Sebeok, ed., pp. 81–106. Philadelphia: American Folklore Society, 1955.

Lopez, Donald S., Jr. "Belief." *Critical Terms for Religious Studies.* Mark C. Taylor, ed., pp. 21–35. Chicago and London: The University of Chicago Press, 1998.

Lowth, Robert. *Lectures on the Sacred Poetry of the Hebrews.* 2 vols. G. Gregory, trans. London: J. Johnson, 1787. Repr. Hildesheim: Georg Olms Verlag, 1969.

Marks, Herbert. "Pauline Typology and Revisionary Criticism." *Modern Critical Views: The Bible.* Harold Bloom, ed., pp. 305–21. New York, New Haven, and Philadelphia: Chelsea House, 1987.

———. "The Twelve Prophets." *The Literary Guide to the Bible.* Robert Alter and Frank Kermode, ed., pp. 207–33. Cambridge, MA: The Belknap Press, 1987.

McGinn, Bernard. "Revelation." *The Literary Guide to the Bible.* Robert Alter and Frank Kermode, ed., pp. 523–41 Cambridge, MA: The Belknap Press of Harvard University Press, 1987.

Mearms, William Hughes. "Antigonish." Accessed 9 September 2010 from http://en.wikipedia.org/wiki/William_Hughes_Mearms.

Merton, Thomas. "St. Paul." *Chapters into Verse: A Selection of Poetry in English Inspired by the Bible from Genesis through Revelation.* Robert Atwan & Laurance Wieder, ed. Oxford and New York: Oxford University Press, 2000.

Metzger, Bruce M., and Michael D. Coogan, ed. *Oxford Companion to the Bible.* Oxford and New York: Oxford University Press, 1993.

Miller, J. Hillis. *The Ethics of Reading.* New York: Columbia University Press, 1987.

Molloy, Michael. *Experiencing the World's Religions: Tradition, Challenge, and Change.* Fourth Edition. Boston: McGraw Hill, 2008.

Monk, Leland. *Standard Deviations. Chance and the Modern British Novel.* Stanford: Stanford University Press, 1993.

Works Cited

Morford, Mark P. O., and Robert J. Lenardon. *Classical Mythology.* 7th ed. New York and Oxford: Oxford University Press, 2003.
Nasrallah, Laura. *"An Ecstasy of Folly": Prophecy and Authority in Early Christianity. Harvard Theological Studies* 52. Cambridge, MA: Harvard University Press for Harvard Theological Studies, 2003.
Noll, Mark A. *America's God: From Jonathan Edwards to Abraham Lincoln.* Oxford: Oxford University Press, 2002.
Ovid. *The Metamorphoses.* Horace Gregory, trans. and intro. New York: New American Library, 1958.
Paine, Thomas. *The Age of Reason.* Radford, VA: A & D, 2007.
Palmer, E. H. "Introduction" and trans. The Qur'ān. Vols. 6 and 9. *The Sacred Books of the East.* F. Max Müller, ed. repr. New Delhi: Motilal Banarsidass, 1965.
Patai, Raphael. *The Hebrew Goddess.* 3rd ed. Detroit: Wayne State University Press, 1990.
———. *Sex and the Family in the Bible and the Middle East.* Garden City, NY: Doubleday, 1959.
———. *The Seed of Abraham: Jews and Arabs in Contact and Conflict.* Salt Lake City: University of Utah Press, 1986.
Pindar. *The Odes of Pindar.* 2nd ed. Richmond Lattimore, trans. Chicago and London: University of Chicago Press, 1976.
Plato. *Phaedrus.* Benjamin Jowett, trans. Accessed 7 September 2010 from http://classics.mit.edu/Plato/phaefrus.html.
———. *The Republic.* Francis Macdonald Cornford, trans. and intro. New York and London: Oxford University Press, 1945.
Prickett, Stephen. *Narrative, Religion and Science: Fundamentalism versus Irony, 1700–1999.* Cambridge: Cambridge University Press, 2002.
Pritchard. James B., ed. *The Ancient Near East: An Anthology of Texts and Pictures.* Princeton: Princeton University Press, 1958.
Raglan, Lord. "The Hero of Tradition." *The Study of Folklore.* Alan Dundes, ed., pp. 142–57. Englewood Cliffs, NJ: Prentice-Hall, 1965.
Rank, Otto. *The Myth of the Birth of the Hero.* Phillip Freund, ed. New York: Vintage Books, 1964.
Rée, Jonathan. "Narrative and Philosophical Experience." *On Paul Ricoeur: Narrative and Interpretation.* David Wood, ed. and intro., pp. 74–83. London and New York: Routledge, 1991.
Richards, I. A. "The Philosophy of Rhetoric." *Philosophical Perspectives on Metaphor.* Mark Johnson, ed., pp. 48–62. Minneapolis: University of Minnesota Press, 1981.
Riffaterre, Michael. "Compulsory Reader Response: The Intertextual Drive." *Intertextuality: Theory and Practice.* Michael Worton and Judith Still, ed., pp. 56–78. Manchester and New York: Manchester University Press, 1990.
Robbins, Jill. "Sacrifice." *Critical Terms for Religious Studies.* Mark C. Taylor, ed., pp. 285–97. Chicago and London: University of Chicago Press, 1998.
Rosenberg, Joel. "1 and 2 Samuel." *The Literary Guide to the Bible.* Robert Alter and Frank Kermode, ed., pp. 122–45. Cambridge, MA: Belknap Press of Harvard University Press, 1987.
Said, Edward W. *Beginnings: Intention and Method.* New York: Basic Books, 1975.
Sandars, N. K., trans. and intro. *The Epic of Gilgamesh.* Rev. and repr. Baltimore: Penguin, 1972.
Sophocles. *The Three Theban Plays: Antigone, Oedipus the King, Oedipus at Colonus.* Robert Fagles, trans. Bernard Knox, intro. New York: Penguin Books, 1984.
Stenger, Victor J. *God: The Failed Hypothesis.* Amherst, NY: Prometheus Books, 2008.

Stevens, Wallace. *The Palm at the End of the Mind: Selected Poems and a Play.* Holly Stevens, ed. New York: Vintage Books, 1971.

Stoyanov, Yuri. *The Other God: Dualist Religions from Antiquity to the Cathar Heresy.* New Haven and London, Yale University Press, 2000.

Taves, Ann. *Fits, Trances, & Visions: Experiencing Religion and Explaining Experience from Wesley to James.* Princeton, NJ: Princeton University Press, 1999.

Taylor, Mark C. *After God.* Chicago and London: The University of Chicago Press, 2007.

———. *Tears.* Albany: State University of New York Press, 1990.

Thomas, D. Winton, ed. *Documents from Old Testament Times.* New York: Harper & Row, 1961.

Torey, Zoltan. *The Crucible of Consciousness: An Integrated Theory of Mind and Brain.* Cambridge, MA, and London: The MIT Press, 2009.

Tracy, David. *Blessed Rage for Order: The New Pluralism in Theology.* New York: Seabury, 1975.

———. "Writing." *Critical Terms for Religious Studies.* Mark C. Taylor, ed., pp. 383–93. Chicago and London: The University of Chicago Press, 1998.

Turbayne, Colin Murray. *The Myth of Metaphor.* Rev. ed. Columbia: University of South Carolina Press, 1970.

Twain, Mark. *Letters from the Earth.* Bernard DeVoto, ed. New York: Fawcett World Library, 1962.

———. *Mark Twain and the Three R's: Race, Religion, Revolution—and Related Matters.* Maxwell Geismar, ed. and intro. Indianapolis and New York: Bobbs-Merrill, 1973.

———. *The Bible According to Mark Twain.* Howard G. Baetzbold and Joseph B. McCullough, ed. New York: Simon & Schuster, 1995.

Vermes, Geza, trans. and ed. *The Complete Dead Sea Scrolls in English.* Rev. ed. London and New York: Penguin Books, 2004.

Vielhauer, Philipp. "Introduction: Apocalypses and Related Subjects." In Edgar Hennecke, *The New Testament Apocrypha: Writings Relating to the Apostles; Apocalypses and Related Subjects.* Vol 2. Wilhelm Schneemelcher, ed., R. McL. Wilson, trans., pp. 581–642. Philadelphia: The Westminster Press 1965.

Virgil. *The Aeneid.* Allen Mandelbaum, trans. New York: Bantam Books, 1971.

Ward, Keith. *The Big Questions in Science and Religion.* West Conshohocken, PA: Templeton Foundation Press, 2008.

Westbrook, Deeanne. "Paradise and Paradox." *Mappings of the Biblical Terrain: The Bible as Text.* Vincent L. Tollers and John Maier, ed., pp. 121–33. Lewisburg: Bucknell University Press; London and Toronto: Associated University Presses, 1990.

———. *Wordsworth's Biblical Ghosts.* New York: Palgrave, 2001.

Weston, Jessie L. *From Ritual to Romance.* Garden City, NY: Doubleday, Anchor Books, 1957.

White, Hayden. *The Content of the Form: Narrative Discourse and Historical Representation.* Baltimore and London: The Johns Hopkins University Press, 1987 (1992).

———. *Tropics of Discourse: Essays in Cultural Criticism.* Baltimore and London: Johns Hopkins University Press, 1978 (1987).

Wood, David, ed. "Introduction." *On Paul Ricoeur: Narrative and Interpretation,* pp. 1–19. London and New York: Routledge, 1991.

Wright, Robert. "One World, under God." *The Atlantic* 303, no. 3 (April, 2009).

Young, Dudley. *The Origins of The Sacred: The Ecstasies of Love and War.* New York: St. Martin's, 1991.

Index

Abraham (Ibrahim), 11, 15, 57, 58, 71, 78, 83, 92, 93, 95–96, 106, 139, 140, 142, 143, 144, 145, 149, 150, 151, 159, 160, 164, 169, 172, 177, 186, 196, 221n12, 223n13, 223n18, 227n7. *See also* Abrahamic religions; Akedah; covenant: with Abraham

Abrahamic religions, 2, 78, 106, 139, 143, 144, 154, 172

Adam, 24, 28, 57, 78, 79, 82, 106, 121, 127, 130, 134, 150, 151, 152, 153, 167, 209, 228n17

Adonis, 34, 99

Ahura Mazda, 24, 34, 99, 225n1, 226n11

Akedah (the Binding of Isaac), 95–96, 97, 101, 223n10, 223n11

Akkadians, 57, 61, 108

alien abduction, 203, 218n7, 231n15

Allah (God), 14, 15, 18, 28, 48, 53, 66, 67, 88, 106, 109, 119, 122, 134, 147, 148, 149, 154, 155, 169, 173, 176, 186, 187, 206, 209, 220n14, 222n27, 224n2, 228n14, 229n5, 230n5, 231n16

Amorites, 57, 143, 177, 179, 231

analogy, 6, 8, 22, 32, 37, 106, 145, 185, 215n9

Anath, 117. *See also* Baal

angels, 41, 42, 43, 44, 61, 67, 78, 83, 84, 88, 113, 117, 122, 123, 127, 130, 131, 168, 169, 171, 175, 176, 196, 198, 199; Gabriel, 42, 51, 83, 106, 123; Michael, 42, 46, 47, 50, 128, 226n20; Uriel, 42, 123, 130

Angier, Natalie, ix

Anshar, 115

Apocalypse, 15, 19, 21, 31, 34, 35–36, 39–47, 217n5, 218n6, n7, n8, 231n17, n18, 232n8; as literary genre, 39–40, 197–98; characteristics 41–42; end of history, 114–117 123, 131, 153, 160, 169, 211–14; four horsemen of 50, 52; John of Patmos' Revelation, 197–200; mode of prophetic experience, 200

Apocrypha, Bel and the Dragon, 93; 2 Esdras, 1, 35, 42–44, 46, 65, 115, 130–31, 135, 146–47, 149; Wisdom of Solomon, 35, 36, 132, 218n8

Apollo, 52, 70, 90–91, 94, 128, 155, 156, 182–83, 187–88, 195, 205, 230n6

Aquinas, St. Thomas, 150

Asimov, Isaac, 230n7

Aslan, Reza, 2, 15, 113, 175, 178, 186, 220n15, 222n27, 225n5, 229n8

Asherah, 23, 58, 59, 66, 71, 73; Yahweh and, 73, 75

Auerbach, Eric, 95, 223n11

Augustine, St., 11, 17, 150, 208, 209, 216n16, 116n19, 228n17
Baal, 51, 52, 58, 59, 62, 63, 66, 70, 71, 72, 73, 75, 76, 99, 160, 185–85; as bull, 102, 219n8, 220n5; child sacrifice and, 97
Babel, Tower of, and language, 112–15, 117, 225n12
Babylon, 42, 219n12; exile in, 75, 122, 123, 225n6; whore of, 44, 46, 47, 82, 86, 115, 117, 199–200, 221n25, 222n28. *See also* Babel, Tower of, and language; Babylonian narratives
Babylonian narratives, 3, 14, 15, 17 19, 22, 23, 24, 25, 26, 36, 37, 51, 52, 61, 63, 72, 194, 222n6; Hammurabi and the law code, 57, 108–9. *See* creation
Baglio, Matt, 226n15
Barfield, Owen, 70, 216n23, 219n11
Barnstone, Willis, 28, 64, 73, 87, 153, 218n9, 221n23. *See also* Pseudepigrapha: Enoch
belief, 13, 15, 16, 136, 137–54; economic metaphor, 138–42; St. Paul's definition of faith, 138–42
Bernstein, J. M., 45
Bible, The Old Testament (Hebrew Bible)
  Amos, 61, 105, 301
  1 Chronicles, 114, 175
  2 Chronicles, 104
  Daniel, 56, 62–63, 65–66, 68, 175, 200, 238, 314
  Deuteronomy, 97, 105, 142n8, 144n21, 170n4, 179, 180, 270, 296n8
  Ecclesiastes, 20, 34, 54, 55, 56, 87, 113, 129, 130, 135, 166, 194, 203
  Exodus, 4, 18, 31–32, 49, 52, 53, 58, 63, 66, 68, 78, 93, 94, 95, 96, 97, 101, 102, 106, 108, 109, 111, 141, 161, 162, 164, 179, 202, 208, 210, 219n2, n4, n8, 220n5, 222n3, 227n5
  Ezekiel, 39, 43, 44, 50, 51, 53, 76–77, 93, 97, 106, 182, 185, 197, 198, 218n3, n10, 219n2, 221n11, 231n7
  Ezra, 99. *See also* Apocrypha, 2 Esdras
  Genesis, ix, 14, 17, 19, 24–25, 27–28, 29, 33, 52, 58, 62–63, 64–65, 71, 72, 77–79, 80, 92, 93, 94, 96–97, 105, 106, 112, 121, 139–40, 141–42, 151, 157, 158, 164, 167, 177, 192, 193, 195–96, 214, 221n16, 229n21, 230n3
  Habakkuk, 51
  Hosea, 38, 71, 74–76, 77, 80, 152, 160–61, 181, 185, 103, 220n5, 231n6
  Isaiah, 39, 44, 52, 62, 70, 71, 76, 126, 149, 160, 163, 165, 166, 173, 185, 187, 195, 219n2, 225n6, 231n7
  Jeremiah, 59, 76, 97, 106, 156, 160, 163, 166, 176, 178, 182, 183, 184, 186, 220n8, 230n3, 231n7
  Judges, 19, 96, 162–63
  Joel, 54, 196
  Job, 12, 19, 42, 43, 51, 53, 63, 98, 107, 122, 127, 130, 144, 164–65, 195, 214, 217n3
  Joshua, 58, 66, 142, 175–76, 177, 231n17
  Jonah, 178–80
  1 Kings, 72, 102, 184, 185, 220n5
  2 Kings, 51, 112
  Leviticus, 79, 81, 109, 110, 208
  Micah, 182, 183
  Numbers, 68, 108, 127, 179, 192
  Proverbs, 34–35, 195, 213, 216n22
  Psalms, 34, 71, 159, 161, 209
  Ruth, 77, 217n3

INDEX

1 Samuel, 21, 121, 163, 175, 189–91, 220n9, 223n7
2 Samuel, 91, 95, 127, 230n4
Song of Solomon, 84, 231n8
Bible, The New Testament
  Acts, 120–21, 129, 148, 196
  1 Corinthians, 1, 84, 88, 116, 129, 133, 145, 153, 181, 191, 192, 199, 219n11
  Ephesians, 120, 129
  Galatians, 121
  Hebrews, 11, 13, 225
  James, 244
  John, Gospel of, 4, 11, 25, 55, 67, 89, 99, 101, 102, 105, 124, 129, 133, 147, 148, 149, 159, 161, 162, 168
  1 John, 197, 208
  Luke, Gospel of, 67, 70, 83, 85, 86, 88, 132, 145, 148, 159, 168, 173, 182, 183, 221n24, 226n22
  Mark, Gospel of, 84, 88, 101, 132 133, 147, 148, 149, 168, 174, 187, 196, 230n3
  Matthew, Gospel of, 14–15, 32, 36, 49, 82, 85–86, 88, 102, 132–33, 145, 148, 150–51, 159–61, 168, 169 171, 172 173, 174, 202, 223n18, 226n21, n22, 229n4, n7, 230n9
  Revelation, 2, 18, 19, 31, 33, 34, 39, 41, 42, 44, 45–48, 50, 51, 52, 53, 61, 67, 82, 86, 99, 106, 114–17, 128, 129 135, 146, 167, 197–200, 203 211, 222n28, 225n13, 116n20, 227n10, 232n8
  Romans, 67, 120, 133, 145, 146 147, 149, 152, 169
  1 Thessalonians, 67, 173
  1 Timothy, 152
Bierce, Ambrose, 137, 150, 174, 224n20
Binding of Isaac, The. *See* Akedah

Black, Max, 216n11
Blonsky, Marshall, 140, 227n6
Bloom, Harold, 2, 84, 216n20, 218n13, 223n8
Boethius, 32, 151
Book, the, 2–3, 5, 15, 20, 42, 43, 45, 46, 48, 67, 82, 106, 113, 159–60, 162, 163, 165–68, 172, 176, 180, 181, 186, 206, 209, 211, 213, 225n13; as history, time 31–32, 154; merging of time and space, 114–15, 117, 150–51. *See also* plot
Borges, Jorge Luis, 113
Bultmann, Rudolf, 123–25
Burke, Kenneth, 6–7, 8, 9, 216n15, n16, 217n8

Calvin, John, 150, 229n18
Campbell, Joseph, 33, 53, 54, 55, 61, 211, 217n10, 219n9, 221n17, 222n3
Canaanite narratives, 23, 52, 70, 71, 72, 73, 75. *See also* creation
Cassirer, Ernst, 11
catachresis, 10, 216n17
Certeau, Michel de, 10, 138, 139, 143–44
cherubim, 44, 50, 51, 52, 73, 219n2, n3, n5
circumcision, 78; as initial wound, 152–52; as sign of covenant, 139–41, 143–45, 154, 227n4, n5, n8; spiritual, 145–46
Clark, R. T. Rundle, 55
Clark, Stephen R. L., 5, 206
Clarke, Isabel, 181, 201, 210
Corbett, Edward P. J., 5, 215n10, 216n17
covenant, 38, 65, 92, 131, 142–43, 151, 157, 227n5; with Abraham, 58, 71, 83, 96, 139–40; evolution of, 145–46; with Jacob 139; and marriage contract, 74–78, 185; original, 151–52; and plot, 151–54

creation, ix, 17–30; creators, 24–29; procreators, 22–24
Crossley-Holland, Kevin, 19, 21, 23, 26, 37, 223n15. *See also* Norse narratives
crucifixion, 99–101, 133, 147, 159, 160, 161, 168, 174, 223n17, 227n2
Cyrus, the Great, 122, 225n6, 226n14

Dagon, 66, 163
David, King, 41, 42, 45, 58, 80, 91, 95, 100, 127–28, 161, 174–75, 190–91, 223n7, n18, 229n8, 230n4
Davies, A. Powell, 123, 225n3, 226n10
Dawkins, Richard, 206, 231n1
Dead Sea Scrolls ("Community Rule"), 119, 153, 225n7
death, 229–36 passim; in cyclical view, 21 34, 36, 55, 56; difficulty of definition, 103, 106, 121, 146–47, 152, 224n1, 228n20; and evil, 119, 120–21, 134, 152; God's plot and, 153, 161; language and, 138; in linear view, 34–35, 36, 56, 134–35; and madness, 187–91; privileging of, 35–36, 39–48; as punishment, 28–29, 127, 151, 165, 166–67; Satan as, 129, 132; and sex, 64, 82, 83–84, 152. *See also* dualism
Demeter ("Hymn to Demeter"), 59, 60, 123, 201
demons, 123, 132–33; demonic possession, 132, 133, 226n15. *See also* Satan
Dever, William, 73, 218n1
Dionysus, 34, 71, 82, 99, 100, 102, 103, 123, 182, 187–92, 230n3, 231n10
doom-eagerness, 2, 16, 31, 47, 48, 200, 211; as "mortiferous religiosity," 215n3

Doria, Charles, 11, 19, 22
dreams. *See* prophecy, prophets
dualism, 64, 195–224; afterlife, 201; confirmed in resurrection, 196; good and evil, 195; ideas from Babylon and Persia, 199–200; life and death, 195; light and darkness (insight and blindness), 195–96; mystery religions and, 202–3; Platonic contributions, 201, 203, 205; reversal of values, 202; soul and body, 201, 203; spirit and matter, 195–96, 203, 320; and St. Paul, 196; truth and falsehood, 195; two ages, 64, 65, 67, 77n6; the two trees, 206–7; universal conflict of the two, 195, 213–14; Zoroastrian dualism, 200

Eco, Umberto, 224n4
economics of belief, 8, 138–42, 143, 144, 152, 154, 227n3. *See also* reward and punishment
ecstasy. *See* prophecy, prophets
Eden. *See* garden
Egyptian narratives, 19, 22, 24, 28, 220n2, 226n17
El, 70, 71, 72, 73
Elijah, 37, 51, 72, 112, 184–85, 192, 231n12
Elisha, 51, 112, 185
Ellerbe, Helen, 228n17, 232n4
End Times, 3, 15, 16, 19, 31–48 passim, 56, 67, 106, 131, 144, 212, 225n4, n7; language of, 114–17. *See also* apocalypse; Last Judgment; time
enemies, of gods, 44, 49, 53, 61, 65, 130, 131, 162–63, 163–65, 167–69, 190, 200, 225n7
enemy, 40, 41, 46, 49, 61–62, 127–29, 162–63, 166–69, 175; adversary, narrative function of, 53–54, 129. *See also* evil; Satan
Eucharist, the, 99, 103, 133, 224n20

Euripides: *The Bacchae*, 102, 103, 187–89, 231n10; *Medea*, 217n11
Eve, 24, 28–29, 38, 57, 71, 78, 82, 152, 153, 167, 209; Adam's rib, 28, 153
evil: and divine justice, 129–31; metamorphosis of, 131–34; in monistic thought, 40, 121–22; the problem of evil, 126–31, 226n19. *See also* dualism; Satan; sexuality

faith: and ethical behavior, 96, 122, 140, 228n15; leap of faith, 138, 228n4; St. Paul's definition, 9, 137; test of, 122. *See also* belief
Fall, the, 24, 33, 77–79, 126–27, 151, 153, 167, 228n15; in the Qur'an, 134
family, 16, 23, 34, 69–88 passim, 145; fathers and sons, 89–102 passim
fate. *See* predestination
Fates, 156, 169, 177. *See also* predestination
flood narratives, 24, 32, 52, 63–65, 72, 79, 94, 109, 164, 165, 179, 209
food for gods, 92–94, 97, 98, 102, 117, 135, 153, 199, 101, 222n6, 231n16
Forsyth, Neil, 24, 32, 53–54, 62, 63, 120, 129, 131, 165, 166, 167, 168, 219n5, 226n19, n22, 229n21
free will, 136, 148–51, 156–57, 221n26, 228n17. *See also* Pelagius; predestination; responsibility
Freud, Sigmund, 89–90, 91, 216n17, 217n6, 222n1, n2

Gaia, 22, 23, 24, 28, 62. *See also* gods, metaphors for: mother

garden, Garden(s), 29, 33, 59, 88, 106, 126, 151, 195, 222n6; eternal, 36–37, 117, 135, 138, 154; place in plot, 33–34, 37
gender, 126, 127; grammatical, 7, 11–12, 69, 82, 88, 216n21
Gerhart, Mary, and Allan Melvin Russell, 6
Gideon, 268–69
Gilgamesh, 55, 58, 100, 132, 217, 224n24
Girard, René, 148–50, 154, 155
gods, metaphors for
  author, 3, 8, 31–34, 106–17, 129, 150, 154, 162, 169, 181, 196, 109, 212, 213, 214, 226n5
  bull, bull calf, 55–56, 69, 73, 82, 97, 98, 102, 164, 188, 219n8, n9, 220n5
  cloud rider, 51–52, 73, 93
  creator and procreator, 7–8, 17, 22–29, 33, 39, 87, 99, 107, 121, 122, 125, 127, 135, 166, 216n2, 217n4, 226n11
  father, 6, 7–8, 12, 23, 49, 51, 53, 69–73, 80, 91, 95, 97, 99, 100, 101, 102, 103, 129, 172, 197, 216n23, 217n9. *See also* sacrifice; sons of God
  hunter, 56, 97–98
  husband, 12, 55, 69, 74–77, 85–87, 186, 220n8
  king, 7, 9, 12, 44, 45, 47, 48, 55, 61–63, 70, 71, 85, 162, 199–200, 205
  lamb, 45, 46, 47, 86, 98, 99, 101, 102, 103, 114, 115, 117, 222n28
  lion, 7, 38–39, 43, 45, 102, 131
  mother, 97–98, 217n9, 226n9, 228n19
  shepherd, 12, 56, 57, 58
  storm, 43, 52–53, 62–67, 199, 219n5; rain as divine semen, 22, 27, 52, 55, 70, 71;

INDEX

gods, metaphors for—*continued*
vegetation, 34, 35, 55, 60, 100, 123, 124. *See also* mystery religions; resurrection; seed
warrior, ix, 5, 12, 15–16, 23, 49–68, 97, 124, 211. *See also* holy war; gods, weapons of
gods, mounts of, 46, 47, 48, 51–52, 53, 62, 67, 73, 107, 199, 219n3, n6. *See also* cherubim
gods, names and titles of. *See individual names*
gods, weapons of, 52, 56, 63, 65, 163; flood and fire, 63, 65, 109, 179, 209; stones, 175, 176, 177, 231n17
golden calf, 97, 98, 102, 164, 219n8, 220n5
Goldsmith, Steven, 19, 114, 115, 116, 218n7, 219n12
Gombrich, E. H., 17
González, Justo L., 127, 150
Gordon, Cyrus H., 70, 71
grand narratives, 3, 14, 19, 29, 31, 32, 215n7. *See also* Book, the
Greek narratives. *See* Euripides; Hesiod; Homer; Morford; Oedipus

Hades, 21, 36, 37, 42, 46, 50, 56, 60, 138, 195. *See also* Sheol
Haleem, M. A. S. Abdel, translator, the Qur'an, 215n8, 224n2
Hammurabi's Law Code, 57, 108–9, 111, 224n5, n7
Hare, John, 207, 208, 232n5
harlot: Baal worship as, 75–76; harlot-bride, 74–75, 76–81, 185; harlotry, 46, 47, 221n11; ritual "prostitution," 75. *See also* Babylon: whore of; marriage metaphor
Harries, Karsten, 6
Harris, Sam, 2, 134, 227n2
Harris, Stephen L., 36, 57, 61, 63, 64, 70, 73, 96, 108, 123, 159, 222n3, 228n12

Haught, James A., 234n4
harvest (of souls), 36, 46, 169. *See also* seed
heaven, 37; as armed camp, 48, 49–50; behavior of citizens, 44, 46, 200; description in Revelation, 40–45, 199; as Gardens, 87–88; kingdom as throne room, 39, 48, 49–50; new heaven (and earth), 41, 44, 47, 145
Hebrew Bible, 2, 3, 11, 160; on use of term "Old Testament" 216n20
Heidel, Alexander, 23, 61, 72, 219n7
Hera, 55, 70, 73
Hermes, 26, 59, 223n9
Herodotus, 106
Hesiod: destruction fragment, 10; Pandora narrative, 26–27, 28; *Theogony*, 17, 22–23, 26, 62, 82, 92, 217n11; *Works and Days*, 26–27, 37, 38, 50, 70, 207, 209
holy madness, 181–203, 229n1; and the production of knowledge, 183, 186, 188, 192, 193–94, 195, 200–202, 231n18
holy war, 65–68, 111, 164, 210, 220n15, 222n3, 230n8
Homer, 124; "Hymn to Demeter," 60, 123; *The Iliad*, 52, 53, 55, 66, 70, 177, 230n6; *The Odyssey*, 21, 37, 50, 56, 59, 60, 98, 102, 117, 136, 153, 156–57, 195
horses of heaven, 45, 50, 51–52, 60, 107, 199, 219n6. *See also* gods, mounts of
houris, in Gardens of Paradise, 48, 87–88, 135, 222n28

immaculate conception, 83, 159–60, 221n19, 119n4
immortality, 34, 35–37, 39, 41, 60, 83–84, 87, 116, 124–25, 127, 134–36, 138, 139, 145, 146–49, 153, 154, 167, 194, 221n21, 223n16, 224n1, 228n20, 231n10

INDEX

Irish narratives, *The Tain,* 89, 222n2

Jabes, Edmond, 143, 151, 152
Jacob, 15, 58, 139, 141,142, 157–59, 164, 169, 226n17; Jacob's dream, 139. *See also* covenant
James, William, 2, 110, 120, 167
Jaynes, Julian, 92, 93
Jefferson, Thomas, 231n1
Jericho, 66, 67, 142, 162
Jerusalem, 37, 38, 39, 59, 99, 101, 120, 129–30, 135, 145, 163, 173, 202, 218n3, 219n8; as bride, 44, 47, 48, 76–77, 85, 86–87, 93, 115, 185–86, 221n11; New Jerusalem, 19, 37, 43, 44, 114
Jesus, 11, 14, 15, 34, 36, 40, 45, 48, 50, 51, 55, 67, 82, 83, 88, 102, 103, 106, 120, 126, 129, 132, 133, 134, 145, 147, 148, 149, 152, 154, 167, 168–69, 172, 174, 176, 196, 198–99, 212, 213, 221n24, 223n16, n17, n18, 225n3, n4, 225n6, 226n16, n20, n22, 227n23, 228n14, 229n8, 230n3, 231n14, n16, 232n11; as bridegroom, 85–87; determined life of, 133, 159–62; as Lamb of God, 99–102. *See also* immaculate conception; sacrifice
jinn, 88, 122, 186, 221n26
Johnson, Mark, 5, 216n11
Joseph, husband of Mary, 82, 160, 112n18
Joseph, son of Jacob, 158–59, 169, 192
Judas, 133, 160, 161–62, 169, 227n23
Juno, 73
Jupiter, 70, 73, 100, 206, 213
justice, divine, 35, 41–42, 96, 107, 108, 109, 121, 125–34 passim,
166, 207; and predetermination, 156–62 passim

Kermode, Frank, 1, 18, 31, 34, 217n5
Khosrokhavar, Farhad, 215n3
Kierkegaard, Sören, 95, 96, 97, 138, 223n12
Knox, Bernard, 156
Kohler, Kaufmann, 218n4
Kott, Jan, 99, 103, 224n19
Kramer, Samuel Noah: *History Begins at Sumer,* 28, 219n12, 224n5; *Mythologies of the Ancient World,* 56, 71, 219n15; *Sumerian Mythology,* ix, 14, 57, 216n21

Lacan, Jacques, 215n5, 217n18
Lactantius, 128–29, 130, 132, 226n18
LaFleur, William R., 223n17, 227n4
LaHaye, Tim, 212–13
language, figurative, 1–16, 29, 63, 96, 135, 138, 140, 106; Babel and the fall of language, 112–13, 225n12; of End Times, 114–17; of gods, 106–17, 172; of prayer, 171–80; of holy madness, 181, 203
Last Judgment, 36, 43, 46, 47, 115, 131, 154; day of wrath, 46
Lattimore, Richmond, 72
law codes, 107–12; *lex talionis,* 108
Lenardon, Robert J., 51, 60, 91, 102, 123, 124
Leviathan, 62–63, 66, 128, 217n7. *See also* serpentine enemy
levirate, 80, 221n21, n22
Lévi-Strauss, Claude, ix–x, 26
Lindsey, Hal, 212, 232n9, n10
logocentrism, 3, 215n4
Lopez, Donald S., Jr., 137, 138
Luther, Martin, 150

madness. *See* holy madness

INDEX

Marduk, 23–24, 26, 28, 51, 52, 62, 63, 128, 205, 206, 225n6
Marks, Herbert, 84, 183–84
marriage: Jesus as bridegroom, 85–87; marriage contract and the covenant, 74–75, 77, 141–42; in New Testament, 83–85; sacred 55, 59; St. Paul's anti-Song of Songs 84. *See also* gods, metaphors for: husband; marriage metaphor
marriage metaphor, 69, 73, 74, 185–86
McGinn, Bernard, 200
Merkabah (throne/chariot), 51, 219n7. *See also* gods, mounts of; horses of heaven
Messiah, 41, 43, 44, 45–46, 47, 114, 131, 159, 225n6
metaphor: classical definition, 215n10; form of, 5; interactive aspect, 7–8, 74, 186, 216n11; knowledge of metaphysical, 5–6; limit language, 6–7. *See also* gods, metaphors for
Metzger, Bruce M., 220n6
Miller, J. Hillis, 10
model, scientific, 4–5, 215n9
Molloy, Michael, 219n1
monism (cosmic), 40, 119, 121–22, 116n19; and divine justice, 129–31; the problem of evil, 126–29
Monk, Leland, 32–33
Moore, Malcolm, 232n8
morality and religion, 82, 207–11
Morford, Mark, 224n3
Morford, Mark P. O., and Robert J. Lenardon, 91, 102, 123, 124
Mosaic Code, 106, 108–12, 143, 145–46; death penalty, 108–9
Moses, 15, 58, 67–68, 81, 101, 106, 108, 109, 141, 159, 160, 162, 164, 169, 178, 198, 216n10, 220n16, 223n18, 227n1, 228n14, 229n8

Mother Earth, 23, 24, 29, 55, 62. *See also* gods, metaphors for
Mother of Books, 2, 15, 106, 113, 117. *See also* Book
Muhammad, 15, 18, 51, 66, 67, 106, 122, 148, 169, 178, 186–87, 220n16, 223n18, 227n1, 228n14, 229n8
muses, 17, 70
mystery religions, 35, 123–25, 129, 146, 187, 193, 226n22
mythology, the two mythologies, 14, 54–61; Cain vs. Abel, 57–59

narratives: grand, 3, 14, 19, 29, 31, 32, 33, 45, 215n7; appearance of chance in, 32–33, 150–51; narrative inevitability, 31–33
Nasrallah, Laura, 181, 182, 193, 196, 200, 229n1
negative morphemes and the sacred, 8–9, 138, 216n15, n16, 217n8; apophasis, 216n15; and parapraxis, 9–11
Nephilim (*bene Elohim*), 70, 72. *See also* gods, metaphors for: father; Watchers
Noah, 63, 65, 84, 112, 209; and sons, 79–80
Noll, Mark A., 232n6
Norse narratives, 22, 23, 26, 49–50, 51, 62, 218n2, 223n15. *See also* Odin
nothing, 6–9, 10, 11, 21, 22, 23, 29, 216n13, 217n8; creation from (*ex nihilo*), 9. *See also* negative morphemes and the sacred

Odin, 21, 23, 26, 49–50, 51, 62, 63, 100, 206, 223n15
Odysseus. *See* Homer: *The Odyssey*
Oedipus, 89–92, 103, 156, 157, 159, 160, 161,162, 169, 189, 195, 196, 222n1, n2, n5, 230n3
Orphism, 123, 125, 217n4

Osiris, 34, 55, 99, 100, 103, 226n17

Paine, Thomas, 229n6, n7
Palmer, E. H., 222n27, 224n8, 229n5
Pandora. *See* Hesiod
parables: in New Testament, 85–86, 148, 169, 173, 196, 221n24; in Qur'an, 149, 228n14
parapraxis, 9–11, 216n19
Pascal, Blaise, Pascal's wager, 138, 139, 227n2
Passover, 101, 102
Patai, Raphael: *The Hebrew Goddess*, 68, 73, 216n22, 217n9, 219n2, n3, n6, 220n5, 222n28; *The Seed of Abraham*, 11–12, 70, 88; *Sex and the Family*, 71, 75, 220n3, n4, 220n8, 332n10, 221n13, n15
Paul, St. (Saul), 9, 84, 88, 100, 138, 145, 146, 149, 150, 153, 167, 191–92, 193, 199, 202, 225n3, 231n16; conversion of, 191; dualism and, 116, 120–21, 133, 152; on marriage, 84
Pelagius, 228n17
Pentheus, 102, 103, 187–89, 190, 230n3, 231n10
Persephone, 34, 60, 70, 71, 100, 123
Pharaoh, 58, 63, 65, 66, 100, 141, 158, 162, 179, 192, 229n6
Philo, 193, 217n9
Plato: Christianity, Islam and, 125–16, 208; dualism and, 125–26, 146, 226n12, n13; "Euthyphro," 65, 207; *Phaedrus*, 181; *The Republic*, 125–26, 146, 216n12
plot, 3, 16, 31–33, 36, 37, 40, 42, 45, 47, 106, 113, 150–51, 153, 211–12, 218n1; covenant and, 153–54; prayer and, 174–80; prophecy and, 155–69; spatial and temporal dimensions, 18, 19, 29, 31, 217n2. *See also* Book; gods, metaphors for: author

prayer, 171–80
predestination, 137, 148, 149, 150, 151, 153, 160, 118n18, 229n5. *See also* free will
Prickett, Steven, 3, 215n7
Pritchard, James B., 17, 34, 37, 94, 135, 194, 227n24
Promised Land, 38, 66, 67, 93, 100, 139, 142, 145, 148, 175, 199
prophecy: and apocalypse, 19, 114, 218n7; dreams and visions, 196–97; holy madness as "prophetic experience," 181–83, 191, 229n1; predictive, 155–69, 172, 174, 175, 176, 177, 181; prophetic irony, 195–96; and symbolic behavior, 183, 185. *See* holy madness; plot
prophets, false, 46, 179, 182–83, 191, 199, 201, 202, 231n16; angry, alienated, 178, 179, 183–86, 199, 230n4
Pseudepigrapha
Enoch (The Book of Enoch), 218n9
2 Enoch (The Secrets of Enoch), 8, 25, 37, 64, 72, 87, 153, 218n8, 221n23, 227n1. *See also* Barnstone, Willis
Gospel of Judas, 227n23
punishment. *See also* reward and punishment
Pythagoras, 123, 225n8

Qur'an, by sura and page
Sura 2: 25, 110, 147, 149, 220n8, 231n1
Sura 3: 15, 105, 106, 134, 147
Sura 4: 228n12
Sura 6: 149, 186
Sura 7: 122, 134
Sura 9: 31, 66
Sura 17: 48, 53, 66, 67, 109, 220n16
Sura 18: 105
Sira 21: 186
Sura 22: ix, 122

Qur'an, by sura and page—*continued*
Sura 24: 110, 173
Sura 29: 173, 228n14
Sura 33: 230n5
Sura 35: 35, 48, 154
Sura 37: 4, 186
Sura 38: 48
Sura 52: 48, 87, 146
Sura 53: 219n1
Sura 54: 220n14
Sura 55: 88, 106
Sura 57: 229n5
Sura 67: 87
Sura 68: 187
Sura 72: 88
Sura 75: 149
Sura 96: 106
Sura 98: 137
Sura 102: 36

Ra, 19, 22–23, 24
Raglan, Lord, 53, 221n17
Rée, Jonathan, 215n7
responsibility, 121, 126, 156–60. *See also* free will; predestination
resurrection, 34, 35–36, 39, 40, 41, 42, 43, 48, 55, 67, 83–84, 88, 99, 100, 102, 103, 120, 123, 129, 131, 133, 134, 149, 155, 159, 160, 176, 224n17, 226n14; in mystery religions, 123–25
reward and punishment, 16, 34–35, 43, 125, 126, 127, 164, 171, 195, 207, 209, 211. *See also* economics of belief
Richards, I. A., 216n11
Riffaterre, Michael, 161
Robbins, Jill, 97, 223n10
Roman narratives, 23, 38, 63–64, 231n13; Ovid, *Metamorphoses*, 20, 24, 27, 28, 38, 63–64, 69; Virgil, *Aeneid*, 37, 50
Rosenberg, Joel, 189

Russell, Allan Melvin, 6

sacrifice, 50, 56, 72; of the first-born, 94–97; as food for the gods, 192–94, 223n9; gods as, 102–3, 223n17; Lamb of God as, 99–102; sacred violence and father-son relationship, 16, 89–92; two mythic types of, 60, 97–99, 222n3. *See also* Akedah; Jesus
Said, Edward W., 143
Samuel (prophet), 21, 71, 163, 189–91, 192, 195, 230n3, 231n12
Satan (Devil), 40, 46, 84, 131, 133, 160, 226n10; as death, 132, 134, 162; and dualism, 126–27, 131; as enemy, 54, 128–29, 265, 226n20; as falsehood, 151–52, 168–69; in Qur'an (Iblis), 77–78, 122; satanic verses, 222n27; as serpent, 47, 131, 167–68, 226n16; as son of God, 164–65. *See also* demons
Saul, King, 21, 121; tragedy of, 189–91, 195, 198, 230n3
seed, good, evil, 36, 73, 98, 130–31, 148, 150, 167, 169, 209
serpentine enemy (dragon, serpent), 46, 62, 63, 128–29, 131, 167–68, 226n16; Tiamat and *Tehōm* (the deep), 62
sexuality, 77–79, 83, 86, 126–27, 151, 208, 229n21; as biblical subtext, 78; and death, 64–65, 152; justification for slavery, 79–80; sex in heaven, 87–88; uncovering nakedness, 77, 79–80, 81, 127. *See also* unclean
Shakespeare, 20, 135, 138
Sheol, 21, 35, 37, 42, 50, 56, 138, 165, 194, 195. *See also* Hades
sin, sexual nature of, 78, 82, 84, 127, 152, 220n4, 221n25, 228n17. *See also* sexuality

Smyth, John Vignaux, 216n14
Solomon, 175, 218n8, 221n12. *See also* Apocrypha: Wisdom of Solomon
Sophocles, *Theban Plays*. *See* Oedipus
sons of God, 71, 72. *See also* gods, metaphors for: father
soul. *See* dualism
Stenger, Victor J., 207, 209
Stevens, Wallace, 3, 18, 205, 206
Stoyanov, Yuri, 123, 127, 128, 131, 225n6, 226n11, n14
Sumerian narratives, ix, 23, 28, 36–37, 55–56, 57, 58, 60, 63, 70–71, 107, 108, 216n21
Sybil, 333n13

Taves, Ann, 230n1
Taylor, Mark, 4, 10
Tertullian's paradox, 138
Thomas, D. Winton, ix, 23
Tiamat, 22, 23, 24, 26, 52, 62, 128, 129, 217n7
time, 17–29 passim, 31–48 passim
tongues, talking in, 190, 191–92. *See also* prophecy
tooth fairy, 201, 203
Torey, Zoltan, 5
Tracy, David, 2, 36, 143
trees, of life and knowledge, 33, 39, 78, 106, 109, 126, 127, 151, 152, 153. *See also* garden
Turbayne, Colin Murray, 7

Twain, Mark, 87, 116, 117, 163, 172, 174, 105, 206

unclean, 81, 101, 132–33, 225n13

Vermes, Geza, 119, 153
Vielhauer, Philipp, 40–41, 197, 198, 218n7, n8
virgin birth, 82–83, 160, 221n17, n18, 119n4
visions. *See* prophecy; prophets

Watchers, 64–65, 72, 221n20, n23
weapons. *See* gods, weapons of
Westbrook, Deeanne, 228n19
White, Hayden, 215n6
Wood, David, 28, 46
Wright, Robert, 225n3

Xenophanes, 5, 206, 223n16

Yahweh (God), passim. *See subject entries, e.g.,* gods, metaphors for: sacrifice, *etc.*
Yeats, William Butler, 20, 116
Young, Dudley, 14

Zeus, 17, 23, 26, 50, 51, 52–53, 55, 59–60, 61–62, 63, 65, 70, 71, 72, 73, 82, 91, 92, 100, 102, 128, 177 187, 205, 206, 207, 216n23, 219n8
Zoroastrianism, 123, 125, 134, 217n4, 225n5, 226n11; Magi, 226n11